FORTY YEARS ON

Photo. Elliott & Fry.

FORTY YEARS ON

BY

LORD ERNEST HAMILTON

WILDSIDE PRESS

CONTENTS

ILLUSTRATIONS

CHAPTER I

To those who may raise the objection that the title of this book is not quite in keeping with the heading of the opening chapter, I would merely observe that the title is meant to strike a polite average between the first and last post of observation, and is therefore not the cowardly evasion that it might at first sight appear. I may add, in further explanation, that it is intended to be a quotation from the last verse of the famous song, and not the first verse—a distinction which many will appreciate. In the last verse the singer claims one gain as against several losses, but sighs in doing it, as well he may; for, though length of memory in another may have some value for the general public, it must always be but a shaky compensation to the possessor for the shortness of wind which buys it. Nevertheless, the long-winded and the short-memoried may be glad to read of the be-haloed days of yore, when Plancus was Consul and the grass grew green on the top of the hill; while the short-winded and the long-memoried may not be sorry to conjure up once more visions of forms and features which were once familiar but which have long since passed on ahead.

I must admit at the start that I do not approach

B   1

my subject in the spirit of a blind *laudator temporis acti*. There must always, of course, be a certain glamour about the long past, which perhaps raises it above its true value, partly because it has slipped away from us, but mainly, I think, because long-past days were the days when limbs were strong and wind was sound and golden apples hung within reach. Apart from the natural regret which we must all feel at the loss of such things, my own view is that the world has, on the whole, gained more than it has lost during the past half-century. I know that few of my contemporaries will agree with this heresy, but, none the less, I must adhere to it. Of course, in certain directions, there have been irreparable losses—not merely money losses, but losses of the sacred customs and traditions which moulded the lives of preceding generations, and which, in a large degree, have helped to make England what it was and what, alas! it will never be again. For all these vanished glories and joys we shed the sad tear, not so much because they represent a personal loss, but because, with their passing, England as a nation seems shorn of some of its most distinctive features. It would almost seem as though one of the stripes had been ripped out of the Union Jack.

All ill winds, however, blow good to somebody, and in other directions there have certainly been gains. Men and women of the upper classes are more enlightened than when I first remember them; girls are more natural; conversation is

less vapid; sentiments are more real, and humbug
is less fashionable. In the Sixties, which is the
first decade of which I have any clear recollection—and it is wonderful how clear that recollection is—a strong vein of humbug, both of self and
others, ran right through Society with a big S.
The affectations of the middle century, in fact—
although moribund—were by no means dead, and
the elderly practised them without shame.

It has been suggested that the affectations of
early Victorian days were a natural rebound from
the coarseness of the Georgian period. In the
depths of the country, where things move slowly,
this Georgian coarseness survived long after
London had shaken it off. The mere foxhunter
of early Victorian days was, we cannot but
believe, a very coarse fellow indeed. Surtees has
bowdlerised him in his immortal works—and quite
properly too—but, reading between Surtees' lines,
it is not difficult to guess at the gross boorishness
of his Jug Boystons, Jack Spraggons and Lord
Scamperdales. Out of the saddle and at close
quarters, these gentry must have left much to
be desired.

In an over-eagerness to prove their aloofness
from the manners of these rude sons of the chase,
the Victorian fops of the Dundreary type went to
the other extreme and made themselves ridiculous
by an extravagant affectation of refinement. They
lisped; they drawled; they pronounced their
" r's " like " w's." They waved scented handker-
chiefs in the air and eschewed all games and

3

sports as being rough and coarse. Gaiety burlesque drew a far from exaggerated picture of this
type in the famous verse :—

" Au revoir, ta-ta,
    I heard him say,
  To the Lady Crambanally
    While bidding her good-day.
  I'll stwike you with a feather,
  I'll stab you with a wose,
  I'll shoot at you with wafers
  And give you fearful blows ! "

In the Sixties, though foppery was on the wane,
and had its contemptuous scoffers among the more
virile school, there were still, among the older
generation, many surviving specimens of the
Dundreary idiot. There were also their feminine
counterparts, who strove, with only partial
success, to outshine the Dundrearys in effeminacy.
One of the chief, and not the least ridiculous
affectation of the cult was the deliberate mis-
pronunciation, where possible, of every word in
the English language. Septuagenarians might
still be heard describing how " The dear Dook was
obleeged by the heat to set in a gyarden cheer,
under the laloc trees, drinking tay out of yellow
chaney coops, while his leddy on the balcōny ate
cowcumbers and reddishes off goold plates brought
to Oxfordsheer from Roome," etc, etc. Even
the middle-aged, through the force of example,
adopted some of these mispronunciations. They
spoke of terriers as " tarriers," and of yellow as
" yallow," but the young eschewed them altogether. Certain names, however, such as Pall

4

Mall, Berkshire and Derby, have permanently taken on the corrupted vowel sound.

The mid-Victorian girls were as natural as their mothers allowed them to be, but the habit of artificiality was still too strong to be entirely shaken off in one generation. Nevertheless, the girls, even though not quite natural, were very sweet. Their complexions were clear and fresh and wholly innocent of the modern disfiguring pastes and powders. The most strenuous precautions were taken to preserve these complexions in their original purity. The first gleam of sunshine, no matter how weak and watery, was the signal for every young woman and girl to hoist a parasol. Lawn tennis, hockey, golf and other similar exercises, where maiden cheeks have to be exposed to sun and wind, were of course unknown. Croquet and archery were the most violent forms of exercise allowed. No girl or woman could swim. Swimming would have been considered highly immodest, as swimming necessitates a swimming costume. When ladies did bathe, which was seldom, they did so in conventual seclusion. Enveloped from head to foot in thick blue sackcloth, they crept into the sea under the shelter of huge hoods which extended from the bathing machines to the water. Here they pranced at the end of a rope for some minutes and then emerged. Any man trespassing within eye-distance of this immodest exhibition of the female form was branded a barbarian in the first degree.

On dry land, feminine forms were pinched and

trussed into all sorts of odd shapes suggestive of anything rather than the work of the Creator. The natural female shape was considered an indecency, and immense pains were taken to camouflage it in every way possible. Feminine beauty was not perhaps more admired than it is to-day, but it was certainly more discussed and was invested with higher importance. The charms of reigning beauties formed one of the regular topics of dinner-table talk. They were called " professional " beauties in those days. They were not numerous, but their reigns were long. Mrs. Asquith, in her Autobiography, gives us a list of such beauties in the Eighties, and, after singing their merits, laments the fact that she can see no beautiful women to-day. This is hardly understandable, because there are un-questionably many more beautiful women about to-day than there were in the Eighties. It could hardly be otherwise with the expansion in all directions of that indefinite body known as Society. The fact of the matter is that to-day female beauty is taken as a matter of course and is not made a song of as it used to be. There are any number of beautiful women in London Society about whose beauty no fuss is made at all. In the Eighties their charms would have been shouted from every housetop in Belgravia and Mayfair. They would have been set on pinnacles on which they would have remained till they were grand-mothers, objects of feminine gush, while men made love elsewhere.

6

THE SIXTIES

While registering my opinion that the women of to-day are on the whole just as beautiful as the women of the Eighties, the Seventies and the Sixties, and perhaps more so, for they are more like women and less like penwipers, I must make one exception in favour of the late Duchess of Leinster, in my opinion incomparably the most beautiful woman I have ever seen—one other always excepted. All Lord Feversham's daughters were beautiful—astonishingly beautiful—but, if the four Yorkshire sisters had stood in competition before Paris, I think he would have given the apple to Lady Hermione, afterwards Duchess of Leinster. As a child of sixteen or so, when she and her sisters used to play about in Belgrave Square, her beauty was so dazzling as to be almost unbelievable. It was not only that she was divinely tall and absolutely flawless in shape, feature and complexion—a very rare combination—but she also had on her face that look of radiant goodness which, for some mysterious reason, is seldom seen on the faces of any except those doomed to an early death.

Drawing-room conversation in the Sixties was mainly anecdotal, as indeed it must always be in a Society which has no knowledge of the practical side of life. The raconteur, from whom people now flee as from the plague, was then in great request. Even he, however, would only tap his stock of anecdotes on occasions worthy of the effort. Election results were discussed with feverish interest, but only in the light of pure

party. No attempt was ever made to analyse
party propaganda. For the rest, conversation
revolved round the simple topics of food, health
and the weather, and in no case was any attempt
made to soar above accepted generalities. Few
indeed, in mid-Victorian days, had the temerity
to exploit original ideas. The intellectual level
of the day did not demand any such excursions,
and such as made the attempt were eyed suspici-
ously. Although health and the weather were
generally recognised as suitable subjects for
dinner-table talk, at moments when conversation
was flagging, undoubtedly the most popular subject for discussion was food; for, whereas in the
former case Society merely passed on the views
of the doctor or the gardener, on the question of
food it could air first-hand opinions. It was also
very well up in its subject, to which much study
and attention were devoted. The meal known as
" dinner " was little short of a religious rite. It
was no longer the disgusting orgy that it had been
in the early nineteenth century, but it was still a
function to which everything else in the day was
subordinate. People went out specially to get
up an appetite for dinner. They refrained from
doing this or doing that for fear of " spoiling
their dinner." Other meals were of no account.
They were, I think, even looked upon with dis-
favour as poachers on the preserves of the final
great gastronomic function. None of the old
school would look at five-o'clock tea for fear it
might imperil their powers of enjoyment later on.

THE SIXTIES

In a Society so naïve and simple-minded as that of the Sixties, the professional classes, as may readily be imagined, ran joyous riot. No layman had sufficient knowledge to question, in the smallest particular, the dogmatic utterances of the doctor, the parson, the lawyer or even the gardener. Doctors, I think, were held in the highest reverence of all the professionals. Their status was almost that of magicians wielding mysterious and supernatural powers. They exercised unchallenged sway over every affluent household. As a direct consequence, sickliness became the fashion of the day. Robust health was looked down upon as vulgar. Mothers with the greatest reluctance admitted that their children were not diseased. " Oh, no; he (or she) is not *really* strong," was the common form of apology for red cheeks and large appetites.

In spite, however, of the many little weaknesses which are inseparable from an age in which practical knowledge is looked down upon as savouring of the middle-classes, Society of the Sixties had many joyous aspects for the few who had the *entrée* to the best houses. I was but a diminutive onlooker of the doings of those days. My joys were the never-failing and never-changing joys of childhood in every age. I trundled hoops and chased butterflies; but, young as I was, my mind is quite clear as to the happy-family fashion in which the great world lived. Society, of course, was very small and very clearly defined. Everyone knew everyone else in that exclusive circle,

9

and as well might the Pope of Rome have tried to enter Mecca, as the self-made millionaire to find a footing in that sacred throng. Although many within the guarded gates were very rich, there was no glaring parade of wealth. Tastes were very simple. The artistic sense among the upper classes was quite undeveloped and yet, to a certain extent, the ends of art were achieved unconsciously. Shiny chintz covers draped chairs and sofas both in town and country, and gave to the living-rooms a certain air of freshness and distinction which even the hideous wall-papers could not entirely dissipate. Furniture was solid and very ugly. Sheraton and Chippendale ware was pronounced " gimcracky " and pushed away out of sight in lumber-rooms. White paint and pale shades of green or blue were shuddered at as being " so cold." Chocolate or maroon was preferred. Reds of all shades were in great request as looking " warm." Tables were concealed under crimson plush covers, and up the corners of walls ran gilded laths.

Amidst these surroundings, long-whiskered men lounged about in peg-top trousers and loose coats fastened by a single button under the chin. Out-of-doors they wore Glengarry caps. The ladies wore crinolines and flounces and the same loose jackets buttoned under the chin. On their heads, when out-of-doors, they wore very shallow flat hats with curly brims. No more disfiguring female dress has ever been devised by the ingenuity of man.

The men and women who, thus attired, gathered round our hearth stand out very clearly in my memory. The Jocelyns and their family; the Elchos and their very large family; the Pophams; Hugh Greville; Alfred Montgomery and the husbands of my four eldest sisters, Lichfield, Durham, Dalkeith and Mount-Edgcumbe. All of these came and went in constant rotation and are clearly photographed upon my mind, but the two figures that, from the first, dwarf all others are those of my father and mother. As the youngest of a family of thirteen, and twenty-four years the junior of my eldest sister, I have naturally no recollection of youthful parents. From the very first my father and mother stand out on the screen of life as old people, but as old people who overshadowed all competitors as objects of adoration—my father stalwart and magnificent, the handsomest man of his day, a little aloof, perhaps, but all the more adorable on that account; and my mother the very embodiment of Christian charity, refusing to believe evil of any and shedding sweetness and kindliness on all around her. These two, so utterly different the one from the other and yet each with so compelling a personality, hold the stage unchallenged through all the changing scenes of my early life.

These scenes changed with exciting frequency. When I first opened my eyes upon the world, we were in occupation of Brocket Hall, which my father rented from Lord Palmerston. Although we left this charming place when I was five, and although I have never revisited it, my recollection of the house and immediate surroundings is very clear. I can see, as though photographed, the house with its divided staircase, the lake, the home-farm across the lake and the bridges at each end. Of stirring incidents, however, my mind seems barren. The most outstanding seems to be that of Jack Durham [1] (then Jack Lambton) kicking the donkey-boy. I must have been five at the time, and Jack Lambton, although my nephew, was three years my senior. We were, I remember, watching the donkey pumping up the water for the house. The boy in attendance thought good to encourage the donkey's efforts by kicking it in the stomach. Jack Lambton watched this procedure in silence for a minute or so and then, without a word, seized the donkey-boy by the collar and kicked him as hard as he had been kicking the unfortunate donkey, but in a different quarter. Whether the boy, who must have been some years older than Jack, made any resistance, I cannot remember. But the incident is interesting as marking Jack Durham, even at that early age, as the fearless champion of the weak and the sworn foe of all dirty dealings.

When I was five, we migrated for three years to Beaudesert Park, which my father rented from Lord Anglesea. As in the case of Brocket, the topography of Beaudesert is very clearly imprinted on my mind, but once again no incident seems worthy of record except, perhaps, the inci-

[1] John, third Earl of Durham.

dent of my nurse throwing the slop-basin at the nursery-maid.

Our nursery occupied a corner room on the top floor and was connected with the lower regions by a small turret staircase. On the memorable evening in question, our tea-table was laid, but the tea did not arrive with its customary punctuality. The delay would seem to have incensed our worthy nurse more than the occasion warranted, for, when the nursery-maid eventually appeared through the door of the turret stairs bearing the tray, she was saluted by the slop-basin, hurled at her head with accurate aim and considerable force. The girl placed the tray in safety, wiped the blood from her face and then gave vent to a suitable flow of tears. There, as far as I know, the incident closed. Why the girl made no complaint is more than I can say, but it is possible that the nurse knew things about her which would have squared accounts had she complained.

At the above scene, as may be supposed, I gazed in open-eyed amazement, wondering what it all meant, for the nurse in question was a particularly kind woman whom my brother and I absolutely adored. The explanation, as we afterwards found out, lay in the brandy-bottle. The good nurse had occasional recourse to this bottle, which, instead of exhilarating, as it should have done, produced exactly the opposite effect, and made her, for the time being, a danger to her neighbours. We children, too, suffered occasionally from unaccountable fits of fury born of brandy, but we bore no ill-will for them, although wondering a good deal what it all meant. I remember well that, when this nurse's time came to leave, I tried hard to recall all the acts of violence from which I had suffered at her hands, so as to soften the pang of parting from one whom I loved so dearly.

Apart from this one incident, Beaudesert is chiefly associated in my mind with the singing of pretty little Mrs. Popham. Mrs. Popham had a very sweet voice and sang, to a guitar accompaniment, little songs of which the words and music were her own. By comparison with modern drawing-room performances these songs would now seem simple and crude, but they certainly had a sweetness and pathos about them which the modern song misses. Mrs. Popham's singing of them made a lasting impression on my youthful mind. I never tired of hearing the following ballad sung, sitting in rapt silence beside her, as directed by the words of the song, which are, of course, supposed to be addressed to a child :

" Sit beside me; I will tell
    Why my heart is always aching,
Why I gaze across the vale,
    Watching shadows circles making.

" In the winter, years ago,
    Long before you can remember,
All the earth was white with snow
    In the month of cold December.

" I was waiting at the gate,
    Watching, sick at heart and weary;
He was never home so late,
    Crossing o'er the mountain dreary.

14

"Never since that winter's day
  Has my heart been free from sorrow,
For beneath the snow he lay,
  No one found him till the morrow.

"That is why I look so pale,
  Why my heart is always aching,
Why I gaze across the vale,
  Watching shadows circles making."

The beauty of the musical setting and the sweet quality of the singer's voice gave a charm to these simple words which can hardly be described. My other favourite, " They told me the old house was haunted," had a happier ending :

"They told me my heart would be broken,
  My young life be withered away;
But in answer I gave them a token
  Of what I had found there that day.
For though the wild fir trees were creaking,
  And ghosts were in every part,
I found what I long had been seeking—
  A heart I could take to my heart."

That was the song of Littlecote, where the ghost of Wild Dayrell was supposed to haunt all the successors of that Judge Popham into whose hands the property had passed after the trial and acquittal of Dayrell on the charge of murder.

In 1866 my father was appointed Lord-Lieutenant of Ireland and we left Beaudesert for the Viceregal Lodge. This to my small-boy's mind was a tremendous event from which I anticipated every sort of pleasurable excitement. These hopes were not fully realised. Small boys of eight are a misfit in Viceregal functions, so that it was little of the Court festivities that I saw during my father's first term of office. There were certain supreme moments, however, when my brother and I found that we were not without an official value. When State " Drawing-Rooms " took place we were brought forth from our schoolroom obscurity and given temporary official rank as pages to our mother. Gorgeously attired in white satin breeches, blue poplin tunics slashed with silver braid and tin-bladed swords, we proudly took up our position behind the throne. We dearly loved these full-dress functions. The excitement of seeing the Dublin ladies file past for presentation never palled. When we recognised friends or acquaintances among those presented our excitement was doubled. Undoubtedly, however, our greatest joy was when, as occasionally happened, one of the Dublin ladies became overcome by bashfulness at the prospect of being kissed by the Lord-Lieutenant. It was the custom of the Court that every lady presented should submit to a salute from the Viceregal lips. This rite was as time-honoured and invariable as the baptismal ceremony, and yet no Drawing-Room ever passed without one or two of the victims being overcome by a sudden access of modesty. It was never the young or pretty ones who raised objections, but always some mature dame or damsel of many Dublin winters. These would back and shy and giggle and simper till in the end Gustavus Lambert was forced with the aid of his underlings to drag them squealing up to the throne, there to receive the Lord-Lieutenant's reluctant kiss upon their wrinkled cheeks.

16

HERMIONE, DUCHESS OF LEINSTER.

We two small pages used to welcome these displays of modesty with frantic enthusiasm.

On the occasion of one Drawing-Room, when the ladies were disappointingly forward, and when proceedings were therefore a trifle dull, my brother discovered that there was just room for two small boys to creep in between the throne and the wall behind it, and there to curl up and go to sleep. It did not in the least disturb us that we emerged from our resting-place with our beautiful liveries coated with the dust of ages. Those who had charge of our morals were very much disturbed, and dusted our coats (and our breeches too) with a vigour which convinced us that in the long run it was more profitable, even though more wearisome, to stand.

Gustavus Lambert, the Chamberlain, whose duty it was to lead the recalcitrant Dublin ladies to the sacrifice, was a singularly striking and picturesque figure, for, when not in official uniform, he invariably wore a tight blue frock-coat with cross bars of braid, and Hessian boots. He had a very dignified bearing and a very tightly waxed moustache which, in combination with his Hessian boots, made him an object of ceaseless gladness to my eyes. Lady Fanny, his wife, who was a Conyngham by birth, was little less striking in her own way. A very handsome woman of the Spanish type, she had a predilection for dresses of Zingari colours which, in those days of expansive crinolines, produced some fine colour effects. They had a galaxy of extremely good-looking daughters.

CHAPTER II

ONE of the first figures of public interest to which long memory carries one back is that of Queen Alexandra, who, as Princess of Wales, visited my father at Dublin Castle in 1867. H.R.H., as I remember her, was then a vision of smiles, side-ringlets and general loveliness. It is no more than the bare truth to say that in the Irish metropolis she won all hearts, and, among them, that of an insignificant but adoring boy of eight and a half.

My small, and probably dirty, hands were at that time badly disfigured by a number of warts. The application of caustic to these warts had turned them brown, which cannot have added to their attractiveness. H.R.H. took the most solicitous interest in my complaint and examined my repulsive little hands with the tenderest care. After listening to a recital of my woes—for my warts were a source of great shame and distress to me—she promised that she would charm them away for me. A certain rite was gone through, to the best of my recollection with hazel twigs, but, be that as it may, the fact remains, that from that day on my warts began to disappear and have never shown any tendency to return.

18

It is not to be wondered at that I worshipped with a lasting adoration the lovely Princess who had worked this Hans Andersen miracle on me.

H.R.H., in common with other members of the Royal Family, had the gift of never forgetting a face and seldom forgetting an incident, no matter how trivial. When, some fourteen years later, the Prince and Princess of Wales came to stay with my father at Barons Court, I was duly presented and made my bow. H.R.H. graciously shook hands with me and then, retaining my hand, said : " But where are the warts ? " I explained that her magic had effected a permanent cure, at which she was greatly pleased.

The next occasion on which I came in contact with their Royal Highnesses carries with it less pleasing recollections. In 1885 the Prince and Princess of Wales paid a friendly visit to the city of Cork, and part of my regiment formed the escort while the remainder kept the streets. My own troop was stationed in Patrick Street, where an immense crowd had collected. On the approach of the Royal carriage, to my horror and unspeakable indignation, the entire crowd gave vent to a chorus of boos, hisses and shrill howls of execration, to which H.R.H., wholly undismayed, replied with her invariably sweet and winning smile. So far from disarming the crowd of its malice, this turning of the other cheek seemed only to incense it the more, for presently onions began to fly through the air and, finally, a miniature wooden coffin was thrown with accurate aim into the Royal carriage and landed almost on H.R.H.'s knees. A more despicable and cowardly return for a visit which was undertaken solely with a view to doing honour to Cork can hardly be imagined, and I can answer for it that there was not a man in my troop who would not gladly have turned the point of his drawn sword upon the howling crowd and charged. In the absence of orders, however, we were powerless to move. Personally I was able to find a certain comforting safety-valve for the indignation which was boiling within me. I was riding a thoroughbred charger named Gainsborough, one of whose peculiarities was that, if I laid my hand on his quarters, he would instantly lash out viciously behind. Never was this slightly inconvenient habit of more loyal service than on the day in question. I backed him to where the crowd was thickest, laid my hand innocently on his quarters and in an instant the crowd in the immediate neighbourhood was scattered like chaff before the wind. Half a dozen times I repeated the performance, and then Gainsborough's opportunities for loyal gymnastics were at an end, for that part of Patrick Street was effectually cleared.

The subject of Gainsborough and his peculiarities leads me by natural channels to another incident which was less satisfactory to my self-esteem. One of the playful beast's habits was to give three tremendous buck-jumps whenever I mounted him. On ordinary occasions this display of spirits rather amused me and had no disturbing effects. One day I was ordered to escort the Duke of Albany through the streets of Liverpool with the Rupert Lane squadron, the squadron to be in full dress. This order meant that my charger had to be decorated with a heavy gold-embroidered cloth, since obsolete, but known in those days as a " shabraque." I inspected my mounted squadron on foot and then proceeded to mount my own horse, who, as usual, delivered himself of his three regulation buck-jumps. To my horror I discovered on the instant that the presence of this thick hanging-cloth absolutely prevented my getting any grip of the saddle. The first buck-jump disturbed my equilibrium; the second practically dislodged me from the saddle, and the third shot me neatly on to my back in the mud of the barrack square. The incident would, in any case, have been distressing, but, in all my best clothes, it was little short of a tragedy. We had only just time to arrive at our destination as it was, so that to change my tunic was out of the question. All that I could do was to get myself rubbed down with a cloth and to mount again with the marks of my discomfiture only very partially effaced. Of this fact the small boys of Liverpool soon gave me loud and hilarious proof. This, however, was not the worst. My place, as commander of the squadron, was close to the left door of the Royal carriage. I had once before had the honour of escorting H.R.H. from Egham to

Claremont on the occasion of his marriage, and, with the peculiar gift of his family, he at once recognised me and made friendly inquiries as to the unusual condition of my tunic and pantaloons. As we trotted along, I told him my sad story. I have seldom seen anyone laugh more. The populace was cheering lustily on both sides of the street and, between his acknowledgments, H.R.H. would, from time to time, turn his eyes upon me as I trotted gloomily at his side with my drawn sword at the carry, and would be momentarily convulsed with mirth. The *Liverpool Courier* next day remarked that H.R.H. was looking particularly well, and for this bright and sunny aspect there is no doubt that I was largely responsible.

A striking figure in the Viceregal days of 1866–68 was that of Lord Strathnairn, better known as Sir Hugh Rose of Indian Mutiny fame. This old Scottish warrior, desperate fire-eater though he was reputed, and I believe justly, to be, was the very reverse in appearance. He had a mildly benevolent countenance, deeply lined, and crowned by hair of most unmilitary length, which fell over his face in long straggling locks, suggestive of a Skye terrier. His manner was almost ladylike in its urbanity and, in place of affecting a military attitude, he habitually stood with his hands limply crossed in front of him. He spoke in a weak, husky voice, and his whole manner, speech and appearance suggested an amiable, absent-minded old lady rather than

22

a dashing general. And yet he was known to be a leader of iron will, of indomitable courage and of pitiless severity when circumstances called for severity.

At the time I remember Lord Strathnairn he was C.-in-C. of the forces in Ireland. His staff worshipped him and, better than any of us, knew how deceptive was his ladylike manner, for his habit was to lead them to and from a field-day straight across country at full gallop, taking every fence exactly where it came in his path. The moment, in fact, that he was mounted, every suggestion of the amiable lady died an instant death, as anyone can judge for himself by a study of the remarkable statue in Knightsbridge, of which every turn and twist is true to life.

Lord Strathnairn took a great fancy to me, at that time a small boy of some eight summers, and my greatest delight was to be allowed to ride behind him during an inspection of troops.

On one occasion the 92nd Gordon Highlanders had a field-day and inspection in the Phœnix Park. By virtue of the fact that my great-grandmother had been the famous Duchess of Gordon who raised the regiment, I was in the habit of sporting a Gordon tartan kilt alternately with one of Royal Stuart tartan, my right to wear which was based on even more remote family ties. Lord Strathnairn, always full of little kindnesses, had made me, on my eighth birthday, a very handsome present of a silk

Gordon tartan plaid, and, shortly afterwards, invited me to accompany him, in the capacity of supernumerary A.D.C., during his inspection of the famous regiment. Full of delight, mingled with a bursting pride, I mounted my pony in all my new glory, silk plaid, eagle's feathers and all, and, accompanied by a guardian groom, rode out to the Phœnix Park to await the arrival of Lord Strathnairn, who was expected from the direction of the Royal Hospital. Presently he arrived—as usual at full gallop—and I fell in behind him as he trotted down the line. My new silk plaid had a heavy fringe, and, the moment I started trotting, this fringe tickled my pony's quarters so distressingly that he gave them a vicious hoist in the air and shot me clean over his head before the whole regiment. Even to this day I remember the overwhelming sense of shame with which I picked myself up and ignominiously limped on foot down the interminable row of grinning Highlanders.

In his last years Lord Strathnairn became very absent-minded. At one Foreign Office reception which he attended, he asked everyone he knew to dine with him on the following night, and then forgot all about it. Next night, some thirty-seven hungry and expectant people disembarked from various vehicles at the front door of his tiny house in Charles Street. As there were no preparations made and nothing in the house to eat, there was nothing for it but to return the way they had come. The guests immediately concerned were not nearly so amused at the incident as were their friends who heard about it next day.

As may be gathered from the above incident, Lord Strathnairn was particularly fond of entertaining and boasted a very excellent cook. It was not his habit to forget his dinner-parties as he did in the case of his unhappy Foreign Office friends, but he sometimes forgot whether he was dining in his own house or another's. On one occasion, when dining with Lady A., and in a particularly absent-minded mood, he suddenly turned to his hostess and said : " My dear Lady A., I really must apologise to you for this extremely nasty dinner. I cannot imagine what has come over my cook. I have never known her so disgrace herself before."

In the midst of a disconnected jumble of childish memories—memories in which there is no chronological order but occasional very clearly-cut incidents—the Viceregal cricket season of 1867 takes foremost place. It is not the actual ebb and flow, success or failure of the cricket matches that I remember, for in these things I took no interest at the time. My recollection is focused on the flannel-clad figures that these cricket matches brought into prominence. Three of these figures are as clearly photographed in my mind as though the days that I am writing of were the days before yesterday, instead of being nearly sixty years away. The three figures are those of Baby Stewart, R. H. Mitchell and

Charlie Buller. All these three, I remember, wore little pork-pie Zingari caps, with the I.Z. monogram in front, cotton shirts buttoned close up to the neck, and finished off with a little Zingari tie in a bow, and, invariably, a Zingari belt with a snake clasp. A flannel or a silk shirt open at the throat would, in those days, have been considered highly indecorous, nor would anyone appearing without a belt and tie have been considered as fully dressed.

My clearest vision of the Baby Stewart of those days pictures him in the Portico drawing-room at the Viceregal Lodge, singing in his fine tenor voice the solo in the Zingari battle-song, with all the rest of the team joining in the chorus. The I.Z. club of those days was a very small and exclusive affair and its members esteemed themselves highly. It is difficult for any modern cricketer who is entitled to wear the red, black and gold to realise the pride of membership and esprit de corps that filled the breasts of those earlier members. The rule (now wholly disregarded) which forbids the wearing of any rival cricket colours was then rigidly enforced. At the Viceregal Lodge the members of the team used to come down to dinner with a broad red, black and yellow ribbon across their waistcoats, after the fashion of the Garter ribbon.

So Baby Stewart, as I say, sang the solo of the Zingari war-song, looking very young and handsome in spite of his big side whiskers, and the rest of the team stood round in all the glory of the club colours and lustily bellowed the chorus to the tune of the " Red, White and Blue " :

> " So to-night let us pledge our devotion
> 'Neath the folds of the red, black and gold."

Baby Stewart, though a good singer and generally an ornament of Society, was at no time a cricketer of unusual prowess. The giants of the team were R. H. Mitchell and Charlie Buller, and as these two were, at the time, the respective champions of Eton and Harrow, partisan feeling ran very high as to which of the two was the better cricketer. I was, of course, far too young at the time to form any judgment of my own, but I believe neutrals did not hesitate to award the palm to Buller, who was generally reckoned in those days to be only second as a cricketer to young W. G. Grace.

Charlie Buller was one of the most remarkable and certainly one of the most fascinating personalities that have ever flashed across the path of Society. At the time I am writing of he must have been about three or four and twenty, and came nearer than anyone I have met to the lady-killing, man-felling, fictional hero of the Guy Livingstone type. My mental picture of him is very clear. He was considered the handsomest man in England, but I remember that, to my childish mind, whose conception of manly beauty was, I think, mainly based on a portrait of Abednego in one of A.L.O.E.'s books, he was not particularly good-looking. He was about five feet ten in height, with a square massive head, of the Roman Emperor type, covered with curly brown hair. He had a well-cut Roman nose, humorous eyes that were always half-laughing, and a rather womanly mouth. His neck was thick and immensely muscular and his torso that of a Hercules. This massive formation of the head, neck and shoulders gave him, to my mind, a slightly top-heavy appearance, but that he was not top-heavy was proved by his clearing 5 ft. 6 ins. in the high jump at the Harrow School sports. His manner was that of a sleepy cat and his voice a gentle purr. His physical strength was prodigious. All sorts of stories were afloat as to the amazing feats of strength of which he occasionally showed himself capable. I myself have seen him, in later days, twist a kitchen poker about in his hands as though it were a piece of picture-wire. One of his favourite recreations was to put on the gloves with the leading heavy-weight prize-fighters of the day. From what I have been given to understand, the professionals did not derive the same enjoyment from this exercise as Charlie Buller did, for the latter's punch was like the kick of a horse. The ladies were said to go down before him like thistles before a scythe, and he had room in his heart for all. The extraordinary attractiveness of the man, to men no less than women, is evidenced by the fact that his regiment (the 2nd Life Guards) twice paid his debts—a case without a parallel in the history of the Army. His hopeless want of ballast, however, made the end inevitable. He gradually drifted downhill. No excesses seemed able to impair his amazing constitution, but his chronic impecuniosity, coupled with a certain disregard of recognised rules, pushed him by degrees out of the Society that had once raved so wildly over him. He tried his fortunes in many countries, and from time to time would reappear in London, flash like a meteor across the path of his old friends, and vanish again as quickly as he had come. The last time I saw him was at Byfleet shortly before his death. I was playing golf, when a shabby figure suddenly emerged from a thicket and accosted me by name. I had no difficulty in recognising Charlie Buller, the one-time darling of Society. He was much thinner than of old, but still amazingly handsome and full of his old irresistible cheeriness. He told me that, for years past, he had been making a living as a professor of boxing in America, but had been forced to give it up on account of his heart. I asked him to dine with me in London that night, and he accepted the invitation but did not turn up. I guessed the reason. A few months later I heard that he was dead. Few beings have ever lived so bountifully endowed by nature as was Charlie Buller.

CHAPTER III

My father, when he came of age, had inherited,
among other things, Bentley Priory, Stanmore,
where his grandfather had dispensed princely
hospitality to William Pitt and all the *fin de siècle*
bucks of the eighteenth century. This great-
grandfather of mine—known in the family as the
" Old Marquis "—is deserving of a word of notice.
He was an extremely good-looking man and
highly esteemed by Pitt for his mental attainments, but he had a leaning towards an ostentati-
ous display of magnificence, which, in these days,
would be thought both vulgar and ridiculous.
The housemaids who made his bed had to wear
kid gloves, and the footmen had to dip their
hands in a bowl of rose-water before handing him
a dish.   His second wife had to be ennobled by
Pitt before he would condescend to marry her.
Both at the Priory and at Hampden House, Green
Street, he entertained in the most sumptuous
and extravagant fashion.   On one occasion, at
a reception at the London house, the guests on
arrival found him surrounded by a bodyguard of
young ladies of fashion all clad alike in classical
costume, and so scantily that some of the guests
fairly gasped.   Each wore on her breast a band

on which were inscribed the three letters I.H.P. Speculation was rife as to what these letters might signify. Finally it transpired that they stood for *In honore Prioris*, the Prior, of course, being the Old Marquis. One of the aforesaid damsels—Lady C. B.—was asked by a friend if she was really as naked as she appeared to be. " Yes," replied the maiden, with candid simplicity, " I really am."

The personal adventures of the Old Marquis were many and varied. The particular adventure by which he became possessed of a single diamond of great size and beauty, which is still in the family, has been so often recounted that there is no need to repeat it here.

With the opening of the new century, Nemesis began to overtake this votary of pleasure, and the house of laughter and frivolity became the house of mourning. The Old Marquis had married, as his first wife, the beautiful daughter of Sir Joseph Copley of Sprottborough, Yorkshire. This lady, after presenting him with six children in quick succession, died of consumption. In 1803, Harriet, the eldest of the daughters, a handsome girl with bright brown hair and a brilliant complexion, who was engaged to the third Marquis of Lansdowne, succumbed to the same disease at the age of nineteen. Five years later, Claud, the second son, a brilliant and athletic youth, followed in his sister's footsteps. Catherine, the second daughter and the most beautiful of a beautiful family, had, at a very early age, married the great Lord Aberdeen. Sir Thomas Lawrence has left us two portraits of this girl, taken at different ages. She had raven locks, slumberous laughing eyes, a very winning expression—which in the later portrait has given way to a fixed look of tragedy—and the fatal brilliancy of colouring for which all the family were remarkable. She died four years after Claud, leaving three daughters. Only Lord Hamilton, the eldest son, and Maria, the youngest of the family, were now left, for the first Lady Catherine had died in infancy. Maria, according to Lawrence's two portraits, was a lovely girl with a bright sunny face, and auburn curls falling over her shoulders. She was the Old Marquis' favourite child, and, as the others passed away, his love for his last-born seems to have become so intense that he had little other thought in the world. His letters at this period are most pathetic reading, showing, as they do, the agony with which he watched over this young girl's health from day to day. So far she had shown no signs of the disease, and everything that money and the medical science of the day could do was brought up into line to fight for her life. It was all of no avail. The doctors of the day believed that the night air was poison and recommended their patients to sleep with closed windows, nightcaps on and curtains drawn round their four-post beds. Death could have asked for no better auxiliary force. Maria died a year and a half after her brother, at the age of eighteen, and was followed to the grave four months later by the eldest son, Lord Hamilton.

LADY CATHERINE HAMILTON.

The whole generation had now been wiped out by consumption in the short space of eleven years, and the Old Marquis, a broken-hearted and desolate man, never held his head up again. He joined his family in the churchyard at Stanmore four years later.

Unfortunately the Copley curse was not yet dead. Catherine had left three girls, who are described as being so startlingly beautiful that crowds used to collect and follow them on their daily walk from Lord Aberdeen's house in Grosvenor Square to the Park. All three died of consumption before they had reached maturity.

The Hamilton-Copley alliance—disastrous as it had proved in the case above cited—did not end with the marriage of the Old Marquis to the lovely Catherine Copley. The Old Marquis married, as his second wife, his cousin, Cecil Hamilton. He obtained a divorce from this lady, who, curiously enough, subsequently married Sir Joseph Copley, the brother of her predecessor, the first Lady Abercorn. Three children resulted from this marriage, of whom one married the third Earl Grey. All three, however, died childless, so that, for the second time, the Copleys became extinct. The male line had died out in 1719, but the name had been adopted by a brother-in-law named Moyle, who took up his residence at Sprottborough Hall. Moyle-Copley's two children have already been dealt with. The daughter married the Old Marquis, and the son married the Old Marquis' second wife after she had been divorced. Both these collateral lines died completely out in the second generation, with the exception of my father, his brother and his sister, who thus became the sole survivors of the Moyle-Copley blood. The name of Copley has since been added to the name of Watson, but that combination was not perpetuated, and it has now been added to the name of Bewicke.

The extraordinary thing is that, although my grandfather (Lord Hamilton) had died of consumption, and although his mother, his brother, all his sisters and all his nieces had died of consumption, he left three children who showed no trace of the disease. My father, his brother Claud and his sister Harriet all lived to a good ripe old age. Of my father's thirteen children only one developed any symptoms of consumption, and the next generation—a generation of Victorian dimensions—has been wholly immune. It is fairly safe then to assume that the Copley curse is dead.

Lord Aberdeen, the widower of the beautiful Catherine Hamilton, married my father's mother a year after the death of her first husband (Lord Hamilton), and, by this second alliance with the family, became my father's guardian during his long minority.

Lord Aberdeen took up his residence at the Priory, from which my father used at first to walk the six miles to Harrow School and back attired in tight green trousers with brass chains under his boots. Later on, however, he and his brother Claud occupied the house next to " the Park " at Harrow.

Six months after my father came of age—after a minority of fourteen years—he married Lady Louisa Russell and continued for some years to live at the Priory. This delightful place, however, was within easy driving distance of London, and my father's numerous friends found the house so pleasant to stay in, and so difficult to say good-bye to, that, in the end, he was forced, in the interests of self-preservation, to sell the place and migrate elsewhere. All its art treasures were stored in the Pantechnicon till such time as another permanent residence at a safer distance from London had been decided upon. This ideal residence was never found. While it was being sought for, my father found lodging for his family by occupying furnished country houses—first Dale Park, then Brocket, then Beaudesert, and lastly Eastwell. This last was rented from Lord Winchilsea at the expiration of my father's first term of office in Dublin, and remained our country residence till he returned to Dublin for the second time in 1874.

Eastwell was not appreciated by the adults of the family, but my brother Freddie and I adored it. The vastness of the park, the solitude and silence of its giant beech-woods, and the wonderful variety of its scenery presented us with practically unlimited opportunities for adventure and exploration. For the adults, however, its very vastness was its condemnation. The house stands on the edge of the park, and by no means on the most attractive edge. The one and only road through the park cuts off the thin slice on which the house stands. The rest is out of reach of ordinary mortals. The beautiful stretches of wood, hill and valley at the Chollock end were inaccessible to ladies, and only accessible to men for whom long walks over rough grass had no terrors. There were, and are, no paths.

Distance meant nothing, to my brother and me in those schoolboy days at Eastwell. Our entire time was spent in long exploratory rambles; and yet, so immense is the park that we had not yet fully mastered its geography when we left at the end of five years. The place still holds very cherished memories for us, even though those memories are nearly fifty years old, and twice since we left have my brother and I journeyed down there to revisit those old haunts of our careless, tireless and intensely energetic boyhood. Each visit has tended to confirm our early recollections of the wonderful grandeur and beauty of the northern end of the park. We might also add the testimony of our very adult legs as to its immensity.

So much for our country life. Up to my twelfth year the London season was spent at Chesterfield House, in those days a very imposing residence. The two colonnades, which now jut out so ludicrously at right angles to the corners of the building, at that time ran parallel with the front of the house, or, to put it more accurately, were a continuation of that front and connected it on one side with the laundry, which stood where Lord Leconfield's house now stands, and on the other with the stables, the site of which is now covered by No. 1 and No. 2 South Audley Street. Behind was a big square garden running back to Chesterfield Street, and, for the whole distance between this street and South Audley Street, the garden wall dominated the pavement of Curzon Street. A hundred years earlier, that is to say in 1750, when the house was built, it stood in a wilderness of waste lands. According to a picture of that date by Edwin Eyres, there was nothing in the way of buildings between Chesterfield House and the Park. Stanhope Street, South Audley Street and Hill Street simply did not exist, and Curzon Street was but a row of low huts.

The great delight of our small lives at Chesterfield House were the dinner-parties, when the footmen were dressed up in gorgeous pink uniforms with silver epaulettes, heavy silver aiguilettes, white stockings and powdered hair. These splendid figures were a never-failing source of delight to our eyes, and when we had inspected them all at close quarters and admiringly fingered the dangling aiguilettes, we would take up our position on the big marble staircase, from which point of vantage, if we crouched behind the banisters, we could see the entry of the party into the dining-room without being seen ourselves. None of the guests, however, excited our admiration to the same extent that the footmen did.

As far as I remember, the custom of dressing footmen up in coloured liveries for dinner-parties did not survive the Eighties. Thereafter footmen were degraded to dark knee breeches and coats, and lost much of their picturesqueness. They retained, however, for many years their white stockings and powdered hair.

A Court " Drawing-Room " was even more exciting than a dinner-party, for then the State coach would emerge from the stables in all the glory of its pink-and-silver box trimmings, its pink-and-silver coachman in his three-cornered hat, and its pink-and-silver footmen hanging ludicrously on behind. The acrobatic difficulties of these last two were accentuated by the presence in one hand of a long knob-headed mace after the pattern of a bandmaster's baton.

Another carriage little less exciting than the coach was the " Charriot " (pronounced Charyot). The " Charriot," as I remember it, was a facsimile of the coach, except that it was a coupé with two seats only and a glass front. The other carriages in the stables were the " Clarence," a roomy closed vehicle upholstered in drab cloth which seated four inside; the " Barouche," in which the ladies took their air in the Park; the " Sociable," which to my recollection looked exactly like the Barouche, but which, I believe, boasted some subtle distinction of its own; the " Victoria," and my father's brougham, which was always driven by the second coachman. Landaus had not yet come into vogue in those early days.

FAMILY HISTORY

I think we were very happy at Chesterfield House. We kept green frogs and silkworms, which we fed respectively on flies from the windows and on mulberry leaves from the tree in the garden. The silkworms behaved very well and made lovely little cocoons of silk for us.

In the mornings we rode in Rotten Row (it was considered very bad form in the Sixties to talk of " the Row "), and in the afternoons we played in Hamilton Gardens—generally with the Tankerville children. Twice a week we were instructed in the rudiments of dancing by a lady whom we always addressed as (and whose name we honestly believed to be) Muddy Muddy Lide, which was our nursery-maid's interpretation of Madame Adelaide. She always brought with her two little French girls, with whom we used, most reluctantly, to gyrate round our enormous school-room, while Muddy Muddy Lide sat ponderously twisted round at the piano, and instructed us in raucous tones over her right shoulder :

" *Baisses les épaules, Frédéric. Glisses les pieds, Ernest, au lieu de gigotter comme un saltimbanque. Ah! Mon Dieu! Mon Dieu! Quels petits chameaux!* "

Then my mother would look in through the door and ask, full of smiling pride :

" *Les petits font de progrès, Madame Adélaïde?* "

" *Mais oui, Madame la Duchesse; assurément ils font de progrès. Voyez donc comme ils sont gracieux, tous les deux.* "

I doubt, however, if even a maternal eye could

39

have discerned anything *gracieux* in our ungainly leaps round the room.

The little French girls, as I remember, were perfectly self-possessed, and tried to enliven our exercise with polite conversational remarks to which we, as became uncouth young Anglo-Saxons, replied in half-shy and half-sulky monosyllables. For this lack of gallantry we could not even plead the excuse of unfamiliarity with the language, for, thanks to a succession of French nursery-maids, and a succession of winters spent in the south of France, we could, when we so pleased, gabble the language fluently enough.

We thoroughly enjoyed our rides in Rotten Row—two small boys in kilts accompanied by an immaculate groom named Sam Dyer, whose very pleasant face and manners were unfortunately marred by alcoholic tendencies which eventually led to his downfall. Our joint stud consisted of two Shetland ponies named Poppy and Tommy. Poppy was the pink of respectability and always behaved with decorum, but not so Tommy, who invariably shot his rider off the moment we reached the tan of Rotten Row, after which he would trot sedately back to the great gate of Chesterfield House and there set up a shrill trumpeting till the gate was thrown open to him by old Morley, our corpulent but faithful janitor. I think, in spite of this bad behaviour, that Tommy must have had a lurking sense of decency under his shaggy forelock, for, to the best of my recollection, he never attempted to get rid of either of us till we reached the soft tan. Then either my brother or myself (we took it in turns to ride him) was quickly on his back and Tommy trotted home. We had not far to fall, the tan was soft, and Tommy never trod on us or kicked us, so that, except for the ignominy of it, we did not in the least mind being kicked off.

One summer (I cannot fix the exact date) after cannily weighing the matter backwards and forwards in my mind, I resolved on a desperate plunge, and betted my brother six marbles that I would reach Albert Gate on Tommy's back before he did. After a few minutes of cautious reflection, he closed with the bet, which I am sorry to say remained to the end undecided, as neither of us ever reached Albert Gate on Tommy's back. Tommy saw to that. Finally, Tommy was sold as incorrigible, and for the future we took alternate rides on Poppy, to the general disappointment, I have little doubt, of the frequenters of Rotten Row, to whom the daily excursion of our kilted forms over Tommy's head must have been a familiar and exhilarating sight.

When my father's lease of Chesterfield House was up, Mr. Magniac bought the property for building purposes and we migrated to Hampden House, Green Street, which remained in the occupation of the family for some fifty years. Curiously enough, the house was already associated with the family, for it had been the town residence of my great-grandfather, the " Old Marquis."

In the meantime, while we were being shuttle-cocked about from one hired place to another, Barons Court, our real home in Ulster, wasted its sweetness on the desert air, for it was seldom that the family went near it. The furnished places in England condemned it to a forlorn grass-widow-hood which it was far from deserving.

It was not till 1878—more than sixty years after he had succeeded to the title—that my father was at last persuaded to acknowledge Barons Court as his permanent country residence. By that time he was in his seventieth year, and I think his lifelong dream of " a place in England " had grown faint. He felt himself too old to undertake a serious hunt for another furnished place and, although one or two were visited—including Shillinglee, afterwards the home of my fifth sister—he finally resolved that, for the rest of his life, Barons Court should shelter the family.

In those days, although the gardens, lakes and park at Barons Court were, as in my opinion they still are, unrivalled for peaceful beauty, the house itself was severely bare of all but the very neces-saries of life. Home-made furniture, white-painted and relieved by a green line, was all that many of the bedrooms could boast of. Drugget carpets served in the passages and stairs, and dimity curtains shaded the bedroom windows. At convenient spots in the long intricate passages, huge baize-lined hampers acted as storage depots for peat fuel. It was not till the winter of 1879

42

that the earnest and persistent representations of the whole family prevailed upon my father to beautify the house at Barons Court with the Priory statues, books, pictures and furniture which for so many years had lain hidden in the Pantechnicon.

From that time on Barons Court became not a palace by any means, but a respectably furnished house to which guests might, without shame, be invited to enjoy the very excellent woodcock shooting, and there my father lived the greater part of each year till his death six years later.

It is a curious fact that although my father never unbent towards the people among whom he spent these last years of his life, and invariably treated them *de haut en bas*, he nevertheless inspired them with an unbounded admiration which very nearly approached worship.

" The Deuk's a nice affable kind of a man," I overheard one say of my brother.

" He is that," replied his companion; " but give me the ould Deuk. Sure he'd look at you as though you were the very dirt under his feet."

I might add that the actual phrase used was " ould the Deuk," that being the invariable form of words round Barons Court, the idea being that, as one speaks of old Mr. Brown or old Sir Thomas, so he should speak of old the Duke, or old the Duchess.

The veneration in which my father was held by the country people around almost surpassed belief. One day, some little time after my father's death, three of my brothers and myself paid a visit to an old pensioned retainer who received us with many manifestations of delight.

" Sure," he said, " it's the proud man I am to see so many of ould the Deuk's *ancestors* standing round me this day."

It was quite clear, in spite of the slight mixture of genealogical terms, that our only value in his eyes lay in our relationship to our father.

When the late Duke of Clarence visited my father at Barons Court in 1883, it was found quite impossible to make the people realise that he was superior to my father in rank, or to accord him any of the reverence due to royalty.

" There's but one Deuk," they declared with Unitarian insistence; " there's others may call themselves so, but they're of no account." Shades of Norfolk and Buccleuch !

CHAPTER IV

ALTHOUGH, as I have said in the preceding chapter, Barons Court did not become the permanent family residence till 1878, we used, prior to that date, to pay it occasional flying visits, to which my brother Freddie and I always looked forward with feverish excitement.

It was a far cry to Barons Court in those days, for though the Irish Mail left Euston no later than it does to-day, we did not reach Newtown Stewart till 3.45 the following afternoon, instead of at ten o'clock in the morning, as at present. During the lengthy passage of the Channel, my brother and I were always placed on our backs on the floor of the ladies' saloon, with a red plush bolster under our heads. In this position we complacently chewed ginger-root, while our nurse was heroically sick from pier to pier. We were both immovably good sailors, but I am afraid we took an unholy joy in the sufferings of our fellow-travellers, without the diversion of which we should have found the passage very tedious. So greatly did we look forward to the discomfiture of the other occupants of the ladies' saloon that, the moment the sea came in sight, we would crane our heads out of the train windows and dance with delight if the waves were white-crested. Inhuman little brutes ! I believe, however, that a subtle analysis of our minds would have revealed the fact that vanity at our own immunity, in contrast to the others round us, was at the bottom of our elation. We did not then realise that the majority of passengers are immune, and that it was only because we were housed with the habitual sufferers that we stood out as such heroes. We honestly believed in those days that everyone on the ship was sick except ourselves.

The short journey from Kingstown to Westland Row, the drive across Dublin, and the reception by obsequious gold-capped officials at Amiens Street, were all things of unmixed joy, but then came the interminable journey to Newtown Stewart, which was anything but a thing of joy. We ate cold chicken and drank light claret poured out of wicker-covered bottles into very shaky glasses. My brother and I generally got through a tin of butterscotch as well. But even these pastimes did not materially shorten the endless journey with its long, purposeless waits at squalid little stations. When Omagh was at length reached we were in our own country and all our weariness left us. The brown rushing Mourne and the purple back of Bessie Bell were old friends, only dimly remembered perhaps, but still very friendly and " homey," and they never left us till the picturesque little town of

46

BARONS COURT

Newtown Stewart leaped suddenly into full view as the train emerged from a short tunnel.

The whole of the four-mile drive from the station to the house was vibrant with mild excitement, for the people, the cottages, the fields and even the gates were utterly different from everything we were accustomed to in England. When, however, the carriage plunged from the bleak countryside into the first of the Barons Court woods, and the rabbits were seen scurrying away from the sound of the wheels into the bushes, our excitement passed beyond the mild stage. The climax was reached when the carriage swept round the bend past the entrance lodge, and the placid waters of the Lower Lake could be seen stretching away up the steep wood-choked valley towards the house. Three successive buck-jumps from the carriage followed as we crossed three steeply-bridged burns, and then the round island of Philip McHugh, with its encircling cloud of cawing rooks, hove in sight. All these things, until seen, were but dim memories in our child minds, confused as they were by the quick changes of our nomad existence, but the moment they were sighted they became intensely familiar and filled us with an entrancing sense of home.

On the whole, however, such of our nursery days as were spent at Barons Court were not exciting and have left but a blunt impression. We not only never left the park, but our exercise ground, as far as I remember, never extended beyond the gardens and the adjacent Middle

Lake, so that the greater part of the park was to us, at that age, unexplored ground.

I remember one very hard winter when the Middle Lake was so hard frozen that carts from the home farm crossed it and a huge bonfire was lighted in the centre.

Through that same winter my brother and I lodged and boarded a tortoiseshell butterfly who answered, or was supposed to answer, to the name of " Butty." Butty was first caught in late autumn flapping torpidly on a window-frame, and, in pity of his plight, we built him a very handsome house with our box of wooden bricks. He had a drawing-room and dining-room, with a fine, two-flight staircase leading up to his bedroom. Every evening, before we retired for the night, Butty was helped up the staircase to his bedroom with a pencil, to which he obligingly clung. Next morning we helped him down again to his dining-room, where he had his breakfast of sugar and water. He was not very active, but he lived all through the winter, and when the spring sunshine came, we let him fly away. He must have had some fine tales to tell to the next generation.

Nursery days were followed by days of governess control, and our knowledge of Barons Court became a little more extended, but not by much. The two home farms and our model villages of Letterbin and Ballyrennan were the only places outside the confines of the park proper that our duties or our pleasures ever led us to. The expeditions to the villages had no charm for us, for they were generally of a charitable nature and associated with the carriage of large wicker-covered jam-pots filled with jelly, puddings or soup. The home farms were more interesting, for each boasted a water-race, a mill-wheel and fascinating sluice-gates which could be raised or lowered with most exciting results. We generally left the farms pleasantly wet from head to foot.

On one historic occasion I remember, in those governess days, we made the ascent of Bessie Bell, the mountain which rises behind the house on the east side. The back of the journey was broken by means of " outside " cars, but the last stages, up to the heather-crowned summit, had to be done on foot. I remember that all who took part in the expedition talked for days after as though they had scaled Mount Everest or, at any rate, the Matterhorn, and my pride at having been one of the party was unbounded. As a matter of fact Bessie Bell is a round-topped hill whose summit is only 1400 feet above sea level and 1200 above Barons Court House.

The Bessie Bell episode stood out in those days because it was one of the few occasions on which we left the beaten track of our daily exercise. Victorian governesses were not adventurous. Excursions beyond the margins of gravel highways held vague terrors for them. They meant, for one thing, damp shoes, which were known to be the root of all evil, and torn clothes, which were a scandal to the well-regulated; so off the

E 49

footpaths and high roads we were never allowed
to stray. The lakes, too, at which we looked
from a distance with such longing eyes, had
nameless terrors for our guardians, as being
bottomless pits into which small charges suddenly
disappeared for ever. So these, too, were given
a wide berth. It was only when Harrow life
began, and we experienced that glorious relief
from constant supervision which is the privilege
of the public-school boy, that my brother and I
began to realise the unlimited possibilities for
enjoyment that Barons Court Park offered.
The park is long and narrow and fills the bottom
of a valley, the steep sides of which are thickly
wooded with fine timber. At the south end a
clear brown stream, about six feet wide and one
foot deep, burrows its way into the park under
an arched stone bridge. After a tranquil and
uneventful course of some 500 yards it broadens
out into the Upper Lake, a small but very lovely
piece of water, fringed by yellow reeds with high
woods behind. At the foot of the Upper Lake
are some very massive sluice-gates through which
the clear brown stream, in enhanced volume,
continues its journey towards the sea. It is
by now some ten feet in width, and for half a
mile wends its way through the only flat ground
in the park, passing under three bridges of wood
and stone, and gathering strength as it goes,
till it reaches the Middle Lake. The Middle
Lake (half a mile long) and the Lower Lake
(three-quarters of a mile long) are really one sheet

of water, for they are on the same level, but they are separated by a long narrow channel spanned by a fine stone bridge. The terraced garden runs down from the house to the edge of the Middle Lake, and there, concealed in a large clump of rhododendrons, stands the boat-house, the starting-point of almost all our school-boy expeditions. The boat-house at Barons Court differs from all other private boat-houses that I have seen in that it is high and dry on land and has no boats in it. This is, perhaps, because it is in Ireland. All the boats are on the placid waters of the lake, either moored alongside the miniature wooden pier which juts out from the edge of the bulrushes, or else dancing at anchor some thirty yards out with the wavelets lapping musically against their sides. The boat-house itself has a peculiar and entrancing smell composed, in equal parts, of tar, paint and fish-scales. It contains an untidy but fascinating miscellany of coracles, paddles, landing-nets, fishing-rods, trimmers, eel-pots, bait-cans, etc., which, like Tennyson's stream, go on for ever, while one generation after another of those who use them passes away. The same may be said of the boats. When we were boys, the fleet consisted of three ancient but smartly-painted rowing-boats, two flat-bottomed home-made boats, a sailing-boat (which was never used) known as " Crazy Jane," a canoe and four coracles. Of this curious assortment our favourite, by immeasurable distance, was a roomy craft which bore the

traditional name of " The Ladies' Boat." The
Ladies' Boat was a short tubby boat in which
one could with safety have danced a fandango.
At the same time she was so light, by reason
of extreme age (and rottenness) that she would
skim over the water without any effort on the
part of the rower in any way commensurate
with her size. Her shortness too and her light
draught made her particularly handy for working
up the winding creeks that in places cut through
the reeds, when we were so minded, so that one
may safely say that practically the whole of
our life on the Barons Court lakes was spent
in the Ladies' Boat. This wonderful old boat
was, even in those days, reputed to be sixty
years old, having been built for my father on
Loch Laggan in Inverness-shire; and she is still
going to this day, looking in her annual coat of
oak-grained paint as smart and spruce as the
day she was launched, and gaining every year
in lightness and handiness.

In this old boat, many years ago, my brother
and I first probed the hitherto forbidden mysteries
of the Middle and Lower Lakes. We pushed up
the creeks formed by the confluent burns, through
the long protecting screens of yellow reeds and
bulrushes; we explored the island, with its
ruined castle and historical legends, and we
christened with high-sounding names all the little
landing-piers, formed out of large, loose, flat
stones which my father had caused to be built
here and there about the lakes. We took, in

fact, forcible possession of the lakes, the boats
and boat-house, and of Hugh Gormley, who was
the official guardian of all these things. Most
of our time during the holidays was spent on
the water. We fished for pike to a certain extent
with trimmer and rod, but our main interest
was in exploration and navigation rather than in
sport. After peopling the island and various
parts of the shore with imaginary inhabitants,
we instituted a fast but slightly-irregular mail-
service between the landing-piers afore-mentioned,
each stage having to be covered in a scheduled
time which left little scope for resting on one's
oars. In order to prevent the engines from becoming utterly exhausted under this high pressure
it was always arranged that they and the steering
gear should change places between each stage.
When a strong sou'-wester blew straight down
the lakes, the delivery of mails on the return
journey was indefinitely postponed, for our practice was to leave the boat at the foot of the Lower
Lake till the wind changed, or for poor Gormley
to row laboriously back against wind and wave.

Occasionally the engine and steering departments failed to work in harmony, and, when this
happened, there was a temporary dislocation
of the mail-service. On one occasion, as the
result of a difference of opinion between the two
departments, a short but lively naval engagement
took place on the Lower Lake, but luckily without
serious casualties to either side. Our most
historic battle, however, occurred one morning

at the boat-house, on dry land. My brother had been running the mail-service by himself, and, having completed the *grand tour* in scheduled time, was proudly approaching the home station. In a desire to help him to manœuvre the boat alongside the little pier, I tried to grapple one of the rowlocks with a boat-hook, but in so doing inadvertently poked the point of the boat-hook through my brother's cheek. In quite unnecessary vexation at this trivial accident he sprang ashore and, seizing a sickle lashed to a pole which was conveniently leaning against a tree, he made a retaliatory sweep at my legs. With a convulsive bound in the air I avoided the blow, and, having thus saved my legs, I made use of them to run with all my powers up to the house, pursued by my bleeding and infuriated brother. Luckily he was hampered by his weapon, whose mission in times of peace was to cut weeds, and I reached the shelter of the house unwounded. Half an hour after we were as good friends as ever, although for many years to come there was hot argument between us as to who had won the battle. He claimed the victory because he had put the opposing force to flight; whereas my argument was that the only casualties were on his side, and that mine was merely a strategic retirement carried out in good order and without loss. The point is still in dispute to this very day.

One of the first and most gratifying discoveries of our enlarged outlook was that no fewer than sixteen burns, great and small, tumbled down to the lower waters of the lakes through the park woods. Some of these burns were full of unsuspected beauties and attractions—rocky pools, waterfalls and so on. The largest and most picturesque was unfortunately afflicted by so offensive a smell that we gave it the name of Cholera Burn. It was some years later before we learned that the cause of the smell was that the burn, in its upper reaches, passes through the precincts of the home farm. All these sixteen burns, each of which had its peculiar characteristics, we got to know by heart. We grew to learn every detail of their windings, their pools, their rapids and their shallows, and in this knowledge believed that we were alone—and probably with justice. Adults do not concern themselves with a minute survey of petty burns. But to us they were a revelation and a ceaseless joy. One of our favourite amusements was to build an artificial dam below some deep pool and then, having amassed a mighty reservoir, to kick the dam away and accompany the released rush of water the whole way down till it became merged in the greater volume below.

Although all the lakes had a charm for us, the Lower Lake was always our favourite. This is an exceptionally beautiful piece of water and with a distinctive character of its own, for, though double the size of the Middle Lake, its waters are much calmer. The thickly-wooded hills which fence it in tend to keep all ruffling breezes from its surface. Only the south-west wind, which blows straight down its length, can raise its waters into waves, and very big waves these sometimes are, crested with foam. But, with all other winds, its waters are like glass, with only the shadow of an occasional squall flitting across its surface.

In late October, when the surrounding woods, reflected in the water, have taken on their autumn tints, the beauty of the Lower Lake has to be seen to be believed. From the round-topped, alder-clad island in the centre, with its faithful reproduction in the glassy water, and from the yellow reeds that fringe the shore to the purple crest of Bessie Bell showing above the tree-tops, everything seems to point to this one spot as the chosen home of eternal peacefulness and beauty.

Barons Court, in our schoolboy days, was an unpretentious place, but I think on that account all the more adored by my brother and myself. We honestly believed that there was no place in the world to compare with it, either in natural beauty or as a playground. We went there very seldom in those days and almost always in the spring, viz. the Easter holidays. The winter climate was considered too damp and the summer climate too stuffy. My dreams of those halcyon days are therefore always associated with the month of April, and with daffodils, primroses, short mossy turf, cawing rooks and baby rabbits. The window of the bedroom I occupied looked out upon a stretch of smooth flat grass to the north of the house, beyond which a long slice of the Lower Lake showed up through a gap in the pine trees. On this stretch of smooth flat grass, in the early morning hours, proud cock pheasants would strut about in the dew below my window and wake me with their enchanting spring crow. Even now the crow of a cock pheasant takes me back with a rush to those far-off days and to the unbelievable gladness that filled my soul when, on the first day of the holidays, I leaned out of my window and sucked in the fresh morning air with its faint flavour of peat smoke. That room is now a changed thing, garnished and swept and decked out with smart trappings. It must always remain a delightful room because of its position and the view that it commands, but, in my eyes, the better part of its glory left it when the white-painted furniture, tartan table-cloth and worn drugget carpet gave way to its present splendour. Boys, I think, are rigidly conservative and bitterly resent the removal of old landmarks with sacred associations. I know we did.

In the halcyon days the garden precincts were enclosed by a four-foot fence of flat pointed palisades, home-made and painted a vivid green. One of the gates through this fence was almost under my window. It opened with a creak and shut with a clang, and it made music to my ears sweeter than any opera, and almost as sweet as the crow of the cock pheasants, or as the more distant call of the water-hens from the edge of the lake. When this fence was replaced by a modern wire fence which took in a great deal more ground, my brother and I felt the blow most keenly. It took us several years to get accustomed to the new fence with its dull, wrought-iron gates which neither creaked nor clanked.

In the matter of boats we were even more conservative. My father bought a brand-new blue boat from the Thames, very smart and very superior, and proudly launched it on the Middle Lake, but, from the very first, my brother and I turned the eye of cold disapproval on it. It was an interloper and we would have none of it. Our old favourites were all painted in grained oak with a green line round. The colour of the new boat was voted a jarring note. It was moored alongside the little wooden pier in a tempting situation, but on the other side of the pier, next the bulrushes, lay the Ladies' Boat, in the berth which had now been hers for thirty years, and, where these two were in rivalry, there could be but one issue. The blue boat's life was a dull one.

In due course came the inevitable break-up. My brother left Harrow and went to France in preparation for the Diplomatic Service, and thenceforward my holidays were spent alone. It was not the same thing. The gingerbread was there but the gilt was off it. I am not ashamed to say that, in all our boyish adventures and enterprises, his was the master mind. He had, of course, the advantage of two years over me, but, altogether apart from this, he had an inventive genius which was never at rest and which, for originality of outlook, I have never known equalled.

All our undertakings were of the most innocent and childish nature, and were never, I think, in any way malicious, but it must be owned that we had little respect for the intrinsic value of property, so long as it suited the purpose for which we required it. I remember, on one occasion, when a south-west gale was blowing, my mother, in hopes of putting dangerous enterprises out of our reach, had ordered the boat-house, which contained all the sails and masts for the rowing-boats, to be locked up. We had no suspicion whatever of why the boat-house had been locked up, but, feeling that it would be a pity to waste such a splendid wind, we wandered up to the house in search of something which would take the place of the regular sails. On a table in one of the lobbies we found a shawl which seemed to have been made specially for the purpose, for it was of very considerable size, wonderfully soft, and so flexible that it was easily knotted round the billiard-cue which we requisitioned to act as mast.

The combination of cue and shawl proved a colossal success. We flew before the wind from the head of the Middle Lake to the foot of the Lower Lake, with the shawl bellying gallantly in the wind and the cue bent like a bow. At the foot of the Lower Lake, as may be supposed, we left the Ladies' Boat, either for the wind to change or for Gormley to bring back, and, with mast and sail in hand, walked proudly back to the house, highly pleased with ourselves. Just opposite the bathing-house we met our mother, who, with a cry of horror, pounced upon our late sail and examined it with anxious eyes for holes. It turned out to be a priceless Rumporchuddah shawl, so marvellously fine that, in spite of its size, it could be passed through a wedding ring. We listened to a recital of its virtues without enthusiasm, and were a good deal surprised that our mother showed little interest when we added a testimonial to the effect that it was the best improvised sail we had yet come across. She took very good care, however, that we should not come across it again.

After my brother Freddie had gone to France, my school holidays, whether spent at Barons Court or elsewhere, took on a different character. Pursuits which had thrilled when there were two of us, lost their zest when I was alone. In self-defence I had to fall back on sport, in which we had so far taken but little interest. By the time I, too, had left Harrow and joined the army, Barons Court had become our permanent residence and all my long leave was spent there, but the golden epoch was closed. The call of the lakes was still very strong, and much of my time was devoted to them, but the official sailings of the Ladies' Boat were necessarily abandoned; partly on account of the loss of dignity which they would have entailed on an officer in H.M. army, but chiefly, I think, because I was alone. I took to prowling about with a gun in search of pigeons, wild-duck or snipe—sometimes alone and sometimes in company with old Taylor, the Scotch head-keeper, than whom no better companion on such expeditions ever lived.

Taylor had a genius for tackling difficult situations which was never at fault and which always excited my admiration. On one occasion, when the snow was lying thick upon the ground, he and I had been shooting some little outlying bogs and strips of wood beyond Crockfad. In the late evening, in a very dim light, a woodcock was flushed from a little gorse covert and flew very low across a field close to a farm-house. I fired at it and missed it, but killed a very fine white goose which I had not noticed in the snow. There were about fifteen geese in the flock, and it was a curious sight to see them form up in a perfect circle round their fallen comrade and, with necks outstretched, " keen " a kind of cackling lament over him. I was greatly distressed over the accident and suggested finding out the market price of the bird and paying for it then and there; but Taylor would have none of it. " We'll just give it the man in a preesent," he said sturdily and, seizing the bird by the neck, strode up to the door of the farm-house. In response to a vigorous knock, the farmer, a man named Davidson, opened the door. " His lordship's compliments," said Taylor, " and he'd be verra pleased if you'd accept a preesent of this fine goose which he has just shot "; with which remark he turned on his heel and walked unconcernedly away, leaving the dead bird in its astonished owner's hand. I never learned whether further restitution was made by the Estate, but the probability is that this was so.

Taylor and I and the second keeper, Porter Adams, used to make long expeditions in search of very small bags, for all the coverts close at hand were of course reserved for the big shoots and closed to my forays. I could never understand why Taylor, who was thirty years older than myself and not unacquainted with rheumatism, showed so little enthusiasm over these long, wet, and rather profitless days. There was a certain beat known as " The Grange," fifteen miles off on the Foyle, which was his pet aversion, as we had to wade all day in wet slosh up to the knees. The place, however, was alive with snipe, and legends of great bags made there in old days filled me with ambitious hopes which over-ruled all poor Taylor's protests.

My hopes were never realised. The first time I went there, snipe rose at every step, but almost invariably well out of shot. A network of footprints in the marshes and many quite fresh cartridge cases strewn about made it quite clear that, though the place was supposed to be strictly preserved, I was by no means the first visitor that year.

" Brogan," I remarked to the local watcher,

as a cloud of snipe rose a hundred yards off, " the snipe seem very wild."

" Ah, well," said the old scoundrel, without a moment's hesitation, " the birds is young yet, and not used to the sound of a gun. If you were to come in a month's time, now, you'd have a far better chance."

" Well," I replied, " if the sound of the gun makes them tame, in a month's time they should certainly lie nearly as well as you do, Brogan."

" They should indeed, my lord," he replied, quite unabashed; but, as a matter of fact, I think my witticism missed its mark, for, though the natives say many things that make one laugh, they are not always quick to take English forms of humour.

When the month of October was reached, we used to go down almost every day to the River Mourne just below its junction with the Derg, three miles from Barons Court. The fishing at that time of year was by no means bad, but the fish which we caught were not good eating, being flabby and dark-coloured owing to the flax-water. Some were almost repulsive in appearance. One of the worst and reddest-looking monsters that I ever saw caught met its fate in the following way. Several of us had been flogging the water all day without the slightest response on the part of the fish. Towards evening, the late Lord Hillingdon (grand-father to the present peer) drove out from Barons Court to see what success we had met with. He found us lazy and despondent, and the rods lying inactive on the bank. As he had never fished for salmon, he was very anxious to try his hand, and we accordingly launched him in the boat with old Alec McBay at the oars. All Lord Hillingdon's previous fishing experiences had been with a worm and float, and, knowing no other way of angling, he dangled the fly in the water with a very short line, exactly as if he were fishing for perch. Smiles of derision had hardly formed on our lips before a large salmon leaped from the water, engulfed the dangling fly and careered gaily with it down the river. The excitement both in the boat and on shore now became intense, and when, after a short but fierce struggle, the fish was finally brought to shore, congratulations were showered on the novice who had so signally put to shame all the expert fishermen.

The fish was a sixteen-pound male fish, bright red and of repulsive appearance. Lord Hillingdon, however, could see nothing that was not beautiful in it and, in the pride of conquest, insisted on packing off his trophy then and there to the clerks in his London bank, who, as in duty bound, ate it and were, I believe, very ill for many days after.

The two watchers on the river at that time were Alec McBay and Paddy McAnany. What Alec McBay's real name was—whether Macbeth or McVeagh—I have never learned. Probably it was Macbeth, for McVeagh is an essentially

Catholic name and Alec was a devout Orangeman; but McBay was the name by which he was known and the name to which he answered. McBay's house stood just above the pool known as " The Feddens," and his housekeeping was done for him by his two young daughters—very decent and respectable-looking girls, but with a startling vocabulary at their command. One day I caught a very big fish in the Feddens, which was laid out for admiration on the turf just below McBay's house. Presently out came the two girls, and for some minutes they contemplated the fish in silence. At last the elder one spoke.

" Well, if that's not the biggest ould thief I've seen pulled out of the Feddens for many a long day," she remarked calmly; only " thief " was not the word she used.

" He is that," the younger sister agreed, " and he's well out of that, anyway, the ould thief "; only, once again, the word used was not " thief."

After these few preliminary remarks, the two sisters fairly let themselves go, and my astonished ears were assailed by such a string of terms impeaching the dead fish's morals and ancestry as I had certainly never, up to that time, associated with maiden lips. The extreme respectability in manner and appearance of the two damsels and their calm demeanour throughout increased the amazement with which I listened to this unprovoked outburst.

The practice of showering abuse upon the victim of one's gun or one's rod is a common one in Ireland and is, I believe, intended as a slanting compliment to the sportsman. The greater the villainies which can be attributed to a dead grouse or a dead salmon, the greater the glory of the hero who has slain him.

Paddy McAnany was, of course, a Roman Catholic, as his name indicates, but he and Alec McBay, in spite of religious and political differences, were in reality very staunch friends. Occasionally, however, they would indulge in a little good-humoured banter on the subject of their differences.

" I know right well what an Orange meeting is," Paddy said to the other one day; " you all sit drinking round a table and shout ' To hell with the Pope ' till you're all so drunk you can't shout any more, and then the devil comes along and wheels you all home in his barrow."

" And that's no more than the truth," Alec said, laughing, " and 'twas only the other night, as he was wheeling me home, that he whispered in my ear what good friends you and he was, Paddy, and of the snug place he's keeping for you down there."

" Well, I wouldn't wish to be parted from you, Alec, anyway," Paddy retorted gravely.

The rest of us never touched upon the subject of politics with our various Roman Catholic henchmen, nor, at election times, did we ever canvass them. I believe they all voted against us, nor indeed did they ever make open pretence of doing otherwise; but we thought none the worse of them on that account, knowing the extreme difficulty of the position in which they found themselves. Dan Devine, our native coachman, would invariably wave his whip in the air and shout " Hamilton for ever," in tones of the utmost enthusiasm, when driving me through a Protestant village at election times, but I have little doubt that he always voted against me.

Paddy McAnany was my most devoted adherent in all matters of sport, and I verily believe would have done anything in the world for me, except vote for me. Long after Barons Court had ceased to be my home, and long after I had ceased to represent North Tyrone in Parliament, I went over to Ireland on one occasion to vote for Mr. Emerson Herdman, the Unionist candidate. After making my cross, I returned by train from Strabane to Newtown Stewart, and at Victoria Bridge Station I saw my old friend Paddy McAnany get out of the train, looking a good deal aged from when I last saw him. I called to him, and we greeted one another warmly and with mutual pleasure. After the usual inquiries as to each other's welfare, and just as the train was moving off, some imp of mischief prompted me to say, " Paddy, you old villain, you know you voted all wrong." The moment the words were out of my mouth I regretted them, for the look of distress on poor Paddy's face told only too plainly that my shot had gone home. He was a man of few words and with no skill at all in lying, so he simply remained silent and looked sheepish. I reproached myself, not only for the rest of that day, but for many days to come, with having broken our hard-and-fast rule of never touching on the subject of politics, and what made me do it on this occasion I really can't say; but I can say this: that had I in the smallest degree foreseen the serious fashion in which Paddy would take what I only intended for chaff, I would have gone far before putting him to such embarrassment. I never saw him again. Shortly afterwards he had a stroke and, a year later, he died. He was a good fellow and a staunch friend, and could tie a fly as well as any man in Ireland.

One of our Roman Catholic retainers who undoubtedly did vote for the family, for he proclaimed his vote openly, was an under-keeper locally known as Chairlie Morrison. His real name was Charlie McPatrick Morris, being as he was the son of one Pat Morris, but as Chairlie Morrison he lived and as Chairlie Morrison he died. His death was universally attributed by those of his own faith in the district to the fact that he had voted as he did, for his action was very adversely commented on in the Draguish Chapel on the Sunday following the poll. His death six months later left no doubt in the minds of any of those who had been present in the chapel when his conduct was denounced that the wrath of Heaven had overtaken poor Chairlie Morrison for his impious action in voting for the Unionist candidate.

The beaters at our woodcock shoots in the winter were fairly equally divided as to religion and were all pretty good friends. In peace time, that is to say, when war was not being waged against the woodcock, they were foresters, and some of them were very fond of airing their technical knowledge when the opportunity offered.

"Did you see that woodcock down, Montgomery?" one would ask.

"I did, my lord; she's down just beyond the Picea Pectinata yonder." Next time it would be behind the Abies Nordmanniana.

There were three of these Montgomerys among the beaters, all very handsome fellows and of aristocratic descent, for their family had at one time been big landed proprietors, and they were no doubt direct descendants of old Sir Hugh Montgomery, who was one of the pioneers of the invasion of Ulster from Scotland. The eldest of the three had a wonderfully poetical vocabulary, and would sometimes give the most surprising replies to simple questions.

"Did that hen pheasant fall, Montgomery?" one of my brothers asked of him, after he had discharged both barrels at a very high rocketer.

"She did not, my lord," was the reply, in Montgomery's very slow bass tones; "she's away across the lake lamenting of her wounds."

Another of our beaters, named John Dogherty, was overheard one day addressing the following exhortation to a rabbit cowering for concealment under a clump of bracken: "Come out of that,

69

ye cowardly little divil, and show yourself to the jintlemen, and join in the sport." A tremendous whack with a stick followed, and the poor rabbit shortly afterwards "joined in the sport" by turning two complete somersaults and then lying still.

Our woodcock shoots were very good fun, for, although we never made sensational bags, we had a great many different beats, on all of which there was quite enough shooting to be enjoyable. The best bag ever got was ninety-two woodcock on Bessie Bell. Another good day was when four guns, of whom I was one, got eighty-two woodcock at Tavanagh. I was scarcely more than a boy at the time and, as I shot with "passed-on" guns which did not suit me, my contribution to the bag on that occasion was a light one. Had I been up to the standard of the others we should certainly have beaten the Bessie Bell day. The other three guns were Lord Newport, Sir William Hart Dyke and my brother Claud, all very good shots. Nowadays, alas! the woodcock shooting at Barons Court is not what it was. The woods have grown up, the heather undergrowth has died down and the woodcock have passed on elsewhere.

CHAPTER V

THE SEVEN SISTERS

FROM the days of muscular adolescence at Barons Court, I must now make a backward leap to the days of sailor suits, velvet knicker-bockers and kilts.

The first vision which I can clearly focus of our domestic circle and its accessories during this period seems to rest on three sisters at home, one brother at home, four brothers who came and went, and four elderly and semi-phantom sisters to whom were attached old and formidable husbands. They were not, of course, really old, nor even elderly, but to the eye of six everyone over thirty might just as well be eighty for all the claims that they can lay to youth. My eldest sister, who had married Lord Lichfield—after three times refusing the late Duke of Manchester—was, in point of fact, twenty-four years older than I was, and, in consequence, a somewhat awe-inspiring figure to my callow eye. With every year that passed, however, some part of that awe evaporated and was replaced by a corresponding influx of affection, with the result that, by the time I had reached the age of under-standing, the lovableness of my eldest sister's nature had taken complete possession of me, and blown all my childish awe to the winds.

Of all my four shadowy married sisters, my second sister, Lady Durham, was the most shadowy. Although we were very often at Lambton Castle in early days, she was seldom visible, for reasons which may be briefly described as maternal reasons. In my recollection, therefore, she is not very clearly defined, but the impression which remains is that of a very beautiful woman with the face of an angel, which, from all accounts, was an exact reflection of her nature. She died at the age of thirty-five, having had thirteen children in seventeen years. In those days of Mosaical belief, stupendous families were thought to be pleasing to the Almighty and, if human sacrifices are pleasing, it is not to be doubted that they were. My three eldest sisters had thirty-four children between them.

Lambton Castle was a truly joyous place for children on account of its size and its many staircases and intricate passages, and because it was always more or less crowded with people of the proper age, that is to say, between six and sixteen. It was a wonderful place for " hide and seek " and all kindred games. Our favourite game was known as " stag." A yelping and inquisitorial pack set out in search of the hidden stag and, after having found and forced him to break cover, chased him in full cry down the long passages and staircases till he was finally brought to bay. He then became one of the pack, and

72

another stag volunteered for service. When the pack was in full cry, the game, as may be imagined, was not one to soothe invalids or those engaged in literary composition. George Durham [1] would sometimes emerge from his study with hunting-crop in hand, and send some of the pack yelping away in deadly earnest.

The thing of most joy at Lambton was its colossal hall, one hundred and twenty feet long and as high as a cathedral, and, like a cathedral, with a vaulted ceiling, which, either by daylight or lamplight, was full of dim and ghostly shadows. At one end was a huge stained-glass window portraying the family's private dragon, known as the Lambton Worm, and at the other end two galleries connecting with the first and second floors of the house. A vast place it was indeed in those days, and full of mystery and fascination. Now I believe it has been clipped at one end and brought within more reasonable bounds.

One little trivial incident in those early days at Lambton stands out very clearly in my memory. My brother Freddie and I happened to be there on the occasion of our sister's birthday, and, before leaving London, we had provided for the event by spending all our joint capital in buying a present for her. I can see that present now. It was a hideous sham leather arrangement for holding writing-paper and envelopes—mud-brown in colour, covered with gilt scroll-work and with a hard round top—a perfect

[1] George, second Earl of Durham.

73

gem of mid-Victorian monstrosity. We thought it beautiful and, with a view to adding to the shock of delight which would be hers on seeing it, we resorted to a piece of guile. I went first into her room (she was as usual ill in bed) with a little glass tube which imitated the call of a nightingale, and gave it to her as our joint birthday present. On seeing it and hearing it —to my great consternation—she burst into tears, but quickly recovered herself and kissed me, smiling. Then I gave the pre-arranged signal and brother Freddie entered, proudly bearing our hideous London atrocity. " Ah ! but this is our *real* present," we cried exultantly, and watched for signs of stupefaction at its beauty and costliness. She praised it and kissed us again and said it was beautiful, but even we saw that it had failed to touch her as our little penny glass tube had done. We wondered why at the time, but I think I know now. We never saw her again. A few months later the news came to us at Eastwell Park that she was dead. The thirteenth child had proved too much. The grief in and around Lambton was, I believe, such as is very rarely seen. Men, women and children agreed that, if heaven had gained an angel, earth had certainly lost one. George Durham was never again the same man. A chronic gloom settled on him and was reflected in a face so sombre that it used to frighten us as children. Later on we learned to like it.

It is a curious fact that my third sister, Lady

Dalkeith,[1] with whom I became so closely and happily intimate in later years, hardly came into my early life at all. Her home in Scotland was too far away, and her husband an eldest son who had not yet succeeded, and who was therefore not completely his own master, as the others were. With the other sisters, and with their husbands and children, we were in close and constant touch. In the case of the Mount-Edgcumbes, it was at Cannes that we mainly foregathered, for Mount-Edgcumbe itself was almost as inaccessible as Scotland, and it was rarely that we found our way there. Every winter my fourth sister and my mother made the journey to Cannes for the sake of health, and with them went all the Edgcumbe family and such members of our family as were unattached. while at Cannes, the two families were always close neighbours, for Mount-Edgcumbe [2] had a villa near the Croix des Gardes which abutted on the garden of the Bellevue Hotel, where we stayed, and all our days were spent in passing from one house to the other, and in joint expeditions to the beauty spots of the district. The residential part of Cannes was in those far-off days very small indeed, and the country round quite wild and unbuilt over.

While the Edgcumbes shared our winters, it was the Ansons and the Lambtons with whom we were mainly thrown at other seasons of the

[1] Afterwards Duchess of Buccleuch.
[2] William, fourth Earl of Mount-Edgcumbe.

year. With these two allied families it was our
habit to exchange hospitality on a wholesale
scale which even now fills me with wonder when
I look back upon it. Nowadays such invasions
in force as we were in the habit of making on our
" in laws " would of course be utterly out of the
question, and I fancy they must have been
something out of the common even in the days
of which I write. I think the relations between
my father and his two eldest sons-in-law must
have been more brotherly than fatherly. In
any case, we used at regular and not long-divided
intervals to bear down in full family force on
George Durham at Lambton, or on the Ansons
at Shugborough—a party consisting of father,
mother, daughter, maid, valet and two sons—
and remain with them for periods running into
weeks. They in turn would pay us long and
equally comprehensive visits at Beaudesert, Eastwell Park or the Viceregal Lodge, as the case
might be. While at Beaudesert we were, of
course, in very close proximity to the Lichfields
at Shugborough, being, in fact, only separated
from them by eight miles of Cannock Chase, at
that time a lovely expanse of heather, bracken
and moorland, but now, alas! made hideously
profitable by a number of coal-mines. Beaudesert Park touches one end of the Chase and
Shugborough Park the other, so that to ride
across from one house to the other was an easy
and a pleasant undertaking. In the case of
lengthy visits in bulk from one establishment to

the other, the transport of all concerned—
parents, children, servants and luggage—was
effected in the family carriages. The incoming
guests were usually accompanied by a certain
amount of live-stock in the shape of horses and
dogs. I remember that, on one occasion, George
Durham came to Eastwell with three daughters,
nurse, nursery-maid, valet and groom—the latter
being in attendance on the eldest daughter's
pony, which also formed one of the party. As
this formidable cavalcade journeyed the whole
way from Co. Durham to Kent, it may easily be
understood that the visit was not exactly in the
nature of a flying one.

During the course of this particular visit, the
pony above-mentioned was responsible for bringing about my humiliation in the eyes of the whole
Eastwell stable establishment. The pony had a
great reputation in Co. Durham for speed. I
also boasted a pony of about the same size which
also had a great (and deserved) reputation for
speed. And so it came about that one day it was
suggested from some quarter or another, that the
two should have a race across the plain in front
of Eastwell House to the foot of the Reservoir
hill and back. After luncheon the ponies were
brought round and the entire house-party crowded
out under the portico to watch the race; and off
we started. I regret to have to record that I
was shamefully beaten, being completely out-
jockeyed by my niece. The fact was that I had
had it ceaselessly dinned into my ears by my

parents and others that I must not gallop across the Plain (as we called it) on account of the masses of rabbit-holes with which it was perforated; or, at any rate, that, if I did, I was to keep a very sharp look-out for the holes and steer clear of them. So deeply had this most proper and reasonable order sunk into my youthful brain that, during the race in question, I was far more occupied in dodging the rabbit-holes than in getting back first to the house. Bee Pembroke—or Bee Lambton, as she then was— on the other hand, made a straight point for her objective from the very start, and galloped full tilt over all the intervening rabbit-holes, with a happy indifference to possibilities which was little short of heroic. Needless to say, I finished a bad second, and was greeted on my return with derisive and insulting comments. " Fancy being beaten by a girl ! " my groom muttered contemptuously as I dismounted. I am afraid it is not to be denied that I deserved all I got. It happened to come to my ears that the two grooms had a return match while out at exercise one morning, and my pony won. There is no doubt that he had a great turn of speed, for in the Phœnix Park (where there are no rabbit-holes) I used regularly to race him, over short courses, with all the grooms at exercise in the Fifteen Acres, and, as far as I remember, I always won.

The effect of the triple alliance above outlined between the three families of Hamilton, Anson and Lambton—each of which curiously enough, numbered exactly thirteen—was that we grew up more or less as one gigantic family of thirty-nine with a plurality of residences. " Uncle and nephews " relations, of course, at no time came into play. How could they indeed in my own case, with four of my Lambton nephews and two of my Anson nephews older than myself? We were simply a mass of brothers and sisters of varying ages.

I think my father must have had an unusually strong liking for George Durham, for he twice combined with him in renting Arisaig from Mr. Astley. Those were tremendous days indeed, for the two families—parents included—numbered together no less than twenty-nine, and, though naturally the whole number were never all at Arisaig at once, we were a pretty big pack of youngsters, and must have taken a lot of handling and a tremendous lot of feeding. To the best of my recollection, however, there was never the slightest trace of friction arising out of the dual tenancy. Durham had his sailing yacht and my father had his steam yacht, to which each might have retired in the event of relations becoming too strained, but nothing of the sort ever took place. When the two tenants took to their yachts, they did so in close company and in furtherance of some joint expedition.

There was an interval of two years between the first and the second tenancy of Arisaig. On the first occasion we were perhaps too young to appreciate to the full the extraordinary beauty of the place and its surroundings, but we fully appreciated the excitement of getting there and the novelty of the Highland scenery through which we passed. My brother Freddie and I journeyed up from Euston to Kingussie under the escort of our brother Claud, and from there drove the ninety-six miles to Arisaig—fifty-six miles in the mail-coach from Kingussie to Banavie, and the remaining forty miles to Arisaig in a hired wagonette. I was only twelve at the time and my brother fourteen. Seats had been reserved for us on the top of the coach just behind the driver, and, in spite of the ceaseless rain, we lived every moment of the long drive to Banavie. To us it was a lifting of the veil that shut off fairy-land. The bare rock cropping up through the heather and bracken; the wild little black-faced sheep scampering about like dogs in such very different fashion to the stolid old South-downs to which we were used; the leaping, twisting, musical burns, brown in colour, but so wonderfully clear and uncontaminated compared to the sluggish, turgid streams of Kent; the indefinable but intoxicating smell of the moor-land, and, beyond all else, I think, the absence of the proprietary enclosures which, in the south, form such a bar to youthful enterprise, filled us with a spirit of enchantment that was almost too rapturous for verbal expression. We simply sat and drank it all in thirstily. At Loch Laggan Inn we disembarked for luncheon and were fed on pink-fleshed trout fried in breadcrumbs, scones, honey and fresh salt butter. I remember that brother Freddie and I drank large tumblers of milk. We did not like milk, but we thought it rather a sporting thing to do, and the kind lassie who waited pressed it on us. We all sat at a round table, a very small party of not more than seven or eight, among whom were two Glasgow tourists who did not drink milk, but a good deal of yellow liquid which they produced out of their pockets. We thought it was cowslip wine.

The novelty and joy of that meal must have stamped itself for ever on my brain, for the whole scene rises before my eyes as clear-cut as though it were yesterday instead of more than half a century ago.

When we resumed our seats we found the two Glasgow tourists behind us, and in talkative mood. We much enjoyed some of their naïve comments on the strange fauna of the Highlands.

" See, Andra, yon's a har'," said one of them, pointing to a large lop-eared rabbit placidly munching a lettuce outside a cottage door.

" Oh, aye," said Andra in rapt admiration. We laughed over this remark for the best part of an hour, but even funnier to our minds was Andra's exclamation of " Yon's a hee hull " (high hill), when the towering, snow-clad crest of Ben Nevis first came into view over Fort William.

The little Loch Laggan Inn where we fortified ourselves with the Arcadian meal above described stood, and I imagine still stands, on the shore of the loch which faces Ardverikie, where

my father and mother had spent such happy
and eventful days five-and-thirty years before
our joyous drive from Kingussie, and nearly
ninety years before the date at which I write.
My father had been one of the first to invade the
Highlands from the south in pursuit of the red
deer. He and my mother used, at first, to drive
the whole way from London in the family coach.
Later on, as railways developed, they used to go
as far as Edinburgh by train, and from there
complete the journey in the family coach. This
historic conveyance, long since matchwood and
fungus, held six inside, four outside behind the
horses and two in the " dickie " behind. The
luggage was carried in a tarpaulined tank-like
arrangement on the top of the coach, which was
drawn by four horses and postilions. Up certain
very steep gradients, two additional horses,
which had been requisitioned in advance, and
which were waiting in readiness by the roadside,
were attached in front.

My father's guests at Ardverikie and at the
Black Mount, which he afterwards rented from
Lord Dudley, would appear to have been the
victims of an insane and altogether childish
jealousy in the matter of their deer-stalking
achievements. At that time a wholly artificial
glamour surrounded the sport of deer-stalking—
chiefly, of course, because of its far-away character and its novelty as a sport for Southrons. A
subsidiary glamour, which was a reflection of the
other, surrounded the eating of decomposed limbs

82

of venison. These were sent by the proud slayer to friends in England, and, as the journey then occupied some fourteen days, and the season was summer, they naturally arrived in a condition which would have condemned any other form of meat to the pig-tub. As, however, the meat in question was the flesh of the romantic Highland red deer, people ate it with the help of much red-currant jelly and smacked their lips ecstatically over its acrid smell and taste. Even after improved train services permitted of venison reaching its destination within twenty-four hours, many people still thought that it was the right thing to keep it till it had gone bad before eating it.

Let us, however, come back to my father's Highland guests and their idiosyncrasies. The petty jealousies of these, according to my mother's oft-repeated accounts, would seem almost to have passed the bounds of belief. If Lord A. shot a stag with two points more than Lord B.'s stag, the latter would go to bed and not reappear for twenty-four hours. If Lord B.'s stag weighed more than Lord C.'s, any allusion to the fact was taken as a personal insult and treated as such. As may be imagined, where such conditions prevailed, hardly any of the guests were on speaking terms with one another after the first two days of the visit. On one occasion Lord D. actually took his departure in wrath and went all the way back to London because Lord C. had been allotted a better beat for the following day than himself. Landseer, the artist, who was always one of the party, and who learned all his deer-lore while staying with my father, was just as jealous as any of them and, though a notoriously bad shot, expected to be sent out on all the best beats as regularly as the others. The burden on the shoulders of a Highland host in those days must have been heavy indeed!

Personally, I am not ashamed to confess that I have never been able to get up the very smallest enthusiasm over deer-stalking as a sport. My experience, I must admit, has been limited, but it has been sufficient. Three stags only, in fact, have fallen to my aim. The death of my first victim will be described anon. The death of my second victim came about as follows :—

I was staying at Invergarry with that most charming and interesting of hostesses, the late Mrs. Edward Ellice, and, as a matter of course, I was sent out deer-stalking. I walked, crawled, wriggled and slid for a great many hours over very wet and stony ground, in the expectation, presumably, of arriving by these means within shot of a deer. The expectation was not realised. What the plan of campaign in the stalker's mind may have been was not divulged to me, nor did I make inquiries. I was frankly bored by the whole thing. I followed patiently in the wake of the stalker, mechanically adopting the same painful and ignominious attitudes as my leader, but without the faintest idea of what we were trying to do. There was much levelling of tele-

84

scopes and much holding up of wet fingers to gauge the direction of the wind. In fact, there was an impressive display of science combined with a high trial of muscular activity and physical endurance, which lasted from morn till dewy eve, but which did not succeed in bringing me—a mere mechanical death-dealer—within shot of a stag. Eventually we gave up the chase and turned for home. Side by side the stalker and I strode along over the bent and heather, while I listened with reverence to a recital of the extraordinary difficulties of wind and atmosphere that we had had to contend with during our stalk. I gathered from what he told me that there was a kind of fiendish atmospheric combination at work that day which made it practically impossible to get within shooting distance of the wily stag. He lamented the fact that my first essay under his auspices should have been on such an evilly disposed day. A little elementary instruction on the art of deer-stalking followed. In the midst of an animated explanation of the necessity for absolute noiselessness in approaching the antlered quarry, we suddenly walked straight upon a large stag browsing peacefully like a cow within thirty yards of us, but with his back turned. Instinctively we both dropped to the ground and the stalker slipped the rifle into my hand. I waited till the beast turned his side to me and then shot him. It was impossible to miss him.

We walked home with our spirits uplifted, but

I could not help wondering for the rest of the evening why I had been forced to sweep such long, wet stretches of moorland with my waistcoat, when it was very evidently possible for two men in full and animated conversation to walk up to within thirty yards of a stag and shoot it.

I shot another stag at Invergarry two days later. This time I came upon the beast in more conventional style, that is to say, in the posture to which the serpent was condemned in the Garden of Eden, and if I ate no dust it was simply because there was no dust to eat. The persistent Scotch mist took care of that. As the stalker handed me the rifle, I excited his rage and contempt by drawing his attention to a magnificent golden eagle which was poised majestically over our heads. I was much more interested in the eagle than in the stag, but eventually I brought my mind back with an effort to the business in hand and did the needful.

I must now tell the story of my first stag, which is really rather interesting. I was staying with old Lochiel at Achnacarry, but my visit had necessarily to be a short one, as I was due on a certain day to pass on to Glamis Castle. The first three days I devoted to boating and fishing, but on the fourth day it was decreed that I should go in pursuit of the deer. On the fourth day, however, the weather was so abominable that my stalk was put off till the fifth day. The fifth day turned out to be worse than the fourth, and as everyone agreed that such weather could not continue, it was again decided to postpone my stalk. The sixth day was a Saturday and, as I was leaving on the Monday, it was the last day on which I had a chance of killing an Achnacarry stag. Unfortunately, the weather on the sixth day was even worse than on either of the preceding days. It rained in torrents; it blew a gale and it was bitterly cold. Everyone (myself included) agreed that it would be madness to go out on such a day. It was suggested that it might clear after luncheon, and with that hope I had to appear content. After luncheon, however, the weather was worse than ever. Maclaren, the stalker, was in the house, and greatly distressed that my visit was to come to an end without my having got a stag. So distressed, in fact, was he that he suggested that we should go out in spite of the weather and have a try. The other stalker, who was also at the house, ridiculed the idea of anyone getting a stag on such a day, but this only seemed to make Maclaren the keener. I could see that he was desperately anxious for me to go, and more, I think, with the idea of showing him that bad weather had no terrors for me than from any real keenness on my own part, I agreed to do so. I also undoubtedly had a certain amount of curiosity to see how the thing was done, as I had never been out deer-stalking in my life, though, needless to say, I did not give that fact away.

Out we went then, like good King Wenceslas and his page, " through the cruel weather." We walked a good long way and then started crawling. We crawled like worms on our stomachs for about three hundred yards, till we got to the edge of a corrie, and there, below us, about eighty yards away, were two splendid stags and about sixty hinds. They were all very much bunched up, and the stags were, of course, more often than not, screened by passing hinds. "The second stag," Maclaren hissed into my ear, as he passed me the rifle. "Now, tak' your time, man." I was soaked to the very skin; my fingers were like ice, and right into my eyes drove a blinding rain, so heavy that it actually blurred the outlines of the deer. However, I determined to do my best. I levelled the rifle in the direction of the second stag and then proceeded to wriggle my body into the approved position as laid down by the Musketry Instructions at Hythe, where I had recently passed my course. While I was going through this preliminary exercise, to my unspeakable horror, my rifle went off with a terrific explosion which echoed and re-echoed off the surrounding hills. I closed my eyes and groaned aloud. I felt that I must inevitably have killed —or worse still wounded—at least a dozen hinds, the one heinous sin for which there is no forgiveness from owners of deer-forests and their myrmidons. I was roused from my tragic thoughts by a loud exultant yell from Maclaren, whom I saw leaping down the side of the corrie in the direction of the second stag, which lay on its side stone dead !

How it was done I cannot attempt to explain. It was certainly the most amazing fluke that ever fell to the lot of man. But the explanation of why it happened is simple enough. I had borrowed Lochiel's rifle, which had a hair-trigger, as to which he had not warned me. The only rifle I had ever handled was a Martini-Henry carbine with a four-pound pull-off, at which one had to tug till one's finger and thumb ached. It is not surprising then that, under my frozen fingers, a hair-trigger did not wait for that " steady pressure of the finger and thumb, without the slightest motion of the hand, eye or arm, till the spring is released," which the Musketry Manual laid down and which I was preparing to give it.

Needless to say, I kept my own counsel and gave nothing away, either at the moment or later on. Maclaren must have thought me a wonderful shot, for the rifle went off almost before I had got it to my shoulder. Nor did I give away the fact that this was my first stag, for such a confession is usually followed by a bloody and unpleasant ritual which I was anxious to avoid.

I told Lochiel, when I got home, that his rifle suited me very well.

" Oh, I am glad you liked it," he said. " By the way, I ought to have warned you that it's got a hair-trigger. But I suppose Maclaren told you."

" No," I replied, " he did not; but, as a matter of fact, I think I rather like hair-triggers. They seem to suit my style of shooting."

" Evidently," he remarked; " Maclaren says you shoot stags as if they were snipe."

I was sorely tempted to reveal the truth, and if it had only been Lochiel that I had to deal with, I am sure that I should have done so; but I was afraid of lowering myself in the eyes of Maclaren, and so I held my peace. Lochiel would have enjoyed the story, for he had a quaint and caustic sense of humour that saw the comical side of life in weal or woe, and an original way of putting things that was at times highly entertaining. I met him on a certain summer day in London.

" Hulloa, Lochiel! " I said. " What brings you up? "

" You may well ask," he replied irritably. " Well, the fact is they wired to say my mother was dying, and I came all the way up from Achnacarry; and now I find she isn't dying at all. It really is a most infernal nuisance." I knew exactly what he meant, but it was a quaint way of putting it.

No man ever fitted his surroundings more picturesquely than Lochiel fitted into the beautiful Cameron country over which he held sway. He was in every sense the typical Highland chieftain, tall, stalwart, white-bearded and beautifully in keeping with the place. In his kilt he looked like a figure out of a Raeburn canvas.

To come back to the question of deer-stalking, I have always held, and still do hold, the belief that there is no particular art in it, and that all

the difficulties and discomforts of approach to
which one is subjected are part of the official
hocus-pocus of the brawny cateran into whose
hands one is committed. Lord Southesk—one
of the best shots with gun or rifle in the kingdom
—once told me that while deer-stalking on a very
famous forest in the Highlands, he chanced to
look round just after the rifle had been handed to
him, and discovered the stalker in the act of
waving a handkerchief behind his back. Without
a word, he laid the rifle down and walked straight
home.

Some years ago I was at Arisaig in the spring-
time with two of my brothers, and we occasionally
amused ourselves by stalking deer—needless to
say unarmed. Never once did we fail to get
within shooting distance of any stag we had
marked, unless, of course, the lie of the ground
made any attempt at concealment impossible.
It may be urged by stalking enthusiasts that the
spring-time stag is a more confiding beast than
the autumn stag, and this may well be so, but I
still hold to my belief that nothing more than
ordinary precautions and ordinary common-
sense are required.

I have, in my none-too-enthusiastic pursuit of
the stag, strayed somewhat from the homely
topic of my brothers-in-law; so let me return, for
a short run, to the main track. When I was
eleven years old, the noble company of my
brothers-in-law was reinforced by the addition
of Lord Blandford and Lord Lansdowne, who

married my two youngest sisters in Westminster
Abbey on the same day, and so added Blenheim
and Bowood to the list of affiliated houses.
The marriage took place from Chesterfield House
and was, as may be supposed, quite a big function.
The item of chief importance in connection with
it was, in my mind, the presentation to me by
one of the bridegrooms (I think it was Lansdowne) of a set of pink coral studs in a leather
case. Those studs were to me for many years
afterwards the most precious thing that the world
held, and I wore them with pride at the wedding
ceremony in combination with a red Stuart
tartan kilt and a blue waistcoat with silver
buttons, so that my appearance must have been
distinctly on the gaudy side.

After the Westminster Abbey ceremony, my
fifth sister was the only one left at home, and at
home she remained for many years in defiance
of a succession of offers, many of which were
desirable in the extreme from the point of view of
parents. At the time of her refusal of these
suitors, my mother was very far from strong, and
I know that my sister considered it her duty to
stay by her. My mother, however, grew stronger
and stronger with advancing years, and finally
became so active and independent that my sister
felt that her presence was no longer essential,
and she married Lord Winterton. It is pleasant
to be able to record that she lost nothing by her
self-denial in earlier years, for a handsomer or
more devoted and sympathetic husband than

finally armed her down the aisle cannot well be conceived. Winterton, in appearance, manners and tastes, was the beau-ideal of the English country gentleman, and his popularity in West Sussex, and indeed in every district and in every family where he was known, was simply prodigious.

CHAPTER VI

FOLLOWING in the footsteps of my father and all my brothers, I was sent to Harrow at the age of thirteen, and there went through the usual experiences of all small boys on their first arrival at a big school. For the public such experiences have no interest and I have no intention of recording them. One incident, however, of my first year seems to stand out as worthy of mention. At the end of my second term I left Bowen's house, which was a small one, and went into Rendall's. By brother Freddie had already been an inmate of this house for over two years. To those who have only known this brother of mine in after years it may come as a surprise to learn that, at that period of his life, he was of a distinctly silent and seclusive disposition. He had an extraordinarily original and inventive mind, and I think used, while other boys were more frivolously engaged, to ruminate deeply over his creative schemes, either musical, literary or hydraulic. His enterprise in the last-named department was remarkable, and proved destructive of much bedroom furniture in the various houses we occupied. On one occasion the miscarriage of an ambitious scheme cut off the water

supply from the Viceregal Lodge for some days
and flooded the dairy to a depth of three feet.
This, however, is by the way. The particular
enterprise of which I wish to speak was not
hydraulic, but religious and musical.

There was at that time a boy in Rendall's house
named Shifner, who was a great friend of my
brother's and almost his equal in inventive
originality. Shifner and my brother conceived a
craze for carving little idols out of wax candles,
and gradually other boys in the house took up
the idea, and a regular competition started as to
who could produce the best-carved and most
artistic image. These images, when completed,
were about three inches high, and we called
them pocket Baals, heaven only knows why.
Pocket Buddhas would have been a far more
appropriate name, but we knew little of Buddha
in those days, whereas Baal figured prominently
in most of the first lessons on Sundays. We used
to carry these little images about in our pockets
and exhibit them with pride in school, and even
put in a few finishing touches in cases where the
form-master was not too quick-sighted.

To Shifner must be allowed the credit of having
first conceived the idea of enshrining one of these
Baals in a temple of its own. A small empty
packing-case was procured from the butler.
This was placed on its side, the walls were lined
with crimson paper and the ceiling with sky-blue.
A little toy lamp hung down on thin chains from
a tin-tack driven into the ceiling. Baal—by the

somewhat ignominious process of placing a lighted match under his base—was stuck to the floor of the temple, and in front of him stood a beautiful altar made out of twigs from our firewood covered with tin-foil. On the top of the altar was a ham on a dish out of some doll's dinner service.

Shifner had conceived the temple; it remained for my brother to conceive the ritual. My brother was something of a musical genius. He was a brilliant performer on the piano, had a most remarkable knowledge of harmony, and could at any time have made a handsome living as a musical entertainer of the Corney Grain type. In fact, in my humble opinion, he was distinctly superior in that line to either Corney Grain or George Grossmith senior. He now set to work to compose a Baalistic chant worthy of the occasion. We were all at the time a little cracked on the subject of part-singing—a form of exercise greatly encouraged by John Farmer—and, in compliment to this craze, my brother composed a four-part chant which we sang with no little effect while marching round the deal table on which reposed the temple of Baal. The words of the chant were not very illuminating, for they simply consisted of a repetition of the one word " Blog." In fact the word " Blog " was simply a peg on which to hang the tune.

One evening, while we were marching round the table, Shifner as high priest, with the table-cloth over his head and the poker in his hand, and my brother behind decorated with the hearthrug, the door suddenly opened and the head of the house, followed by the five house monitors, stalked into the room, laid violent hands on our temple and bore it away in pompous triumph.

Next evening the whole house was summoned into Pupil Room, where the head of the house made a speech, or at any rate made the beginning of a speech, for he never got beyond the opening sentence.

" I am sorry to find," he began, " that a pernicious practice has taken root in this house—the practice of Baal worship——"

He got no farther. A yell of laughter went up from one end of Pupil Room to the other and continued in varying degrees of intensity till the close of the meeting.

The close of the proceedings, though entertaining in the extreme for the laity, held some painful moments for the Baalistic clergy, for we were each in turn called out and given " six " with a cane by the head of the house, a distressingly muscular youth. Shifner, as " high priest," received ten.

It is extraordinary what foolish acts wellmeaning boys vested with a little authority are capable of. Prior to the unfortunate speech above described, our musical rite had been a most tin-pot affair in which even the boys in the adjoining room took little interest. The Pupil Room tribunal, however, raised us with a jerk into celebrity. Next day we were all objects of popular interest, if not of envy. " How's Baal? "

one grinning boy after another would inquire. " Oh, going strong, thanks," was our invariable and proud reply.

I believe it was John Farmer who was really responsible for our being led away after strange gods, as it was he who had inspired us with the love of part-singing, which was really at the bottom of the whole thing. The Harrow song-books of those days were full of old German and old English folk-songs arranged by John Farmer for four voices, and very effectively, I think, we used to perform these four-part songs—all, alas ! now crowded out of the school repertoire. In addition to these simple songs arranged for four voices after the German fashion, the " School Twenty," as it was called in those days, was occasionally called upon to attack more ambitious harmonised works composed by Farmer himself, as, for instance, his oratorio " Christ and His soldiers," which he produced while I was in the school, and other compositions of that type. These, after due practice, we used to perform at end-of-term concerts, and I think perform them well. At any rate we took an immense pride in our work and acquired thereby a taste for part-singing which has certainly lasted me through life. From present-day concerts at Harrow all part-singing has been eliminated, which I think is a pity, as a dozen songs bawled in unison one after another are apt to be monotonous.

My first term at Harrow was in a small house, and all we small-house boys used to assemble for the fortnightly house-singing in the music school. My first house-singing was a great excitement to me, for I knew I should be tried for my voice, and hoped I might be selected for honours. The first thing I saw when I entered the hall was a cheerful-looking little man in spectacles, with a round, red, perspiring face, who was sitting at the piano playing muffled chords with an abstracted air. This was John Farmer. The moment the door was closed, his abstracted manner left him and he began bouncing up and down on his seat with all the signs of that tremendous energy which was characteristic of him.

" Now then," he cried, " we'll get rid of the new squeakers first." He struck a few tremendous chords on the instrument, wandered away into all sorts of experimental harmonies and modulations, and finally came to a stop with an emphatic bang. " The Three Students," he bellowed, and struck the opening chords of that good old German air. The whole assemblage sang through the five verses, and then Farmer, after consulting a list at his right hand, called out " Atkinson junior." A small apoplectic-looking boy rose reluctantly to his feet.

" Now then, Atkinson junior," Farmer called out encouragingly, " pipe away your best. You must know the tune by this time."

Very slowly and helpfully Farmer played through the tune, while Atkinson junior delivered himself of a series of strangled and inarticulate gurgles.

" Very good," Farmer cried cheerfully. " Now
then, Armstrong minor, let's hear what your idea
of the tune is." This was one of Farmer's standing
jokes.

As we were taken alphabetically, my name
came about half-way down the list, and by the
time I was called upon I had the tune at my
fingers' ends, and, what is more, I liked it.

" Now then, Hamilton junior." I got up,
feeling nervous but pleased, and I certainly sang
with great enjoyment of what I was doing :

> " There came three students from over the Rhine,
> To a certain good hostel they turned them for wine ;
> To a certain good hostel they turned them for wine."

On the second " hostel " there was a good high
note at which I let drive and made a bull's-eye,
so to speak. All Farmer said was " Next verse,"
and when I had finished that, he nodded to me to
continue. So I sang the whole song through,
feeling particularly pleased with myself, especially
during the last verse, which gave scope for the
pathetic stop to be pulled out :

> " Dead art thou, Lizbeth, cold lip and brow ?
> Ah, God ! I learn how I loved thee now ;
> Ah, God ! I learn how I loved thee now."

From that night on, till my voice broke, " The
Three Students " was my allotted song. It was
one of Farmer's customs to allot a particular
song to each boy, and, when such a song had once
been allotted, no other boy in the same house was,
on any account, allowed to sing it as a solo.

HARROW

The chief incident of interest, however, at my first house-singing was not my own squeaky performance, but something of far more lasting and even historical importance. It was, naturally, the first house-singing of the term and, during the holidays, John Farmer had been at work on a new school song with which he was much in love. The moment the last new boy had been dismissed, he turned to the piano with an air of suppressed but ill-concealed excitement and said : "Now I've got something new for you which I want you to learn. You can learn the tune first and then we'll get the words printed for you. I'll sing it through to you." He struck a single chord, which at that time meant nothing to us, but which to-day brings every Harrovian to his feet as surely as the opening notes of the National Anthem. And then, in his rich baritone voice, he sang :

> " Forty years on, when afar and asunder
> Parted are those who are singing to-day,
> When we look back and forgetfully wonder
> What we were like in our work and our play,
> Then it may be there will often come o'er you
> Glimpses of notes like the catch of a song,
> Visions of boyhood will float then before you,
> Echoes of dreamland shall bear them along."

I am thankful to say that the first verdict of the school was unanimous. The song was good. We only carried away with us fragments of tune and scraps of the words, but we were distinctly pleased with John Farmer's lastest effort. It was characteristic of boys that we gave no credit to

101

Edward Bowen for the composition of the words; the tune was all we bothered about. Even I, though the author was my house-master, saw nothing remarkable in the words. Forty years had to pass before full appreciation came; and then appreciation had in it a touch of melancholy.

> " Forty years on, growing older and older,
>   Shorter in wind as in memory long,
> Feeble of foot and rheumatic of shoulder,
>   How will it help you that once you were strong ?
> God give us ' bases ' [1] to guard or beleaguer,
>   Games to play out whether earnest or fun,
> Fights for the fearless and goals for the eager,
>   Twenty and thirty and forty years on."

The combination of Edward Bowen and John Farmer has become little less famous, in its smaller world, than that of Gilbert and Sullivan. Between them, the two Harrow masters—each a genius in his own way—laid the foundation (and the ground and first floors) of that wonderful collection of school songs in the possession of which Harrow is so conspicuously ahead of all rivals. There have been other combinations—notably that of Howson and Eaton Faning—which have produced songs of equal merit. " Here, Sir," and " Five hundred faces " will go down through the ages as two of the greatest school songs ever conceived; but the Bowen and Farmer combination, both for prolificness and for the sustained high level of its work, must always stand pre-eminent.

We used to think Bowen's words a little mad, but they were not mad, only poetically subtle and

---

[1] The Harrow term for goals.

102

wide of the obvious—too wide, in some cases,
for the consumption of boys. "She was a
Shepherdess" and "Fairies" belong to this type
of song—each a gem of beauty in its own way
both as to words and music, but too cryptic for
general popularity. "Good-night," in my humble
opinion the pick of the whole collection, has a
veiled sentimentality which probably appeals
more to Old Harrovians than to members of the
school. It is also too delicate in structure to be
sung in chorus, and so is only available when
some eminent soloist is on the spot. Behind
these few exotics comes the mass of the more
popular school songs with swinging musical tunes
and clever but intelligible words—"Raleigh,"
"October," "Ducker," "Byron," "Queen
Elizabeth," "Giants," "Come, charge your
glasses," and so on. "Forty Years On," however, is, and always will be, the School National
Anthem. It was not until some ten years after
its creation that it finally assumed that position,
and then, not by any general vote or edict, but
by a gradual consensus of opinion that, as a
school song, it stands alone.

In my earlier days at Harrow the two most
conspicuous figures (from the boy's point of view)
were Willie Grenfell, afterwards Lord Desborough,
and Fred Leyland.

Grenfell was the strong boy of the school.
Those who had the misfortune to come in contact
with his stalwart form in the "footer" field
went down before him like so many cornstalks

before the sickle. At all feats of strength he was unrivalled and, as he was also a very fine long-distance runner, and in both elevens, and also near the top of the school, he occupied a place apart in popular estimation.

Fred Leyland was of a different type. Tall and slight with very broad shoulders and a curious rolling walk, he arrested the eye at once, both on account of his good looks and because of the unusual breadth of his shoulders in comparison with the rest of his build. At all games and sports he was *facile princeps*, and was, moreover, a boxer of considerable merit. His most famous exploit in this direction was in connection with the overthrow of the great local pugilist, "Bottles." Harrow in those days was infested with local bullies of the prize-fighting type, whose principal trade lay in extracting money from small boys either by threats or persuasion, and in carrying on an illicit traffic in cast-off clothes. They were a villainous crew, and, of the whole villainous crew the worst and biggest was a man named Ambrose, popularly known as "Bottles," on account of his remarkable drinking capacity.

Bottles was a huge brute weighing sixteen stone and with a tremendous local reputation as one of the past lights of the prize-ring. He was a foul-mouthed bully and the terror not only of the school, but of the whole country-side. The school authorities, after enduring his unpleasant ways in silence for some time, finally resolved upon his excommunication. The School was summoned to the Speech Room, and there Dr. Butler in his clear silvery tones announced to us with much solemnity that " The man Ambrose is out of bounds." The School did not receive the announcement with the same solemnity. We quite understood that public-houses and certain private paths and by-ways were quite fittingly placed " out of bounds," but the idea of a man being out of bounds struck us as being extraordinarily funny and we laughed accordingly. The Head Master was not pleased.

This, however, is all by the way. My real story is about Fred Leyland and Bottles. Leyland and another were walking on the Ducker Road one day when Bottles in his most truculent mood came lurching up from the direction of the nearest public-house, and proceeded to plaster Leyland with all the foulest epithets that his foul mind had at command. Leyland's reply was to hit the huge bully straight between the eyes. A desperate combat ensued, at the end of which the late ornament of the prize-ring was left practically senseless in the ditch by the side of the road. From that day on his dominion fell from him. He was a pricked bubble. Little boys shouted out " Where's Leyland? " and then ran away. The pride of Bottles was broken and Harrow knew him no more. The authorities took no action in the matter. It was no doubt difficult for them to decide whether knocking a man out was, strictly speaking, an infringement of the " out of bounds " edict.

CHAPTER VII

Most of my holidays, since I had first gone to a private school, had been passed at Eastwell, but one memorable summer holiday was spent at Arisaig, a particularly heavenly spot on the west coast of Inverness-shire which my father, in conjunction with my brother-in-law, Lord Durham, rented from Mr. Astley. During the summer term of 1873 my brother and I, to our ecstatic delight, learned that Arisaig had once more been rented and that our summer holidays were to be spent in a spot which was brimful of the delightful memories of our first occupation two years earlier.

In order to avoid the ninety-six miles drive from Kingussie, which in those days was the only way of arriving at Arisaig by land, and also no doubt from a genuine love of the sea, my father bought a fifty-ton steam yacht named the *Nereid*, in which it was arranged that he and my brother Freddie and I should coast up to Arisaig from Greenock. That trip still holds a hallowed niche in my memory.

I was fourteen and my brother sixteen, ages to which sleeplessness, indigestion or fatigue are unknown. The glorious west Highland coast

106

with its intricacy of islands and inlets was virgin
ground to us, and its romantic beauties made an
impression upon us which no time has been able
to efface. A copy of William Black's *Land of
Lorne* was on board the yacht, and the pages of
this charming work tended to strengthen the
impression which daily grew on us that we were
cruising about in a fairy-land. From that time
on, through the ever-mounting decades, the Land
of Lorne has remained for me a cross between
fairy-land and heaven. It comes to me in my
dreams as the one haven to which all storm-
tossed cruisers press and ultimately reach. Once
there, a peace which passes all understanding
takes possession of my sleeping soul. I am happy
with an inexpressible happiness which has no
justification except that I am where I am. The
centresome of this region of happiness is Arisaig.

Arisaig, as may be gathered from the above, is
no ordinary spot. Imagine a long but narrow
arm of the sea with romantic mountain outlines
on both sides, cut out of the sheer jagged rock;
oak and birch scrub tumbling down from the
edge of the bare rock to the very water's edge;
brilliant clumps of bell-heather growing everywhere among the rocks; innumerable islands of
all shapes and sizes; caves without end; trans-
lucent rock-pools teeming with strange forms
of life; wonderful sea-birds unknown to more
southern shores; a tranquil sea patronised by
seals, porpoises and even occasional whales, and
a boathouse containing no fewer than six Thames

rowing-boats in which to investigate all these wonders. What more could any boy's heart desire?

The house itself was large, and we filled it to the brim. Five Lambton boys and the two eldest girls (now Lady Pembroke and the Duchess of Leeds), four Hamilton brothers, my father and mother and George Durham, with their invited guests, left little room to spare.

We were rich in the matter of yachts that summer, for, in addition to the *Nereid*, George Durham had his own yacht, the *Beatrix*, a schooner of 160 tons, and another brother-in-law, Lichfield, who was my father's guest, arrived in his square-rigged yacht, the *Cyclone*, of about the same size.

The *Nereid*, in which we had made our never-to-be-forgotten trip up the coast, was a comfortable and confidential little boat, but as crazy as Bedlam among anything but Lilliputian waves. My father knew her for a bad sea-boat when he bought her, but, none the less, he determined, during our stay at Arisaig, to attempt in her the passage to the Hebrides across the Minch. This trip was destined to bring some of us very near the gates of heaven. We started in fair weather, but when about half-way across the Minch were met by a furious gale from the north-west. The waves ran mountains high, and it was clear that our only chance of ever seeing the Hebrides, or indeed any other land this side of Jordan, lay in keeping the *Nereid's* nose straight to the waves.

For some little while after the bursting of the storm all went well, or, at any rate, nothing went very badly. Then, suddenly, to our horror, we saw the skipper, who had so far been at the wheel, fling himself down on his knees on the deck and commence an impassioned appeal to the Virgin, leaving the wheel to take care of itself and the nose of the vessel to do as it would. The *Nereid* was a small boat and it took my father but three strides to reach the derelict wheel and seize the spokes. For half a minute or so I believe it was touch and go with us, for the boat's bow had fallen perceptibly away from the waves and the lee gunwale was very near under water; but after a few desperate and nerve-racking plunges, she came back to her true course and the imminence of the danger was past. The situation, however, was still sufficiently terrifying, for the *Nereid* had to stand almost on end to climb the giant waves that raced down on her, and when her nose plunged down on the far side, it seemed as though the next wave must inevitably overwhelm her. By this time the two members of the crew had joined the skipper in his impromptu service, and all three rolled about on their knees alternately howling and offering all sorts of strange bribes to the Virgin if she would come to their aid.

Owing either to in-breeding, or the emigration of the fittest, or to the enervating climate in which they live, the natives of west Inverness-shire are a very inferior race to the Aberdonians or even to their brethren in eastern Inverness-shire. Round Arisaig they are almost exclusively Roman Catholics.

To me, a small, drenched and inexperienced boy of fourteen, it seemed that afternoon that the end was only a matter of moments, for nothing is so infectious as panic, and there was ranting and perspiring panic on the deck at my very feet. But terrified as I undoubtedly was (and I am not ashamed to own that I was terrified), I was not so terrified as not to be filled with pride at the sight of my magnificent father as he stood with quivering nostril and flashing eye, gripping in his muscular grasp the controlling spokes, the correct handling of which meant life or death to us. I remember thinking how like one of the Vikings of old he looked, with his erect head and his thick pointed beard flattened upon his chest by the gale.

My father was physically one of the bravest men I have known. In face of most of the dangers that freeze other men's marrow he was utterly fearless. In two spots only was his nerve vulnerable, and they were two very ridiculous spots. He was terrified of a horse and terrified of a dog. But nothing else frightened him. On the occasion of our passage of the Minch, there can be no doubt that his nerve and promptitude saved the lives of all on board. Luckily the engineer, a Lowland Scot named Alison, also kept his head and his nerve, and these two between them pulled us through.

MY FATHER

Of the human element my father had no fear, and, as he was extremely pugnacious by nature, the wonder is that he did not get into serious trouble; for in latter days, forgetful of his advancing years, he was always eager (a little too eager) to administer personal chastisement to any who, in his opinion, outraged the laws of chivalry, even though they were of half his age. In the days of his youth he was a very useful boxer, and a particularly hard hitter owing to an abnormal development of the dorsal muscle behind the shoulder-blade. During his school days at Harrow he fought a memorable and victorious fight against a much bigger boy than himself which lasted for an hour and a quarter in the cloisters under the old Speech Room. As a young man he was very lucky to come successfully out of a rash encounter (of the knight-errant type) with a certain damsel-baiting ogre who turned out to be a professional boxer. It happened in this way. My father saw a blackguard insulting a girl on the beach at Brighton and, true to his instincts, he leaped in hot-headed to the rescue, and almost before he knew it, found himself engaged in furious battle with an assailant who was knocking him all over the place. Finding that he was out-pointed, my father realised that his only chance was to make use of his superior agility. He retreated under a shower of blows and a torrent of invective to where the shingle sloped up steeply. Once he was established on this slope with his face to the sea, the battle was his. His opponent's blows had no force, for the shingle slipped away from under his feet every time he tried to hit, whereas my father got an admirable purchase for the delivery of his downward punches. The professional stuck gamely to it, but by no means could he succeed in manœuvring himself above my father, who was by far the younger and more active man. Finally, his exertions reduced him to breathless impotence and my father was able to hammer him about as he pleased.

When the passage of time had robbed his natural weapons of their old vigour, my father took to the sword as an arm of offence. He always slept with a rapier at his bedside, and, at the slightest hint of burglars downstairs, he would seize this weapon and face the unknown below with a courage which never failed to excite my admiration. His hunts were never successful, which was perhaps just as well, as a rapier is but a poor affair against a revolver.

When I was about fifteen, an incident occurred, at the recollection of which I sometimes laugh still. I was on the point of leaving Hampden House one morning, when on the doorstep I encountered a stranger who was evidently just about to ring the bell. I asked him in a friendly way what I could do for him, and was informed that he wished to see my sister, Lady ——. In response to further inquiries he informed me that his name was Costello. I sent a servant to let my sister know of Mr. Costello's wish to see her, and, while awaiting her reply, I

Photo. Chancellor, Dublin.

JAMES, 1ST DUKE OF ABERCORN.

exchanged civil banalities with the visitor, who
was unctuously polite, but who gave signs, I
fancied, of a certain nervousness. In the midst
of an appreciative remark on the subject of the
recent fine weather, I chanced to look round and,
to my amazement, saw my father advancing with
giant strides down the hall with his bared rapier
grasped menacingly in his right hand. The
entrance hall at Hampden House is a long narrow
room which runs parallel to the street, so that
Mr. Costello, who was nearer the street than I
was, had no intimation of the approaching storm
till the threatening figure of my father suddenly
filled the doorway and rudely cut short his pre-
diction that rain might be expected before night.
In the twinkling of an eye my friendly conversa-
tionalist was running down the street as though
all the furies of hell were at his heels. My father
stood majestically in the doorway for a minute or
so, like a dog whose antagonist has turned tail, and
then stalked slowly back the way he had come.

It appeared that Costello, who was a Dublin
man, imagined himself in love with my sister,
whom he had never spoken to, but had seen at
some State function. From that day on he had
pestered her with letters of which, of course, she
took not the slightest notice; but he had never
before attempted to address her personally. My
father happened to be in the room when the
servant brought the message announcing the
arrival in the flesh of this persistent but invisible
suitor, and he at once realised that here was the

long-sought-for opportunity for the use of his sword. I may add that Mr. Costello—who, it turned out, was quite mad—did not call again.

When my father went to Dublin for the second time in 1874, he found an outlet for the physical energy which was still so conspicuous in him in the game of cricket—a curious development in a man well over sixty who had so far only a nodding acquaintance with the game. So great was his sudden enthusiasm for cricket that affairs of State had, to a certain extent, to shape themselves so as to meet the requirements of the game. All the A.D.C.'s were selected for their cricket attainments rather than for softer social qualities. Ireland was scoured for cricketing parsons to swell the list of official chaplains. This search was not on the whole a success, but one parson of the name of Byrne was unearthed who was really a very effective bowler.

Another quasi-clerical bowler on the list of honorary chaplains was the late Prof. Mahaffy of universal renown and equal popularity. Mahaffy was the only bowler I ever knew who preferred a wet ball. Rumour had it that, in very dry weather, he had a bucket of water placed where the ordinary bowler has his sawdust. Whether this was really so is to be doubted, but I can testify to the fact that, after rain, he would deliberately roll the ball in the wet grass before each delivery.

Having satisfied himself that his personal staff was well selected, my father, who did nothing by

114

halves, signalised his last year of office by engaging
Wheeler, the crack Leicestershire bat, and Shaw
and Morley, the two famous Nottingham bowlers,
to be at the service of the Viceregal Lodge during
the month of August. Thus equipped, he proceeded to issue challenges on behalf of the Viceregal Lodge team to the Na Shuler, Phœnix and
Leinster clubs—all matches to be played on the
Lodge ground.

During the reigns of less enthusiastic Viceroys,
the custom had been for the Zingari team, which
was housed at the Lodge during its August tour,
to play these Irish clubs. It was a new and
audacious departure for the Lodge itself to challenge such formidable teams, and at first the
challenge was looked upon as a joke. When,
however, it became known that the Viceregal
team included Shaw and Morley, the two best
bowlers in England, it was realised that the joke
would probably be on the other side; and so
indeed it turned out, for the two Nottingham
bowlers proved absolutely irresistible, even to
such redoubtable players as Trotter and Kempster
of Trinity College, and young Willie Hone.

In anticipation of these matches, in which he
always took part, it was my father's habit to
practise regularly at the nets for two hours every
day to the bowling of Wheeler and various
members of the Staff. Curiously enough for a
man who had only taken up cricket when he
was sixty-three, he could play fast bowling very
fairly well. Slows, however, or anything with

a pronounced break, no matter how obvious, utterly defeated him.

The last match of the 1876 season was advertised as Viceregal Lodge and Staff *v.* the Rest. In this match Shaw and Morley had perforce to be included among the Rest, as by no stretch of imagination could they be interpreted as members of the Staff. The result, as may be supposed, was the utter devastation of the Viceregal wickets. When the sixth wicket had fallen for a very inglorious total, a murmur of excitement ran round the ground as my father was seen stalking, bat in hand, out of the dressing tent towards the centre of the ground. The local umpire placed his hand to his mouth and, in an audible whisper, called out : " Whist, boys; it's his Excellency. Bowl saft now." The first over came from Shaw. Alfred Shaw, who bore a marked resemblance to the late King Edward, was, by general consent, the foremost bowler of his day. It was said that, for a bet, he had once pitched six consecutive balls on a half-crown placed ten feet from the far wicket. He could break both ways and vary his pace without any perceptible alteration of his action.

On the momentous occasion in question, Shaw played his part nobly. Four consecutive balls, well pitched up, and just wide of the off stump, were all returned by my father in correct style to mid-off. The last ball of the over was a slow long-hop to leg, off which my father scored a single amidst much loyal applause. He was then called upon to face Morley. Now Morley had about as much idea of " bowling saft " as he had of playing the harp. He was a tall, lithe, athletic young fellow with an utterly expressionless countenance. His style of bowling was to take a short run and then, with his left arm, deliver a bumpy ball, at an appalling pace, straight at the batsman's body. The ball generally broke back six inches and scattered the bails; if it did not, it generally disabled the batsman. Morley seldom bowled through an innings without stretching out some-one on the sward.

On the historical occasion in question, Morley, it must be owned, did his best, which meant that he bowled well up and just wide of the off stump. Try as he would, however, he could not rid his deliveries of that disastrous break back. The Lord-Lieutenant lunged forward in approved style, but he made no allowance for the break, and the first ball went straight into Willie Hone's hands at point. Now Willie Hone was the best field in Ireland. No ball, however hard struck, ever succeeded in evading those two prehensile hands. It was therefore with a gasp of astonish-ment, mingled with relief, that the assembled crowd saw Hone first fumble the ball, then recover it again with a desperate effort, and finally stamp in bitter disappointment as the ball eluded his grasp and fell to earth. Tremendous cheering followed on a realisation of this miraculous escape, and the Lord-Lieutenant once more faced the bowler. Morley, being an absolute machine, delivered once more exactly the same ball as before, with exactly the same result, and once more Willie Hone, after a display of juggling worthy of Cinquevalli, let the ball slip through his fingers to the ground. This time the Lord-Lieutenant's escape was received in thoughtful silence. All might now have been well had Morley been capable of delivering some other form of innocuous ball, but he was not, and once more my father, with exactly the same stroke, played the ball straight into Hone's hands, who, this time, retained it, with a joyful expression of countenance which seemed to say : " Well, thank heaven, I've managed to hold it at last."

My father had not the slightest suspicion of the efforts made by both bowlers and fields to prolong his stay at the wicket, and attributed his failure entirely to Hone's exceptional skill at point.

That year I had been tried several times for the Harrow Eleven, but without success, and another twelve months had to pass before I got my School flannels. But for a happy accident, I might even then have been found wanting. The accident was this. Harrow cricketers of the day were greatly addicted to a straddling " stance," with the legs wide apart and the bat held short, in marked contrast to the Eton style, which was upright with the feet close together. Two notable exponents of the Harrow style were Walter Hadow and A. J. Webbe, both brilliant cricketers, the latter unquestionably the best boy bat of his decade; and, with two such successful examples before my eyes, I felt that I could not do better than follow suit. Boys are essentially imitative. We had no real cricket-coach at Harrow in those days. Old Fred Ponsonby and Bob Grimston took a lot of trouble over our instruction, but no one paid much attention to their advice, for they were both septuagenarians (or, at any rate, we thought they were) and neither had any cricket reputation behind him. Old Bob always wore a tall hat with a flat brim and a strap under the chin, while Fred Ponsonby affected a billy-cock three sizes too big for him. Both were apostles of the stone-wall-defence style of batting and almost shed tears when a boundary was hit. Hartley and Pollard, the two professionals attached to the school, coached us a bit, but they were both old and indolent, and let us go pretty much our own way. What then could a small boy do but imitate his seniors and betters? I accordingly adopted the straddling stance, but with a marked absence of success, for " stone-walling," as it afterwards turned out, was not my *métier* at all.

Among the Viceregal house-party during the cricket season of 1876 was Walter Forbes, the Eton fast bowler, who had captained his school eleven that year and had scored 113 against Harrow at Lord's. This last achievement, coupled with his high reputation as a fast bowler, was quite sufficient for my father, who, staunch Harrovian though he was, could not

resist the temptation of enlisting young Forbes'
services for the Viceregal team. In this way he
and I became fast and abiding friends. To me
came Walter Forbes one day while I was batting
at the nets and said : " Why don't you stand
straight up, hold your bat at the end and make
the most of your height ? " I had no answer to
offer except that it had never occurred to me to
do so. " Well, do it now," he said; and I did,
with results which astonished no one more than
myself.

Some five years later, while playing one day at
Escrick, I chanced to make a good score against
a team which included my late cricket tutor. It
was a very hot day, and Walter Forbes bowled
through most of the innings with his usual untir-
ing energy. When I had passed my century, he
plaintively mopped his perspiring brow and said :
" If I could have foreseen this, Ernest, I should
certainly never have shown you the proper way
to hold your bat."

It is impossible to leave the subject of Walter
Forbes without some reference to his extraordinary throwing powers. Although nearly fifty
years have passed since he threw the cricket ball
132 yards 2 feet in the Eton Sports, that record
has never been broken, nor does it seem likely
that it ever will be. He threw with a very low
arm and, when not out for a big throw, with an
amazingly low trajectory. As a field in the long
country he was unrivalled. From the remotest
corner of the ground, the ball was sent back to

within an inch of the bails with what appeared to be a mere flick of the wrist. The only cricketer I have ever seen who could approach Walter Forbes in rapidity of return is A. P. Chapman, the Cambridge cricketer. Both have very much the same way of picking up the ball and returning it all in one motion. It used to be my great delight to get Walter Forbes to throw stones for my edification. At this exercise he outstripped all competitors even more conspicuously than with the cricket ball. His unusually low delivery had the effect of keeping a thin flat stone absolutely horizontal and with a very low but gradually soaring flight, till it dropped to earth (or water) some 200 yards away—a really beautiful sight to witness.

Although I was the only member of the family to get into the Harrow eleven, my brother George was twelfth man in his year, and in this capacity was indirectly responsible for the loudest burst of hilarity that, in all probability, has ever shaken the confines of Lord's Cricket Ground. People used at that time to drive into the ground and remain seated in their carriages, from which the horses were, of course, withdrawn, and under which hampers of provisions were stored. About one o'clock one day, when the contents of these hampers had been brought to light, my mother turned to the footman in attendance and said: " William, will you find Lord George and tell him luncheon is ready." The footman disappeared and, about a minute later, a roar of delirious laughter went up to heaven from five thousand throats, as a stiff figure in silk stockings, powder and plush was seen slowly making its way across the ground in the direction of "Short slip," to whom he bowed and then returned the way he had come, quite unmoved by the boisterous greetings of the crowd. One of the eleven had been suddenly taken ill and the twelfth man had been unexpectedly called upon to take his place. It was many a day before my unfortunate brother was allowed to forget the incident.

It may come as a surprise to the rising generation to learn that in those days, Harrow was almost always victorious at Lord's. The selection of the team was entirely in the hands of the captain of the eleven, with whose freedom of action no master would have ventured, or even wished, to interfere. The only point aimed at was to get the eleven best players in the school to fight Eton. Now, alas! it is very much otherwise, and Harrow almost always loses.

CHAPTER VIII

By the date of my father's second term of office as Lord-Lieutenant I was old enough to take a certain delight in the pomp and panoply of Viceregal life, and was yet too young to be fully conscious of the strong flavour of Gilbert and Sullivan which lay at the back of it all. I only realised the ludicrous side of the whole thing in later years when I saw others enacting the part of Viceroy. My father had a magnificent presence and a wonderful dignity which was free from the smallest trace of pomposity. He was also the handsomest old man I have ever seen and, with these advantages, was able to carry off a situation which, in less gifted hands, was apt to raise a smile.

Viceregal Lodge life was really very jolly country-house life, with the imitation purple occasionally assumed for State functions. One part of the *menage*, however, which really was worthy of admiration and which, in fact, could compare favourably with any royal equipage, was the stables, presided over by that most delightful of Dublin's permanent officials, Colonel Frank Foster. My father had always affected big black-brown horses, but, naturally, the exigencies of Viceregal life called for many more of these than were required at home. No fewer than twenty-two of these 16.2 black-browns, hardly distinguishable one from the other and all supplied by East of Curzon Street, stood in the Viceregal stables, and it was truly a brave sight to see them parade for some State function. The first two carriages had four horses each, ridden by postilions, while those that followed were drawn by pairs driven by coachmen. Two outriders preceded the leading carriage. The claret-coloured carriages drawn by the big black horses; the heavy silver harness with its Knight of the Garter embossments, and the dark blue and white rosettes at the horses' ears, really formed a most effective spectacle and one of which I never tired. My father's carriage turnout was reputed the best that Dublin had ever seen.

Another department of Viceregal life in which my father was said to excel all rival Lord-Lieutenants was in that of public speaking. His speeches were always short, and were invariably committed to memory, for he had not, I think, any natural fluency of speech. They were perhaps a little grandiloquent, but not more so than was suited to his style and appearance. He spoke very slowly, in sonorous and vibrating tones, standing very upright and pivoting first to right and then to left upon his heels. It was a *tour de force*—wholly artificial, if you please, but none the less tremendously effective in his hands. Imitators beware !

VICEREGAL DAYS

My first lessons in riding over fences were given me in those days with the Ward Union and Kildare hounds. The meets of the Meath were a little out of reach of the Viceregal Lodge except by train. My instructor and guardian, during these hunting expeditions, was one Cassidy, a Dublin horse-breaker, and my instructions were never to jump any fence except in the wake of Cassidy. At these restrictions my youthful spirit chafed, for Cassidy, doubtless weighed down by a sense of his responsibility, was prudence itself, and refused to negotiate any fence which offered exciting possibilities. As though to make up for this enforced restraint, he used to regale me, on the way home, with tales of his desperate exploits in the saddle when not handicapped by the charge of a Viceregal youth. Among other startling feats which he claimed to have performed was the following :—In those days (and possibly still) along the edge of the straight road which runs through the Phœnix Park from the Dublin Gate to the Castleknock Gate was a series of terrific obstacles consisting of horizontal trees fixed on uprights about 4 feet 6 inches from the ground. These obstacles had been built for the purpose of preventing horsemen from galloping along the grass at the edge of the road, and thoroughly well did they fulfil this purpose. Never have I seen one of them jumped, or even attempted, by the most daring riders. Cassidy, however, assured me that, for a bet, he had once jumped the whole series (there must have been thirty or forty of them) from gate to gate. I firmly believed the tale and was for ever urging him to repeat the performance (or even a part of it) for my special edification. Unfortunately, however, the wonderful horse on which he had done the deed was always ailing on the particular day fixed for the exhibition, so that my curiosity remained unsatisfied.

The mention of daring riders in connection with the Viceregal Lodge and the Phœnix Park naturally conjures up memories of Bay Middleton. Bay was not on my father's staff, having been adjudged rather too lively for the post, but he was a perpetual visitor at the Lodge during the cricket season, and always played for the staff by virtue of the fact that he had been A.D.C. to Lord Spencer during the preceding régime. He was a very useful bowler, but his chief value to the team lay in his amazing vitality and his unfailing fund of humour. Under the influence of strong excitement, however, he occasionally became a little unmanageable, which was the reason for his exclusion from my father's staff. He had been trepanned as the result of a bad fall out hunting and, ever after, was subject to moments of pronounced excitability. As he was extremely strong and muscular, and inclined to be a little dangerous when excited, the prudent avoided exciting him. The young and foolish, however, were often tempted to do the opposite, and not infrequently had cause to regret that they had not let sleeping dogs lie.

126

One youth, however, registered so distinct a score over Bay that the story must be told, even though not for the first time.

It was in Lord Spencer's day. Bay was in waiting, and noted with pain that a certain youth was in the habit of appearing in the A.D.C.'s room, after the ladies had retired to bed, in his evening tail-coat, instead of in the orthodox smoking-jacket. In those days men always smoked in special costume, the idea being that the smell of tobacco was so offensive to the fair sex that even the coat of a man who had smoked on the preceding day was contaminated. The older generation even went to the length of crowning themselves with curious be-tasselled velvet caps in order to prevent the nuptial pillow from being desecrated by any of the noxious fumes. Smoking, in fact, in those days, was little removed from a secret vice. Bay Middleton, in deference to these established ideas, pointed out the magnitude of his offence to the erring youth, but without any marked success, for, on the following night, he again appeared in his evening clothes.

" Look here, young fellow," said Bay; " I have warned you once already about coming to the smoking-room in those clothes. If it occurs again, you will be sorry." The youth accepted his rebuke mildly and the party broke up and went to bed. Next night, to everyone's nervous surprise, the offence was once more repeated. " Very well, my young friend," said the now thoroughly aroused Bay; " you have had fair

warning. Now you must pay the penalty."
With these words, he seized the limp and unresist-
ing youth by the collar and deliberately cut the
offending coat to ribbons with a penknife. The
culprit slunk abashed towards the door.

" Good-night, all," he said. " By the way,
Bay, I may as well tell you that it was your own
coat that you've been cutting up. I changed
into it just before I came down."

Bay, who was one of the best fellows in the
world, took the joke in excellent part, and was one
of the first to join in the laugh against himself.

He had the most marvellous control over his
facial muscles. I have seen him stand in a crowd
at race-meetings and other gatherings and, in a
vibrant voice, deliver himself of the most offensive
personal remarks at the expense of his near
neighbours. When these turned round glaring
blood and war, they could find no one on whom
to fix their wrath but a bland-looking gentleman
gazing with vacuous eyes into the distance. It
was clearly impossible to associate the remark
they had overheard with so benign and pre-
occupied a countenance, and so, after a long and
wrathful scrutiny, the insulted one would once
more face to his front, convinced that his ears
must have deceived him.

It is difficult for the present generation to
realise how deadly to feminine organisms the fumes
of tobacco were supposed to be in the Sixties.
Queen Victoria herself headed the crusade against
tobacco, and visitors to Windsor had to smoke

with their heads up the chimney. No one ever smoked after dinner, or indeed in any room except that specially set apart for the purpose, which was usually in the most remote and inaccessible position procurable. At Drumlanrig, in the old days, smokers, having crept down from their rooms, clad in the peculiar livery exacted by the custom of the day, passed through a swing-door leading out of the entrance hall. Here a scarlet band on a white wall guided them down a circular stone staircase. At the foot of this staircase the scarlet band pursued its way through an interminable intricacy of passages, tunnels and swing-doors till, finally, a room at the extreme end of a long projecting wing was reached. Here, and here only, the votaries of tobacco were allowed to emit their deadly fumes. Nowadays, when we see the nostrils of fair ladies shooting forth clouds of smoke in the holy of holies of their grandmothers, and not only surviving, but looking remarkably fresh and pretty, one cannot help wondering whether the horror of tobacco affected by the ladies of the Sixties was wholly genuine.

CHAPTER IX

DRUMLANRIG

DRUMLANRIG CASTLE in the days of Walter
Francis, fifth Duke of Buccleuch and seventh
Duke of Queensberry, was the most princely
establishment in the kingdom. For three months
of the year the Duke and Duchess, with traditional
Scottish hospitality, kept open house. This has
become an expression which is often loosely used
to describe a totally inadequate set of circumstances; but in the case of the Buccleuchs it was
literally true. Anyone and everyone, who was
so inclined, used to invite themselves to Drumlanrig, with all their retinue, and very often with
all their children, and there remain so long as
it suited their convenience. No one was ever
refused or turned away, so long as there was an
empty bedroom in the house. This princely
custom was, as may well be imagined, not only
appreciated but taken full advantage of, and, in
many cases, it was taken advantage of by those
who, had they waited for an invitation, would
have seen but little of the inside of Drumlanrig
Castle. It need scarcely be said that a custom
such as this, splendid though it may be in the
abstract, is sure to be presumed upon by the

mighty army of opportunists, and cannot fail to saddle those responsible for it with many guests who are not of their own choosing and who never would be of their own choosing. The excuse of " no room " was hardly admissible in view of the size of the house, and, besides, any such line of action would have been contrary to the established family principle, which laid down that Drumlanrig had to receive all comers with open arms, whether welcome or otherwise.

If the domestic arrangements of Walter Francis were regal, as one cannot but admit they were, his personal status throughout the Border country was little less so. Partly from tradition connected with the exploits of the " bauld Buccleuch," partly on account of his own impressive personality, but mainly, no doubt, because of his immense possessions, he ranked in his own country as the equal of anyone in the kingdom, whether crowned or uncrowned. " No, not if you were the Duke of Buccleuch himself," became a common expression in cases where an impossibility was asked.

The residential possessions of Walter Francis were not only greater by far than those of any other subject, but were probably greater than those of any crowned head in Europe. In 1878, on the occasion of his jubilee as a landlord, he was presented with an illuminated address signed by no fewer than seven hundred of his tenants in Scotland. To those who are acquainted with the mighty acreage of the Border farms this figure

will convey some idea of the vast extent of his
landed estates. His principal residences in Scotland were Drumlanrig Castle, Dalkeith Palace,
Bowhill Park, Eildon Hall, Langholm Lodge and
Branxholm Hall, the latter being the original
dwelling-place of the Scotts of Buccleuch. Sir
Walter Scott tells us that on the maintenance
and improvement of these places, Charles, fourth
Duke and father of Walter Francis, at one time
employed no fewer than 947 labourers. In
England the Duke's principal country houses
were Boughton House, Beaulieu Abbey, Dunchurch House, Cawston Hall, Ditton House and
a large and beautiful villa on the Thames at
Richmond. This embarrassing accumulation of
country residences had drifted into the possession
of one man through the gradual fusion by marriage of the three ducal houses of Montagu,
Queensberry and Buccleuch. Dunchurch and
Cawston were let and Branxholm was in the
occupation of one of the land agents, but all the
others, as well as Montagu House, Whitehall,
were so kept up as to be ready for occupation by
their owner at any moment. Each of the Scotch
houses was favoured with a certain period of
residence during the year. At the end of the
London season, Langholm was occupied for two
months or so for the grouse shooting. The next
three months were spent at Drumlanrig, and, at
Christmas, the family gathered together at Dalkeith, where they remained till March, when
Bowhill became the family residence till the

DRUMLANRIG

London season began again. Eildon was occupied sporadically during the hunting season, being situated near the kennels of the Duke's hounds. These various places were linked together by estates so vast that it was possible for the Duke to drive from one to the other without being for any great length of time off his own property.

Of the English places, Boughton House, Kettering, was, and is still, the most striking. This house is a miniature Versailles, built for the Duke of Montagu by the same architect, and surrounded—as in Versailles—by star-shaped avenues. It is full of beautiful things. The real emporium of beautiful things, however, is Dalkeith, which contains almost a second Wallace Collection of art treasures. Drumlanrig contains little that is of high artistic value, and yet in the grandeur of its position and surroundings it dwarfs, in my opinion, any other private residence in the kingdom. The late Lord Bath held the same view, and, on the occasion of his first visit to Drumlanrig, told me that, in his opinion, it beat anything in the kingdom for grandeur, not excepting his own beautiful place at Longleat.

Drumlanrig Castle has been described, and aptly described, as standing on a tea-cup inverted in a washing-basin. The Castle itself crowns an abrupt eminence which is, in turn, hedged round by a ring of magnificently shaped mountains some five or six miles distant. The old Duke always spoke of this ring of mountains as the " park wall " and, in honest truth, the description is not altogether inapt. The woods, radiating out in all directions from the Castle, make it difficult to determine when the park proper may be said to end and the open country begin. In the day of Walter Francis there were said to be a hundred miles of grass rides through these woods, all of which were kept mown like lawns.

At the time of my first visit to Drumlanrig, all this splendour left me cold. The young take such things for granted. It is only as years advance that the problem of ways and means presents any live interest and, possibly, excites a wondering admiration. To the youth— and especially the gilded youth—who has so far had to pay for nothing and organise nothing, the crowd of obsequious figures that minister to his daily wants and pleasures are but an essential part of the scheme of nature and excite no more speculation in his mind than the rising of the sun or the budding of the trees in spring. The only item on the daily programme at Drumlanrig that moved me to any wonder was the fruit supply—possibly because, at that early age, I was extremely partial to fruit. Fruit was to me neither forbidden nor unfamiliar. I had, in fact, been used, all my life, to big country houses with their kitchen-gardens attached. At the Viceregal Lodge I had been used to something more, for the garden there is the second largest in the kingdom, but the piles and pyramids of fruit which crowded the dining-room table at

Drumlanrig at every meal were something altogether outside my experience. At the age of
twenty I was particularly fond of fruit and, though
decency demanded a certain restraint in attacking
the aforesaid pyramids, I found consolation at first
for having to tear myself away from some particularly attractive dish of peaches or nectarines,
or some very special brand of grape, in the
thought that I could resume the attack at the
next meal. To my surprise, however, I soon
learned that this was not practicable, for there
was no reappearance of the special brand of
grapes, peaches or nectarines aforesaid. In their
place on the table were new and strange piles of
fruit with which I had no previous acquaintance.
I made timid inquiry and was told that the
custom of the house (no doubt emanating from
the basement) was that no fruit which had once
graced the dining-room table should on any
account make a second appearance there. Under
this strange rule, huge bunches of grapes, with
their symmetry hardly affected by the feeble
assaults of those sitting near them, dived down
into the lower regions after their debut, to be
seen no more. It is clear that a system of
prodigal consumption such as this could not do
otherwise than make stupendous demands on the
Buccleuch fruit supplies. These, however, never
failed to prove fully equal to the demand.
Langholm, Eildon and Bowhill could each boast
large and prolific kitchen-gardens, but the main
sources of supply were, of course, Drumlanrig and

Dalkeith. The latter alone required a permanent staff of forty-two gardeners. The garden at Drumlanrig was even larger, though not favoured by so sunny a climate. It is doubtful whether Walter Francis knew of the unwritten law of the steward's room which made such extravagant demands upon his fruit supplies. It is doubtful whether the knowledge would have interested him in any way. His disposition was towards a happy tolerance of weaknesses and a broad distribution of God's gifts. All home produce was either consumed in the course of ordinary hospitality or given away to charitable institutions. In the case of game this custom entailed ceaseless and munificent gifts controlled by a distributing agency that had no spare time on its hands, as may be judged from the following figures. In 1888 the Buccleuch estates in Scotland produced 7726 grouse, 1121 black game, 2342 partridges, 2961 pheasants and 3639 hares, all of which were either consumed on the premises, or else were given away to farmers, neighbours and hospitals, or sent away to distant friends. Walter Francis was by that time dead, but the custom of the family was still rigidly maintained by William Henry, the sixth Duke, and my sister. Later on, when, under careful management, the grouse and pheasant shooting had been very greatly improved, the numbers killed in a day became so large that there was no alternative but to sell the game or let it go bad. But, even then, the family rule was broken with great reluct-

Photo. W. & D. Downey.

WALTER FRANCIS, 5TH DUKE OF BUCCLEUCH.

ance, and not without, I think, a certain sense of delinquency.

At present, however, we are dealing with the days of Walter Francis. He himself was a curious mixture of the *grand seigneur* and of the simple country squire. He was equally at home with the peasant as with the prince and had only one form of address for both. On grand occasions, when dressed up for the part, he was the beau-ideal of the polished aristocrat. He had a spare but very upright figure, a small square face with little bushy side-whiskers and an invariably humorous and kindly expression. In ordinary domestic life, however, his habits and dress were of the simplest. He always wore a Glengarry bonnet when in Scotland, and, in winter, affected a shepherd's plaid flung across his shoulders in place of an overcoat. On several occasions he was, to his own unbounded delight, mistaken by his own household servants for a shepherd, and accosted as such. On one occasion his own valet made this mistake when passing him in the dusk, and, wishing to be affable, remarked : " Fine evening, Jock." " Oh, aye, it's a' that," replied the Duke.

He took a real delight in the society of his own tenant-farmers, and would sit for any length of time chatting with them on current topics : nor indeed was this taste of his greatly to be wondered at, for the tenant-farmer of the Border counties is a companion in whose society any man may take delight. His fund of general knowledge, his

137

keen appreciative humour and his stock of local
anecdotes are such that it is impossible to be in
his company and not be entertained, in every
sense of the word. Never shall I forget the
wonderful teas which those Dumfriesshire and
Roxburghshire farmers used to provide for us
after shooting. They even now dwell pleasantly
in my memory.

I was very young when I first went to Drumlanrig, having, in fact, only just left Harrow. I
was staying at Langholm with the Dalkeiths and,
having heard much of the wonders of Drumlanrig,
experienced a great wish to see it. I consulted
my host and hostess as to how it could be done.
" Why, write to the Duchess, of course, and say
you are coming," was the reply; " that is what
everyone does."

I followed this advice and at once received a
most cordial reply, begging that I would come
and stay as long as I felt inclined. I arrived and
found the house (as it always was during the last
three months of the year) packed with visitors,
of whom all the males were intent on shooting,
as indeed was I, armed with a new pair of guns.
One of the most outstanding drawbacks of
universal hospitality, in a country house where
there is shooting, is that the host cannot select
his own guns, or, if he does select them, finds
them crowded out by so many self-invited guests
that everyone's pleasure is spoilt. At Drumlanrig
it was by no means uncommon for fifteen or
sixteen guns to assemble after breakfast at the

DRUMLANRIG

top of the red sandstone steps that lead down
from the front door. One and all expected to
be conveyed to the scene of action, with their
loaders and dogs, and, when there, to be provided
with plenty to shoot at. All were gratified of
their wish, for how could any be refused without
a violation of the fundamental principle of the
family—the principle of universal hospitality?
The extent of the shooting-ground was practically
unlimited, but, of necessity, some of it lay at
very great distances and the question of transport
was no light one. It was achieved in those days
by means of big omnibuses with four horses and
postilions. At least four days a week throughout
October, November and December one or two of
such omnibuses would set out from the main
entrance for some distant part of the estate,
packed to their utmost limits with shooting
enthusiasts of all ages from eighteen to eighty.
I have myself, on more occasions than one, been
one of a party of fifteen; but the game-book has
it on record that, on one occasion, no fewer than
twenty-three guns took part in a grouse drive at
Wanlock Head, eleven miles from Drumlanrig!
These over-weighted shooting-parties were, of
course, a nuisance to everyone concerned, but
the only people who never complained were those
who had to provide the entertainment. Others
did grumble freely, forgetting that the fault lay
entirely with themselves, for having pushed themselves in where they were not invited. It is only
fair to add that the grumblers were almost always

old fogies who from long indulgence thought that no one had any right to be there but themselves, and who overlooked the fact that they themselves were open to all the charges which they levelled so freely against the other old fogies.

Over-weighted as these shooting-parties undoubtedly were, and great as were the grumblings, jealousies and mutual hatred of the many old fogies engaged in them, the general atmosphere was one of thorough enjoyment, and luncheon generally succeeded in restoring good humour all round. Not that these shooting-luncheons were by any means in the nature of gastronomic orgies. On the contrary, they were almost Spartan in their simplicity. Abundance of all kind there certainly was, but all of a simple character. It was, is still, and probably always will be a rule in the Scott family that shooting-luncheons should be cold and taken in the open air. No matter how cold or wet it might be, the shelter of a wall and the protection of a game-bag were all that was offered and all that was asked for. The elaborate feasts in tents which King Edward introduced in the south, and which cut so big a slice out of the time available for shooting, found no favour on the Buccleuch estates. The teas, however, in the farm-houses at the end of the day were full compensation for any discomforts of wind or rain. No sooner had we discarded our waterproofs and wrung the rain from our caps than our eyes were gladdened by the sight of piles of scones, baffs and girdle-cakes, flanked by fresh-made butter, heather-honey and a delicious confection known as nub-berry jelly, made from pale red mulberry-shaped berries sometimes called " cloud-berries," owing to their eccentric reluctance to grow at less than a thousand feet above the sea. No matter to what distant corner of the estate the day's sport might have led us, there was always the same sumptuous tea waiting to refresh us after our labours; and while the guid-wife and her daughter plied us with tea and cakes, the farmer would surreptitiously urge the claims of the big decanter standing on the sideboard; nor would he by any means always urge in vain. Why is it that the whisky of the Scottish farmer is so infinitely better than the whisky of the Duke? Or is it only that it tastes better because one is wet and cold and tired? The answer must be left for others. All that I can vouch for is that no whisky has ever tasted to me as the whisky of those hospitable Border farmers tasted.

The rule with the Scotts as to alfresco luncheons out shooting was so inviolable that even when the present King and Queen visited Drumlanrig in October 1899 there was no departure from the recognised custom. Day after day, wet or fine, the King (then Duke of York) would drive ten or twelve miles for the sake of a rough day's blackcock driving (which was the only form of sport that the time of year permitted), and, wet or fine, there was no one of the party who shot so well or who enjoyed himself more, despite small

141

bags, wet weather and cold luncheon under the shelter of a wall.

The Duke and Duchess of York were not, as may be imagined, among the self-invited guests, nor was Arthur James Balfour, who visited Drumlanrig some few years later. Arthur Balfour, who was Prime Minister at the time, was asked to Drumlanrig for the purpose of a big meeting which he was advertised to address at Dumfries. During the previous week Mr. Asquith had delivered an important speech at Dumfries, in the course of which he had, as usual, failed to find merit in any single act or action of the Government during its entire tenure of office. While driving to the Unionist meeting which was designed to act as a counterblast to the other, one of the party said to the Prime Minister :

" Well, Arthur, I suppose you are going to knock holes in all the terrible indictments that Asquith launched against you in his speech last week ? "

" Well," said the Prime Minister calmly, " I hope I may, but the fact is I didn't read his speech. Did he say very dreadful things about me ? "

In reply the other enumerated a number of the scathing charges which Mr. Asquith had levelled against the Government and its leader.

" Ah, thank you," said Arthur Balfour, " I think I shall be able to dispose of those points all right." And there is not the slightest doubt that he did, to the unqualified delight of the

142

DRUMLANRIG

audience of 5000 who heard him. But I could not help wondering what would have been the subject of his speech had our friend not made his chance remark in the motor-car. One thing only is quite certain, and that is that the speech would have been an admirable and telling one whatever the circumstances were, and however suddenly the points to be dealt with had been thrust upon the speaker.

Next day John Bell, the then head-keeper at Drumlanrig, was asked if he had heard Mr. Balfour's speech.

" No," was his unexpected reply; " the fact is I have made it a practice for some years past never to go out after sundown,"—a refreshingly candid admission from a gamekeeper!

John Bell was a fine example of the old Scottish gamekeeper—highly educated, keenly intelligent and meticulously honest. In one particular he stands out vividly in my recollection, viz. as the only man I have ever come across who resolutely refused a proffered tip. I had been shooting at Drumlanrig and, on my departure, presented Bell with the usual tip. Unexpected circumstances brought me back to Drumlanrig a fortnight later, and I had two more days' shooting. Before leaving I extended a sovereign, at sight of which Bell turned his back and thrust both his hands deep into his pockets.

" No," he said, calmly but resolutely, " you gave me plenty before, and I'll take no more."

I persisted, but he was obdurate and finally

143

strode hastily away in the direction of his house, leaving me standing there with my hand foolishly extended. I had, in the end, to send the money by post, and, in reply, received a very appreciative but reproachful letter of thanks.

The extraordinary idea, originated and maintained by Cockney comic papers and Cockney music-halls, that the Scot is a mean fellow to whom the spending of a sixpence is pain, is about as wide of the truth as it is possible for a popular fallacy to reach. In my experience, which is considerable, the Scot, in the matter of generosity, is distinctly ahead of either the English, the Welsh or the Irish; but he is a hater of waste and loves driving a hard bargain. In no section of the British Isles, outside of Scotland, have I come across men of the humbler classes who will do one laborious service without any expectation of reward. I have met that spirit in Western America and Western Canada, but nowhere in the British Isles except in Scotland. The outstanding generosity of the Scot is always in full evidence on the occasion of any national subscription for charitable or patriotic purposes. On such occasions Glasgow's contribution is invariably ahead of that of any other town in the kingdom.

I was at one time, for a year or two, a regular attendant at the Scotch Presbyterian Church in Pont Street. When it so happened that Dr. McLeod was called upon to make a charitable appeal from the pulpit, the response was such as

144

DRUMLANRIG CASTLE.

absolutely to stagger one who was only accustomed to the miserly silver and copper offerings
with which the pious besprinkle the plates in
English churches. It was rare at St. Columba's
to see anything less than gold, while five-pound
notes and cheques rose in such disorderly pro-
fusion from the plate that, in the end, the sub-
stratum of gold was completely hidden. Think
of that, you comic paper artists, who think twice
before putting sixpence in the plate !

I think there can be little doubt that it is the
innate honesty of the Scot which has earned for
him the character of meanness with a certain
class of critic. Conscientious honesty is the most
unpopular attribute that any man can have,
except in the estimation of the immediate circle
that employs him. An unhappily large proportion of mankind, outside the upper ten
thousand, is intrinsically dishonest, and, when
these come in contact with a meticulous honesty
which is outside their understanding, they show
their resentment by plastering it with nasty
names.

A striking example of this very common failing
came under my observation on one occasion when
I was travelling from Jamaica to Colon. At the
same table as myself sat two mining engineers
who were destined for South America on two
totally distinct errands. One was a Scot, whom
I will call Macpherson, and the other was an
Irishman, whom I will call O'Grady. Christmas
Day fell on us during this sea voyage in the

tropics, and at dinner O'Grady called loudly for a bottle of champagne with which to celebrate the occasion.

" Now then, Mac, you have one too," he urged.

" Oh, no," said Macpherson, " I think I'll stick to my usual whisky-and-soda."

Afterwards, on deck, O'Grady commented sarcastically on the modesty of Macpherson's potations. " Fancy that fellow Mac not drinking champagne ! " he said to me; " a regular mean Scotchman, eh ? "

" Well," I replied doubtfully, " who would have paid for the champagne ? "

" Why, the Company that's sending him out, of course," he said.

" And who will pay for yours ? " I asked.

" Why, my Company, of course," he replied, laughing hilariously; " and what's more, it's not the first nor the last bottle they'll pay for by a long way."

CHAPTER X

WHEN Walter Francis, the fifth Duke died, there was no appreciable change in the Buccleuch routine. The Richmond villa was sold, Beaulieu passed to Lord Henry Scott, the second son, afterwards Lord Montagu, and Ditton House went to the Dowager Duchess for her life, and afterwards that too went to Lord Montagu, together with the valuable Clitheroe property in Lancashire. The alienation of these places made no change in the habits of the family. William Henry, the sixth Duke, and my sister continued to tread religiously in the footsteps of their predecessors. Of all the articles of faith which govern the lives of the Scotts of Buccleuch, the first and foremost is a belief in strict adherence to family traditions. Nothing must be done which could in any way offend the shades of past generations. So nothing was changed. Drumlanrig continued to entertain its hosts of self-invited guests with an unabated magnificence. Montagu House, in Whitehall, maintained the same spirit of open hospitality. Every day, throughout the London season, luncheon was provided for all comers. As at Drumlanrig, everyone who chose to walk in was welcome, and very freely did the friends of the family avail themselves of this most sumptuous and convenient custom. The only real change which followed on the death of Walter Francis was an astonishing development in the sporting productiveness of the Buccleuch properties. Walter Dalkeith, the new Duke's eldest son, was full of a boundless energy and a keen enthusiasm for all outdoor games and sports. The shooting at Langholm had for many years lain dormant under the tutelage of an amiable but lethargic Highlander, who preferred ease and anecdote to strenuous work and big bags. Opportunities for ease and anecdote were secured for the old retainer elsewhere and, in collaboration with a new, young and athletic head-keeper, Walter Dalkeith (or Eskdale, as he was then) determined to probe the possibilities of the Langholm moors to their utmost.

In the summer of 1881, before the old Duke's death, my sister wrote to me—at that time a subaltern quartered at Hounslow—asking me to come up to Langholm for a month and shoot grouse. The invitation was unexpected, but, of course, quite irresistible. I knew nothing about shooting grouse; I had never even seen a grouse; to me it was a semi-mythical bird, written about in books and pictured in *Punch* cartoons, but not really existent. However, now it appeared that it was actually to be presented to me in the flesh, and so in due course, in a spirit of delirious exaltation, I took my seat in the Midland express which was to bear me to a land of unknown

wonders and delights. Once Carlisle was passed,
and I had changed into the slow local train which
was to carry me the rest of the way, my eyes
feasted on every yard of this new country with a
consuming interest. When the train left the huge
flat fields of Netherby and burrowed in among
the heather-clad hills, in the midst of which
Langholm lies tucked away, I felt—and with
perfect justice—that a new and hitherto undreamt-
of chapter in my life was being opened. But
not even then did I for one moment anticipate
that, for thirty-five years to come, I would, every
August, with unfailing regularity, make that same
slow crawling journey from Carlisle into those
friendly, familiar and beloved hills that held for
me joys almost too great to be decorously borne,
and certainly far too great to be described. Yet
so it was. Season after season, in response to
an invitation which for thirty-five years never
failed to gladden my expectant eyes, I made my
rejoicing way to Langholm, there to be ever met
with the same warm, boisterous welcome and the
same self-effacing kindness and affection, till
in the end the benty Border hills, with their
towering round crests streaked and flecked with
heather, and fantastically split by precipitous
cleuchs, became for me the most familiar landmarks in the British Isles; Langholm became a
second home to me, and my nephews became more
to me than brothers.

In the first of these thirty-five years, when I
had been deposited, palpitating with excitement,

at the front door of Langholm Lodge, I found myself facing a house of considerable size, but of unpretentious architecture. A hundred yards away the Esk careered musically towards the sea, while on either side a steep-faced mountain rose abruptly to the sky. Woods were on every side, out of which little brown owls were plaintively hooting to the accompaniment of the river. All through that first sleepless night—and for many years to come every first night at Langholm was a sleepless one—these little owls would make pleasant music to me as I lay awake waiting eagerly for the dawn. All too slowly for my eagerness that dawn at length broke; at 7.30 we had breakfast and at nine we were on the moors, walking up the hitherto mythical grouse in military line, and occasionally even laying one low upon the heather. That was the moment of realisation, and it fell but a very little way short of expectation. In fact, I think it is not too much to say that it actually exceeded expectation. There was but one blot on our perfect happiness. We did not succeed in winning the approval of the head-keeper. He was young and energetic, but we were younger and more energetic, and we walked him off his legs, and at the same time missed a good many grouse which we ought not to have missed. His comments were not flattering. When, by happy chance, a bird did fall to our guns, it was retrieved by beautiful but odd-looking dogs which bore no sort of resemblance to any retriever I had ever seen. They were small, with coats like otters, pointed muscular tails and alert intelligent heads, and they galloped where retrievers would have walked. Full of interest and curiosity, I asked what these strange beasts were, and was told that they were Labrador retrievers and the only ones in the kingdom. Labrador retrievers are now familiar objects everywhere, but in those days they were unknown except at Langholm, and it is worthy of note that it was from the two original Langholm Labradors, " Hector " and " Dinah," that the entire modern breed has sprung. For many years Langholm and Drumlanrig enjoyed a monopoly of these beautiful and fascinating dogs; but they then became so numerous that many were given away to friends, and so the breed became distributed about the kingdom. The Buccleuch strain, however, still remains superior to any other, as the best dogs and bitches have never been given away.

As may be gathered from the foregoing confessions, our bags were not of a sensational order. It was only by prodigious efforts of pedestrianism that we were able to amass between thirty and forty brace per day; for it is not to be denied that, though we were good walkers and free shooters, we were very bad hitters. These figures are quite interesting in view of future developments, and as an illustration of how comparatively sterile moors can be made prolific by intelligent treatment.

For six years these annual August gatherings continued to fill us—or, at any rate, one among us—with indescribable happiness. Our shooting gradually improved, but our bags did not advance proportionately, for driving only supplanted the old military line very gradually, and over the dead bodies, so to speak, of the keepers, who opposed the change with every antiquated argument known to ignorance. Walter Dalkeith, however, gradually asserted his will, and experimental lines of butts began to stud the hill-sides and rigs. He himself, with the aid of a pair of new guns which suited him, had developed into a real " class " shot.

Then, in 1886, came the blow which, for the time being, shattered all the happiness of the house of Buccleuch. Walter Dalkeith was killed while deer-stalking at Achnacarry. The accident was a curious one. Dalkeith had just fired at a stag which, as it turned out, he had shot through the heart, but the deer had passed out of his sight, and, in his eagerness to see the result of his shot, he ran down a slope of loose shale, with the rifle still in his hand. His feet slipped and he fell on his back and, in that position, slithered down the incline. The butt of the rifle caught a projecting rock, the rifle was twisted round so that it pointed at his armpit, and the jerk of his finger on the trigger exploded the second barrel. He died within three minutes.

Walter Dalkeith had a most rare and lovable personality. It is quite impossible by the mere use of hackneyed words and phrases to convey any idea of how lovable that personality was, or

Photo. W. & D. Downey.

WILLIAM HENRY, 6TH DUKE OF BUCCLEUCH, AND THE
DUCHESS (LADY LOUISA HAMILTON).

of what it was exactly that endeared him so to all who knew him. Unselfishness, good-humour, simplicity of mind, and that complete absence of anything approaching " side," which is characteristic of all the Scotts of Buccleuch, were perhaps the most conspicuous features in his character. Like all the Scotts of the four generations I have known, he had the faculty of making himself beloved by all classes of society, from the highest to the lowest, and that without any effort or straining after popularity. It is no exaggeration or sentimental figure of speech to say that, when he died, there was general and genuine mourning from the Solway to Edinburgh.

At the time of the deer-stalking tragedy the present Duke was in the navy. He felt his brother's death most acutely, and, for a long while, shrank perceptibly from publicly assuming a position which had been thrust upon him by a tragedy. It accordingly devolved upon George Scott, the next brother, to take temporary charge of the shooting arrangements, and he attacked his subject with an enthusiasm—behind which was real genius—which was destined to effect astonishing changes in the entries in the Langholm game-book. His methods were drastic and revolutionary, and were based on a long and careful study, on each individual moor, of the birds' natural flight. All the old lines of butts, sacred by usage but most unprofitable for purposes of intercepting game, were ruthlessly swept away. New lines were erected in strange and unlikely-looking positions. The family looked on in amused scepticism. The keepers, after publicly prophesying utter disaster, obeyed their orders in a spirit of depressed resignation. All alike looked upon George Scott's innovations as a colossal joke. Those who dared, laughed openly; those who did not, nudged one another and grinned knowingly. After the first experimental drives, however, they laughed and grinned no more. The birds came. Even in the most precipitous and abysmal regions they came, sailing unexpectedly out of the blue straight over the new lines of butts at which so many fingers of scorn had been pointed. Game-book entries soared up by leaps and bounds. The reconstruction of the lines of butts was supplemented by other aids to grouse culture. Heather was systematically burned, boggy bits were surface-drained; a war of extermination was waged against vermin. The grouse responded to these stimulants in a becoming spirit, till entries began to figure in the game-book which were far and away beyond the most imaginative flights of those who had shot under the old dispensation. The climax was reached in 1911. In that year, eight guns, of whom one was a schoolboy with a single 16-bore gun, shot 2523 grouse in seven drives on the Roan Fell, a beat which, in old days, had always been condemned as "completely useless." This wonderful bag might very easily have been increased by 300 brace, had any special efforts been made to establish a record.

No such efforts were made or even suggested. We climbed up to our first line of butts, 1500 feet above the sea, with the idea that, with luck, we might get 500 brace, and our cartridge supply was on those lines. By midday the whole party had run out of cartridges, and a long wait followed while the car was sent back eleven miles to Langholm for a fresh supply. When this arrived, we recommenced operations and shot till about five, when Henry Scott, who was in charge of the party, said that he thought we had shot enough and gave the word for home. Anything in the nature of publicity, self-advertisement or of what is vulgarly known as " swank " is, and always has been, utterly abhorrent to the Scotts of Buccleuch, and the very thought that, if we continued shooting, we should probably create a world's record was enough to determine Henry Scott to sound the " cease fire." But it is beyond question that, even allowing for the long interval of inaction in the middle of the day, we could easily have created a world's record and with a lot to spare.

Some idea of the masses of birds on the wing during this astonishing shoot may be gathered from the fact that, after the fourth drive, Francis Scott and I commiserated one another on having been clean out of the shooting. I was on the left flank and he was next me. As a matter of fact, we each had over eighty birds down that drive, and yet, by contrast with the terrific fusillade from the middle of the line, it really did seem that we were getting no shooting. Jack Dawnay,

in the centre and best butt, had 181 birds down—
a feat which he achieved by a wonderful display
of quick and accurate shooting. The fourth
drive, just referred to—being an up-wind drive—
was the most prolific of the day, but the most
sporting and interesting was unquestionably the
third. This third drive on the Roan Fell is
probably the best individual drive in the kingdom.
The birds are driven two miles before they come
to the guns (always down wind, for otherwise the
beat would not be shot), and generally down a
semi-gale, for the drive is along the top of a
mountain ridge. The butts are on the slope of the
hill and, as the birds are always heavily flanked
from the top of the hill, they come swooping down
on to the guns at a tremendous rate and at
every conceivable angle. There were several
" centuries " got that day in the third drive.
During that year 29,092 grouse were shot at
Langholm and its outlying shooting-box at
Newlands; and in the following year 28,542
grouse were shot over the same ground. In the
latter year, 1912, the Buccleuch moors in Scotland
yielded over 40,000 grouse, and if the reader will
recall the fact that our earlier efforts seldom
realised more than forty brace a day, he will get
some idea of the astonishing progress which had
been registered, during the intervening years,
under the direction of George Scott.

In November 1914 William Henry, sixth Duke
of Buccleuch, died in his eighty-second year,
two years after the death of his beloved wife and

inseparable companion through life. When my sister was on her deathbed, I hurried up to Dalkeith, but was just too late to see her alive. The old Duke took me to her room and told me in his own simple, unaffected way that life was now over for him and that his one wish was to follow quickly and rejoin the faithful partner of all his joys and sorrows. In these days, when married life is so often a short farce and a quick tragedy, it is good to reflect on the unwavering affection, through fifty odd years of married life, of these two. No couple were ever more beloved by their children, their employés and the immense circle of friends to whom they stood for all that was purest and kindest in life. My brother-in-law had a remarkable and singularly lovable disposition. If asked for a special definition, I should unhesitatingly describe him as the greatest gentleman, in the highest sense of the term, that I have known. He was perhaps less of the *grand seigneur* than his father, and it is possible that in that very difference lay his chief claim to special distinction. Although his *ménage* was conducted on the same magnificent scale as that of his predecessor, the absence of grandiosity was so marked as almost to suggest an effort at concealment. There was, however, no effort. All arrangements, no matter how sumptuous, were carried out in a quiet matter-of-course spirit which took everything, quite simply, for granted. It would be misleading to say that ostentation was deliberately suppressed by the

Duke; it simply never came within the range of his imagination. He was as simple-minded and unaffected as a child, as incapable of guile as he was incapable of discourtesy. He had an admirable brain and, when forced to the effort, could make as effective a speech—of a kind—as any man in the kingdom.

Of my sister, I can truly say that she was a consort worthy, in every way, of the man she married. She was the most unselfish woman I have ever met, incapable of thinking or speaking ill of any, ceaselessly thinking out kind actions, and with a conscientious sense of duty which, in the end, forced her to carry greater burdens than her strength was equal to. Had she, at the last, relaxed some of her self-imposed duties, she would without doubt have prolonged her life. They were a wonderful couple.

CHAPTER XI

EARLY in 1878 I joined the 11th Hussars, at that time an exceedingly lively regiment quartered at Colchester. I think this regiment was selected for me partly because it had the reputation of being a particularly smart and efficient regiment, and partly because it was only just home from India and might therefore reasonably be expected to remain some ten years or so in the United Kingdom. In any event the selection was a particularly happy one for me, for a better lot of fellows than the brother-officers among whom I found myself cannot well be imagined. Over almost all these bright souls the " Last Post " has now been sounded, but the recollection of their cheeriness, their daring, and above all of their staunchness in sunshine or storm, will live as long as memory lives. *Treu und fest* is the motto of the regiment, and true and fast these gallant spirits were to the end, till one by one we

> " Wrapped them up in their old stable-jackets,
> And said a poor buffer lay low, lay low."

Peace to their ashes !

Colonel Garnet, who commanded us, was, in a
sense, an anomaly in a regiment such as the 11th
Hussars, for he despised externals, despised all
parade movements, and was himself conspicuously
careless in his dress. Perhaps he had a right to
despise all these things, for, as a leader of cavalry
in the field, he had certainly no equal in the British
army at that time. In the sham fights at Aldershot, later on, it was always a foregone conclusion
that any side of which Garnet commanded the
cavalry effectually rolled up the other side. I
used, in those Aldershot days, to gallop regularly
for the cavalry leaders, and even to my inexperienced mind, Garnet's immeasurable superiority over all the others was at once apparent.
Unlike his opponents, he was always absolutely
cool and collected, detected in an instant any flaw
in their dispositions and did exactly the right
thing to bring them to utter discomfiture. I
never knew him hesitate, countermand an order
or do the wrong thing. It was no uncommon
thing for many of the other cavalry commanders
to send three gallopers, one after the other, each
countermanding the orders of the preceding one,
with the result, of course, that the regimental
officers were at their wits' end to know what to
do; and while they were trying to unravel the
various conflicting orders, Garnet would execute
one of his lightning movements and put the whole
lot—and very often many of the infantry as well
—out of action.

It was a national misfortune when Garnet's

early death robbed the country of a soldier who might have risen to any heights.

At the time I joined the 11th Hussars, the material god of the regiment was, needless to say, the horse, and of that noble animal I at once became a fanatical devotee. In one particular instance, however, my devotion was strained almost to the breaking-point, for my association with a certain troop-horse of ungentle paces, known as F. 33, was so long and so irksome that love very nearly turned to hate.

It was within the walls of the riding school that F. 33 and I first formed an acquaintance which was destined to prove more protracted than was agreeable to one of the parties concerned.

I had already done a certain amount of riding, having, in fact, had a hunter of my own at Sandhurst on which I hunted regularly with the Staff College drag. In spite, however, of this previous experience, I found an unaccountable difficulty in passing out of the riding school. Another subaltern, who had joined at the same time as myself and who was a notoriously poor horseman, passed out within a month, while I was left bumping round, day after day, on F. 33, under a ceaseless flow of scathing vituperation from the riding-master. Puzzled and pained by my lack of success, I, one day, poured out my woes to the subaltern who had joined with me.

" You have a lot to learn yet, my dear fellow," he remarked complacently.

" But, hang it all," I said, " you were always

shooting off on to your back, while I have not bitten the tan once."

" I remarked that you had a lot to learn," he repeated, " but I did not say in riding."

" In what then ? " I asked.

Prescott lighted a cigarette and gazed dreamily up at the ceiling.

" Old X.'s forage-cap is getting shabby," he observed presently.

" What on earth has that got to do with it ? " I asked.

" Everything," was his calm reply.

The hint, without further enlargement, was taken and acted upon. The result surpassed expectation. In place of the old abuse, the most lavish praise now pursued me as I bumped dusty and perspiring round the school, and within a week I was pronounced sufficiently expert to be discharged.

Life at Colchester was, on the whole, unexciting, but, in the winter of 1878, the monotony was pleasantly relieved by the appearance on the scene of an illusive midnight reveller known as " Spring-heeled Jack." This mysterious being was responsible for a series of visitations which shook the nerves of the entire military camp to their foundations. Night after night sentries would be bonneted, cuffed and thrown down by an invisible assailant. Cavalry, infantry and artillery were all alike impartially victimised. In our own Cavalry barracks, the story told next day by the nerve-shattered wrecks who had been on sentry-duty the night before was that Spring-heeled Jack came flying—without any preliminary warning—over the top of the stable buildings, dropped on their shoulders, knocked them down and was gone before they could recover their feet. Other reports were to the effect that a snow-white figure suddenly appeared from nowhere, hurled the sentries about with superhuman strength and vanished into thin air. All accounts agreed that Spring-heeled Jack's movements were absolutely noiseless. The whole population of Colchester, both military and civil, was deeply stirred. Sentries were everywhere doubled and, even then, went on their rounds with shaking knees and perspiring brows. They themselves were firmly convinced that Spring-heeled Jack was the devil. We, in the officers' mess, were just as firmly convinced that it was Lieut. Alfrey of the 60th Rifles. Probably both were wrong. Alfrey was a very big and powerful man, but extraordinarily active. He used to come out with the Essex and Suffolk hounds on a grey polo-pony of about fourteen hands, and it was the prettiest sight in the world to see the two in combination. On approaching a five-barred gate, Alfrey would vault off his pony's back whilst in full career. He and the pony would then jump the gate side by side, after which he would vault back into the saddle and continue the chase until the next gate was reached, when the performance would be repeated.

Our suspicions that Alfrey was the culprit were

163

strengthened when we moved to Aldershot in the winter of 1879. The 60th moved to Aldershot about the same time, and, at once, Spring-heeled Jack made his appearance in the new camp and commenced his old pranks on the night sentries. At Aldershot, the general panic became so great that eventually Spring-heeled Jack was officially proclaimed in General Orders; ball cartridge was handed out to the sentries and these were ordered to shoot the night terror on sight. These measures proved effective and Spring-heeled Jack was seen no more. Whether it really was Alfrey or not I have never learnt, and it would be interesting to have some pronouncement on the subject from his own lips or from his own pen. His equipment was supposed to consist of rubber-soled shoes and a sheet which was white on one side and black on the other.

In the later Seventies, life at Aldershot was inclined to be riotous, and more champagne flowed than was good either for the pockets or the stomachs of those who were quartered there. As an inevitable consequence of this alcoholic tendency, the after-dinner mood was a reckless one, and many insane wagers used to be made between brother-officers or their guests and to be settled on the spur of the moment. One of the most insane of these wagers, and one that occurs to me at the moment, was a bet made by Dalbiac of the Horse Gunners, commonly known as " The Treasure," that he would drive a dog-cart round Cocked-hat Wood against Dick Fort of my regiment on foot. It was agreed that the bet should be settled on the spot and, as the H.A. barracks were almost opposite to the East Cavalry barracks which sheltered my regiment, it was not many minutes before " The Treasure " was back in his dog-cart. Fort in the meanwhile had donned running costume, and off the two started, Dalbiac at a mad gallop and Fort at a slow, plodding jog-trot. The rest of us having seen them start returned to the Mess to await developments. At the end of about ninety minutes, Fort, who was a good runner, reappeared, but not so Dalbiac. A search party was organised and we all started out for the Long Valley with lanterns, and, after a long search and much shouting, to which there was no response, came upon four hoofs and two wheels sticking up in the air from the depths of one of the deep sandy nullahs just short of Cocked-hat Wood. A faint voice from below the wheels informed us that Dalbiac was still alive, and we then set to work to get the horse and dog-cart clear of him. It was a ticklish business, for the horse might very well have kicked his brains out, but we eventually managed it, and then proceeded to extract Dalbiac from the very bottom of the nullah, the narrowness of which had saved him from the full weight of the horse and cart. He was quite black in the face and unable to stand, but we lifted him on to a led pony and managed to get him home, though half-way there he was

seized with a convulsive fit. Next morning
there was a field-day, and, to our utter amazement, there was " The Treasure " as fresh as
paint at the head of his famous chestnut troop.

Dalbiac was, at that time, easily the best
steeplechase rider in the army. He was also a
very remarkable sprinter, and used to make a
lot of money by backing himself to run eighty
yards against any horse over sixteen hands.
He almost always won, but against a pony he
had, of course, no chance. He was killed, poor
chap, in the Boer War, leading a very gallant
but quite insane cavalry charge up a hill against
entrenched Boers.

On another occasion not very long after the
dog-cart incident, I myself made a wager which
was little less idiotic than Dalbiac's. I had at
that time a very beautiful thoroughbred four-
year-old named Monmouth, by Prince Charlie
out of Gaylass. Monmouth was one of the
quietest horses I ever rode, with a mouth like
silk, and, in a rash and I am afraid slightly
alcoholic moment, I backed myself to ride Monmouth bare-backed round Cocked-hat Wood
against Dick Fort on a slow but saddled hunter.
It was a pitch-dark night, and we had no sooner
started than I realised to my horror that the lamb-
like Monmouth, excited either by the strangeness
of the hour chosen for exercise or by the presence
of my dinner overalls on his bare back, was
pulling like a steam-tug and was going exactly
where and how he liked. Like a tornado we

dashed through the West Gate and along the track that led to the Long Valley. Monmouth had a satiny coat as slippery as ice, and very sharp withers, and on to these sharp withers I was now pulled with such steady pressure that I was almost cut in two. I was in very severe pain and absolutely powerless either to check or guide the tearing whirlwind between my legs. All that I could do was to keep my balance, and that was far from easy on account of the horse's slippery satiny coat, and, as I have already said, desperately painful. The darkness was so intense that I could not see twenty yards ahead of me, but presumably the horse could, for no disaster overtook us till quite close to Cocked-hat Wood. What exactly happened then I shall never know. There was a terrific crash : I saw any number of stars and then relapsed into unconsciousness. Like Dalbiac, I was eventually discovered by a search party and escorted home, strange to say, none the worse except for torn overalls and a split stable-jacket.

Another horsy experience of mine at Aldershot had a happier ending. One summer morning Sir Frederick Fitzwygram had my regiment and the 15th Hussars out in the Long Valley for an educational field-day. In the course of our evolutions, General Fitzwygram got both regiments into line and, according to time-honoured custom, sounded first " trot," then " gallop," and, finally, " charge." It was, and no doubt

167

still is, a recognised rule that a charge should automatically cease when a hundred yards have been covered. On this occasion, however, for some mad reason, the two regiments started to race one another and charged for nearly a mile, till the canal finally brought them up short. I made a meritorious effort to stop my troop but, seeing fifty sword-points directed at my back and impelled by the instinct of self-preservation, I finally set spurs to my horse and kept as far out of their reach as possible. The result was that I was the first to reach the canal. Of General Fitzwygram's wrath I need say nothing, nor of the penalties that were put upon the two erring regiments. The offence was indeed somewhat serious, for many horses fell and three were so badly injured that they had to be destroyed. In addition, several men had to be taken to hospital. The one point about the whole affair which interested me was that I had reached the canal first. This set me thinking, and I could arrive at no other conclusion except that my first charger must be possessed of a turn of speed of which I had so far no suspicion, for I had never before extended the horse. In order to put the matter to the proof I determined to enter him in the Hunters' Flat Race at the forthcoming Aldershot summer meeting. In those days it was the easiest matter in the world to qualify any horse for Hunters' races, and I found no difficulty in getting the necessary certificate from the neighbouring M.F.H.

SOLDIERING

The horse in question, whom I had named Cobweb, was a tall, bony thoroughbred chestnut. Heaven only knows how old he was, but I should imagine very far advanced in his "teens," for his teeth were of monumental length and he had hollows over his eyes like teacups. He had the most extravagant knee-action of any horse I have ever seen and, when trotting, nearly knocked his teeth out with every stride. He literally danced.

So, on the day of the race, I had the old horse led down to the paddock, where he attracted no attention whatever as he walked demurely round. The moment, however, that I climbed into the saddle, a wave of ribald hilarity swept over the whole assembly. The old horse no doubt mistook the grand-stand for the saluting-point at a Royal inspection, for he peacocked past with such tremendous gesticulation of the knees that I was almost shaken out of the saddle. Never shall I forget the yells of derision that saluted me as we passed the ring.

"Hi! governor, which way to the circus?" "'Ere. Twenty to one the blinking giraffe," and so on. No doubt we presented a comical sight enough, for it is to be doubted whether any horse with such extravagant knee-action had ever been seen on a racecourse before. I felt bitterly ashamed of myself and cursed my folly in having been such a simpleton as to pit a peacocky old charger against the silky-actioned race-horses that were "lollopping" past me with long, easy strides on their way to the starting-post. Veritable race-horses they actually were, for very few horses that ran in Hunters' Flat Races in those days had even been over a fence. However, the long and short of it all is that old Cobweb won anyhow over the two-mile course, having led the field from start to finish. No one was more surprised that I was, and unfortunately I had not a penny on the race.

Flushed by my success, I next made a match over a mile course against a very fast horse owned by Micky Burke of the 7th D.G.'s, and once again Cobweb won easily. His galloping action, needless to say, was very different from his trot. He galloped, leaning heavily on my hand, with his head low, his back slightly arched and with an immense stride which seemed to annihilate space. In his youth he must have been an extraordinarily fast horse, for, on both occasions, he was practically untrained, and there is no doubt that he was of patriarchal age.

Some years later, when my regiment went from Leeds to Ireland, I gave old Cobweb away to an officer who had risen from the ranks belonging to the regiment that was taking our place. He admired the horse immensely, and I said I would give it to him if he gave me his solemn word that he would shoot the horse when he had done with him and never give him away or sell him. He gave the required undertaking, but I regret to say did not keep it, for he sold the horse into a Leeds cab. I have never forgiven that man, and I never will. Poor old Cobweb's place as my first charger was taken by the famous kicking Gainsborough, of whose exploits I have already written.

CHAPTER XII

From Aldershot my regiment went to Hounslow, which was at that time, by universal consent, the most popular cavalry station in the south of England. We were within ten miles of London, within driving distance of many race-meetings, close to Kempton Park, where by the courtesy of the management we were allowed to train our horses, and we had a cricket ground in the barrack square. We had everything, in fact, that the heart of a soldier can desire, except hunting. For that we were—locally—driven to the Queen's.

Our cricket matches in the barracks were great fun. The teams that opposed us almost invariably came down from London on a coach driven by one of the team, dined with us after the match, and started on their return journey in the small hours of the morning—usually in a musical and contented frame of mind.

For a cavalry regiment we really had a very fair side. Our captain, Kildare Burroughs, was very nearly a first-class cricketer and on several occasions was called on to keep wicket for Middlesex. He and I had many a merry innings together. On one occasion, while we were quartered at Colchester, we established something which I

think must have been a record, for, in a certain
match at Witham, we hit eleven consecutive
" boundaries." We were playing for Essex *v.*
South of England. W. G. Grace was bowling
at one end and Southerton at the other—both
tempting " donkey-droppers." The boundary
was a very easy one—so easy, in fact, that by
preconcerted arrangement, Burroughs and I
agreed to run out and hit at everything which
was at all pitched up. At one period of our
partnership eleven consecutive balls were sufficiently pitched up for our purpose, and every one
went either over or under the ropes. They only
allowed us three for a " boundary," unless it
went over the ropes, so that in many cases we
had to cross over, which made it all the more
exciting. The " old man," as they used to call
W. G., was absolutely delighted at our dis-
respectful treatment of his bowling. He roared
with laughter. Southerton was not so pleased.
My end came in trying to hit the twelfth
" boundary." The ball was a little too short
and I missed it, and was stumped by Pooley.
My total was only thirty-three, but Burroughs
stayed till he had made eighty.

We generally won our matches at Hounslow,
partly, I think, because of the good luncheons
we provided, and partly because we knew the
ground, which was a very bad one. There was
only about an inch of turf above the gravel,
and, as a consequence, the eccentricity of the
projectile was, at times, very marked and very

disconcerting to the batsman. The fast under-
hand "grubs," which were the only form of
bowling I could aspire to, and which had little
value on a true wicket, were enormously helped
by the ups and downs of the Hounslow wicket,
and, aided by these, I once bowled nine wickets
of a strong Eton Rambler team, whose subsequent
comments on the nature of the pitch, and on
"grub" bowlers and bowling in general, were more
forcible than friendly. As a rule, however, the
actual cricket was not taken too seriously, and it
was noticeable that the side which batted after
luncheon developed a certain light-hearted recklessness of demeanour which made for the amusement of the onlookers rather than for high scores.
It need scarcely be added that my nine wickets
afore-mentioned were obtained after luncheon.

The opposing teams, as I have said, always
dined with us and we always did our best to
entertain them hospitably, and generally with
success. We succeeded, I remember, particularly
well with a certain House of Commons team
which included one actual Secretary of State
and several others who were destined to become
future ornaments of the Cabinet. The dinner
was a marked success, and the musical efforts
of the good legislators, as they drove away
through the barrack gate, would certainly have
startled their constituencies.

Once the regiment had, so to speak, a very
bad fall. Among the members of a certain
Zingari team that came down to play us were

HOUNSLOW

Grannie and Esmé Gordon, surely two of the handsomest and most fascinating personalities that the last half-century has produced. Their good looks and their cheeriness were outstanding to the eye of the world, and it need scarcely be said that they contributed in no small measure to the conviviality of our dinner. It was not till after dinner that we learned to our sorrow that the physical endowments of the brothers did not begin and end with a pleasing exterior.

I may mention that it was not our custom after these dinners to sit for long in meditative or digestive repose. Some stimulating exercise, either vocal or muscular, usually followed closely on the drinking of the Queen's health—not by preconcerted arrangement, but simply as the natural outcome of what had gone before. How exactly these things are set in motion no man can say. They just happen. On the occasion in question, we found ourselves challenging the two Gordons, or the two Gordons challenging us (it matters little which) to a variety of acrobatic exercises for which the large Mess premises at Hounslow seemed specially fitted, but for which we had so far neglected to employ them. It is distressing to have to record that, in the competitions which followed, the regiment came off distinctly second best. The Gordon brothers beat us all round.

First of all Grannie challenged our champion at billiards and beat him very heavily. Then he vaulted over the corner of the table, with one hand holding the pocket, which none of us could do. Esmé then challenged any and all of us to jump two chairs placed back to back from an " all fours " position on the floor. He approached the two chairs on all fours like a dog, bucked over and landed on his hands without touching either chair. Several blithe spirits, in the evanescent confidence which is so often noticeable between 9.30 p.m. and midnight, attempted the feat, but only succeeded in losing a quantity of skin and in gaining a number of bruises in exchange.

We had not practised drawing-room acrobatics as a regiment, but there was one trick to which we had devoted a certain amount of study and in which we took a certain regimental pride. This trick consisted in standing with one's back to the edge of an open door, clasping the top of the door with both hands and circling up till one sat astride the top of the door. Our regimental champion at this exercise was Pat Close, who, after having demonstrated the feat to our visitors, challenged them to do the like. To our no little surprise, Esmé Gordon proved equal to the occasion, and managed—not without some little difficulty—to establish himself astride the door. It is not an easy trick to carry through, as anyone can find out for himself by making the attempt, and it has one rather painful moment, when the collar-bone comes in contact with the door-edge. After this Grannie turned somersaults in a chair without leaving the chair, which again proved beyond our powers; and, as there were wagers on all these events, the end of it all was that the Lords Granville and Esmé Gordon left Hounslow Barracks considerably enriched in pocket, while the regiment was correspondingly poorer.

Those were days when every well-regulated subaltern, who was quartered within fifty miles of London, thought it necessary to attend the Gaiety Theatre at least once a week. Here Terry, Royce, Kate Vaughan and Nellie Farren, supported by a much better-looking chorus than any theatre can boast to-day, dispensed burlesque in the old-fashioned jingle rhyme to rows of callow youths in high collars decorating the first four rows of the stalls. That the old Gaiety chorus was better-looking than any present-day chorus is not attributable to any decadence in feminine grace, but simply to the fact that the Gaiety was in those days the only theatre which gave burlesque, and it could therefore pick and choose from the troops of young ladies whose ambition lay in wearing pink tights and in simpering from behind footlights to their admirers in front. They never could sing a note, or dance, or indeed do anything but look pretty, and they invariably wore tights. Nowadays the majority of revue choruses are composed of girls dressed as girls—very lightly dressed sometimes, but still unmistakably dressed as girls. Male impersonators are the exception. In the Seventies, if I remember right, there were never any petti-

coated girls in the Gaiety chorus. All were
invariably male impersonators, with their legs
in silk tights and their bodies in stiff tight tunics.
This fashion certainly lasted without change for
ten years. Nellie Farren herself was invariably
dressed in tights and tunic. No one ever saw
her on the stage at the period I am writing
of in petticoats or as anything but a male
impersonator.

Nellie Farren was unquestionably the most
successful burlesque actress of the past fifty
years. It is true that she had practically no
competitors, for the Gaiety alone provided the
form of entertainment in which she shone, but,
none the less, I think one may safely say that no
one in that particular line of business has ever
achieved the same measure of popularity. It is
difficult to say in what exactly lay the secret of
her success. When I first knew her on the stage,
she was no longer young and was not particularly
good-looking. She could neither dance nor sing
and was handicapped by a weak, husky voice.
And yet her hold on the public was something
" abune by-ordinar," as the Scots say. If by
chance she were ill or unable to appear, all the
counter-attractions of her understudy and of
Terry, Royce, Kate Vaughan and the beauty
chorus combined failed to dispel the overwhelming sense of loss that her absence caused. Some
have thought that the secret of her power lay
in her complete unconsciousness of sex, and there
may be some truth in that, but I think it was

mainly due to her unquenchable vitality and animal magnetism. The moment she was on the stage, a piece which before had hung fire seemed to go with a swing, and yet she never exerted herself or appeared to have any particular desire to please. It was simply her being herself that did it. In person she was of medium size with very well-shaped legs and a curious kind of stiff, strutting gait. She had a round face, very wide-open round eyes, and a little pursed-up mouth. Her expression was one of perpetually surprised amusement and hardly ever changed. She never laughed.

While on the subject of the Gaiety and its chorus, it may not be out of place to record an incident which occurred while we were at Hounslow, and as to which many ill-natured and quite unfounded insinuations were made at the time. The facts were these. It was determined in regimental conclave to give a dance in barracks, and, as we had no acquaintances among the Hounslow ladies, and as a dance can only take place with the assistance of ladies, it was decided to invite down the Gaiety chorus to fill the deficiency. The invitation was accompanied by an offer to put the ladies up for the night, and was formally accepted by C. G., who acted as spokesman for the others, on the express understanding that all those who responded to the invitation were to be treated from first to last with distant respect. The undertaking was gladly given and subscribed to by all the junior officers at Hounslow at the time. Half the regiment was away on long leave, so that there was plenty of accommodation in the absent officers' rooms, to each of which—at their own special request—two of the ladies were assigned.

The entertainment was an immense success. All enjoyed themselves amazingly and, in the early morning, the sleepy ladies went off in cabs to the station, after refreshing themselves with cups of tea discreetly handed into their rooms through chinks in the doors.

This absolutely innocent escapade created a most desperate stir. The *World* was the first paper to take it up, and others followed with all sorts of ridiculous exaggerations and insulting comments. Finally the Duke himself bombarded the regiment with a Note of the most furious and condemnatory type; explanations were called for and threats of dire penalties were held over our heads. All this would have been bearable enough except for the fatuous attitude taken up by street acquaintances. These humorous asses flatly refused to believe that the temporary association of the Gaiety chorus and the 11th Hussars had been as scrupulously platonic as was really the case. We, on our side, were much incensed at the incredulity of the world, for was not our solemn word passed, and were we not before all else officers and gentlemen?

Another incident which called down upon us the wrath of the good Duke was in connection with a cricket match in the barracks against the

HOUNSLOW

Eton Ramblers in 1881. We, the juniors in the
regiment, were considerably annoyed at that
time at being unable to retain the services of our
own band for cricket matches and other similar
festivities. Our band, which was a good one,
was in great request in the neighbourhood, partly
because of its good music and partly, I think,
because of its crimson overalls; and it was
perpetually being sent about all over the country
to play at suburban functions when we ourselves
badly needed it at home. A distinguished team
of Eton Ramblers was expected down to play
against us during the day and dine with us at
night, and we wanted our band to cheer things
up and do them honour. We were told that it
was already engaged to play at the Twickenham
Temperance Society's third anniversary, or
something of the kind, and we were highly, and
I think justly, incensed. In this mood we wired
for the Blue Hungarian Band to come down from
London and play during the afternoon and
evening. The cost, of course, was considerable,
but the thing was really done as a protest against
the alienation of our own band, and—as a protest
—it succeeded beyond belief. The papers were
full of this new instance of the criminal ex-
travagance of the 11th Hussars. The Duke once
more took the matter up in a very stern and
minatory mood, and the culprits were severely
censured. But thereafter we had our own band !
The wrath of the old Duke, when roused, was
loud and plain-spoken, and we all bowed before

it because we loved him and hated to cause him annoyance. He was very fond of our regiment, and the feeling was fully reciprocated by all of us. I personally had a special reverence and veneration for H.R.H., for on one occasion it was his kindly offices that alone saved me from feeling the full weight of the War Office arm. The circumstances were these.

In December 1883, Lord Mayor Dawson of Dublin was advertised to speak in Derry, and as he had lately been giving vent to most seditious and anti-British utterances in his own town, the loyalists of Derry determined to protest against his spreading similar doctrines in the Maiden City. With this worthy object in view a meeting of the well-disposed was arranged in the Prentice Boys' Hall at Derry, and, as I was the only member of my family at Barons Court at the time, I was told off to attend the meeting and lend the support of my presence to the protest. So off I set, feeling that, if I were not the hub of the universe, I was, at least, for the occasion, the hub of Ulster.

At the meeting in the Prentice Boys' Hall many speeches expressive of loyal indignation were delivered; the enthusiasm of those who listened rose with each succeeding speech, till, in the end, it was decided that the only course open to the good and true was to occupy the Town Hall (in which Mr. Dawson was advertised to speak) and so to prevent his delivering himself of his noxious doctrines. No sooner was the suggestion made than it was acted upon. In a body we marched to the Diamond and there took possession of the Town Hall, barred and bolted the doors and prepared to resist the siege which we knew must follow.

In the meanwhile the partisans of the Lord Mayor had assembled at the railway station in their hundreds, and, on the arrival of the Dublin train, the Nationalist crowd marched up with bands playing and banners flying to the Town Hall, which, to their marked annoyance, they found in the occupation of the enemy. In those days the Town Hall was an isolated building standing on the ground now occupied by the public gardens in the Diamond. Round and round this building drove the Lord Mayor in speechless indignation and accompanied by an exasperated mob of admirers, but there was no possible means of obtaining admission except by force, and there was a strong argument against the application of force in the shape of a most determined garrison inside. After a time the Lord Mayor resigned himself to the inevitable and drove off, and eventually held his meeting in the slaughter-house, which we considered an eminently suitable spot; but for the rest of the day the Nationalist crowd surged round and round the Town Hall, shaking impotent fists, and breathing war and threatenings.

About 3 p.m. the demonstration outside grew more distinctly hostile. I was watching the scene with much amusement from one of the

windows when I noticed that the yelling and
booing were punctuated by a number of little
pops which sounded like corks being drawn. I
heard the sound of broken glass from one of the
Town Hall windows, and I saw a man in the
street throw up his arms and collapse in a heap,
and then, for the first time, I realised that
revolvers were being freely used on both sides.
The crowd outside melted away, carrying the
fallen man with them, and, after some seven
hours' incarceration in the Town Hall, we inside—
having learned that the Lord Mayor had returned
to Dublin—sallied forth and marched in provoca-
tive procession through the Nationalist quarters.
At various points we were assailed by bottles
hurled from windows, but no one was seriously
hurt, and about 7 p.m. a detachment of the
17th Lancers arrived from Enniskillen and peace
was restored. The man, however, whom I had
seen shot was killed, and I was not only summoned
to give evidence at the inquest, but was actually
indicted for having headed a riot, while an officer
in H.M. forces, and having caused loss of life.
But for the Duke I should have run a very grave
risk of being turned out of the army, but he
represented that I was only a youth and a mere
puppet in the movement which had resulted in
the unfortunate man's death. I was absolved,
but the escape was a narrow one.

The Duke was not only one of the kindest of
men, he was also one of the ablest. As his
galloper on many occasions during sham fights

on the Fox Hills, I had ample opportunity for gauging H.R.H.'s ability as a generalissimo. There is no question that he stood out from all the Aldershot "cocked-hats" of my time. Of course he never personally commanded either of the opposing sides, but his detection of the slightest tactical error on the part of those who did command was instantaneous. He had the eye of a hawk and the unerring instinct of the born military leader, and he never hesitated to point out their errors to offending Generals in language which there was no mistaking. As a speaker, too, of a certain kind, the Duke was certainly second to none in the kingdom. H.R.H. came down to inspect the regiment at Aldershot before it sailed for India somewhere in the Nineties. I was present on the occasion as a guest of the regiment. At the end of the inspection, the Duke formed the regiment up in quarter-column and made a speech which lasted some ten minutes. At the end of that time I will not say that there was not a dry eye in the regiment, but I will certainly say that a number of the N.C.O.'s and men were very visibly affected. It was a very wonderful speech, manly and vigorous, but at the same time intensely pathetic. The Duke was at that time an old man, and the speech was in the nature of a lasting farewell to a regiment which he loved, but which, in the nature of things, he would never again inspect.

Another member of the Royal family who was a constant and welcome visitor at our Hounslow

Mess was the late Duke of Teck, who was, at that time, in the occupation of the White Lodge in Richmond Park. He was very fond of lunching and dining with us, and, generally, took a keen interest in the regiment. I remember being particularly struck by the fact that he had forgotten most of his German. We had a German in the regiment, and the Prince expressed a wish to see him and talk to him. I myself led him to the man, but, when conversation began, H.S.H. found himself quite unable to express himself adequately in German, and had in the end to revert to English.

The Prince was the soul of hospitality and was always asking me over to the White Lodge. I enjoyed these visits more than I can say, for there was no kinder or more entertaining hostess in England than Princess Mary of beloved memory. During my wanderings about the White Lodge grounds, I would occasionally— but only occasionally—get a glimpse of the present Queen, at that time a pretty but rather shy girl of fifteen.

I think those Hounslow days succeeded in breaking most of the regiment. We were unfortunately situated in the very centre of the racing country. Ascot, Epsom, Sandown, Kempton, Egham and Hampton were all within driving distance of the regimental coach, and at each of these places the regiment thought it necessary to entertain the world. Our regimental races were held the first year at Sandown, and the second at Kempton, and at each of these places, and at Ascot in each year, a huge crimson and yellow (regimental colours) marquee proffered unstinted hospitality to all comers. It was very magnificent but very foolish, and I think we only got ridicule for our pains and little thanks.

I remember on one occasion, when we had our regimental races at Kempton, the Duke of Albany and the Duke of Cambridge had both accepted our invitation to luncheon, and, as a consequence, the long table with its load of elaborate dishes and regimental plate was by common consent left undisturbed till the arrival of the Royalties. I had just ridden the winner of the Regimental Cup, beating the favourite by a length, and I was standing inside the marquee, mildly celebrating the event with Bob Hardy, the owner of the horse, when, to my amazement, five members of a certain regiment burst into the tent, sat down uninvited and began shouting to the waiters to bring them champagne, while they piled up their plates from all the dishes within reach, thereby quite ruining the virgin appearance of the table. In dumb amazement I stood and watched them till—having had all they wanted—they swaggered out again without a word of thanks either to Bob Hardy or myself, or anyone else for that matter. One of these barbarians was the eldest son of a peer, another was his brother and a third was a well-known baronet. Although that incident occurred over forty years ago, it still holds the record in my memory as the most ungentlemanly act I have ever witnessed.

CHAPTER XIII

F<small>ROM</small> Hounslow my regiment went to Leeds, and from Leeds to Ballincollig. At Ballincollig we took over the old Muskerry hounds and hunted the country twice a week. On our arrival we were invaded by a perfect swarm of local horse-dealers—amateur and professional—who assured us that to ride our English horses over their country would be to invite certain death, and who—out of solicitude for our necks—offered to provide us with any number of safe and talented horses from their own stables, the majority of whom—needless to say—were by Victor (compared to whom Solomon must have been a confirmed bachelor) out of a Birdcatcher mare. Firmly but politely, however, we declined these friendly offers, preferring, as we told our well-wishers, to face the certain death which they predicted for us on our English horses, to the expense of new purchases. Fortunately their predictions were not verified. We schooled our horses over the banks at the back of the barracks for a week, at the end of which time they were as safe conveyances as any horses in the country.

As a matter of fact, an Irish bank country is the easiest in the world to ride over. It is very rare indeed to see a fall over a bank; only when the bank is narrow and rotten is there any chance of a fall, and even then it is seldom a bad one.

As an instance of what an extraordinarily easy fence a hunting bank is for a horse to negotiate in safety, I may relate an incident which occurred to myself during our early days at Ballincollig. I was hunting with our own hounds on my second charger, who was only an indifferent performer, when a local acquaintance came up to me and—after a few disparaging remarks at the expense of my mount—volunteered the information that he had at home a certain four-year-old (by Victor, of course) which could jump anything on earth and gallop round the horse I was riding at the moment. Being more or less new to the south of Ireland, I accepted all this as fact, or at least as something approaching to fact, and, on the following day, I rode over to my friend's residence, which was some nine miles distant. A very nice-looking young horse was brought out for my inspection and, after having gone through the usual routine of punching and pinching, I climbed up, and proceeded to gallop him over the neighbouring fields. The horse was a gallant little beast and had no idea of refusing, but he negotiated the banks very clumsily indeed and, though he did not actually fall, scrambled about a good deal. I returned to where the owner stood watching, and explained that, though to my mind the horse had the makings of a good one, he was not exactly what I wanted, which was a made hunter.

" Then you'll not have him ? " he said, a trifle truculently, as I thought.

" No, I am afraid not," I replied.

" Well," he said, " I'm greatly obliged to you for the schooling, anyway. To tell the truth, this is the first day the little harse has ever seen a fence." And I had ridden over nine miles for this !

Hunting had its drawbacks in Co. Cork in the year of grace 1885. When our meets were publicly advertised we were apt to find poisoned foxes hanging from the trees in our best coverts, so that eventually we had to send round private notices of our fixtures. Every sort of obstacle was placed by the light-hearted peasantry in the way of our sport, the reason assigned being, that we hunted " in England's bloody red."

On one occasion, as the field was passing through a very narrow lane, we found the way blocked by three farm-hands brandishing pointed pitchforks. The leading file happened to be a certain Dr. Cross, who lived close by and who hunted regularly with our hounds and was a very good man across country. He promptly clubbed his hunting crop, rode one man down, broke the head of another and sent the third scuttling over the fence into an adjoining field. It was a gallant piece of work, and a notable example of the superiority of cavalry over infantry under certain conditions. I regret to say that, in spite of my testimony in the witness-box as to Dr. Cross' peaceful attitude until attacked, he was heavily

190

fined for assault by a hostile jury. I regret still more to say that he was hanged the following year for poisoning his wife with a view to marrying the governess. The evidence was conflicting and far from conclusive, but he was locally unpopular, and a politically hostile jury hanged him. The prison officials pronounced him to be the bravest man that had ever faced death in Cork Gaol.

On another occasion while hunting with the United Hunt, a very large field was " held up " while trotting along the high-road from covert to covert. The road passed under a railway arch, from wall to wall of which the natives had erected a strong barricade behind which a score of men stood with big stones in their hands. The railway embankment above was lined by thirty or forty more men similarly armed. On this occasion money was the only thing that the " bhoys " were out for, and the tender of half-a-crown procured a free pass through the barrier. To my amazement, almost everyone in the field, which must have numbered quite two hundred, paid up. I was not amongst the number.

In the spring of 1885 we held our regimental races at Cork Park. It appeared that the local humorists thought it would be good fun to see the English officers tumble about and, possibly, break their necks. In this jocular mood they built the fences (flying banks) up to an unprecedented height, and, in a state of pleasurable excitement, assembled in large numbers to watch developments. To their no little annoyance and disappointment—as we afterwards learned—most of our horses got round all right, nor were we conscious of having done anything out of the ordinary. The two days following our races, however, were the days appointed for the Cork Park Spring Steeplechase meeting, and we then learned for the first time of the special efforts that had been made for our benefit, for the Irish jockeys, after walking round the course, one and all flatly refused to ride at the meeting unless every fence on the course was cut down by a foot. This was done during the night and the meeting took place as usual. I had a ride in the Open Hunters' Steeplechase on a horse of Lord Doneraile's named Obadiah, and I can testify to the ridiculous smallness of the fences as compared with those which our regimental horses had safely negotiated on the preceding day. I still maintain, however, despite the strike of the local jockeys, that the fences before being cut down were no more than fair steeplechase fences; in proof whereof I may mention that I successfully rode over them a very hard-pulling mare belonging to a brother officer, which had only just arrived from Epsom, and which had never seen a bank in her life before. In the first race of the day I broke a stirrup-leather after the first fence and, feeling unequal to the task of riding such a tearing puller over the fences with only one stirrup, I pulled her on to the flat-race course which lay inside the other. Here we careered wildly round for two miles or so before I could stop her. At

one point in the flat-race course was a flight of
hurdles. Now, Irish steeplechase fences are very
much smaller than those in use on English courses,
but on the other hand Irish hurdles are much
higher. They are, however, fashioned of very
thin material (deal laths), and are always fixed
at such a slope as to reduce their height by a
third. On the occasion in question, however, the
hurdles, being merely where they were with a
view to preventing traffic, had been fixed perfectly
upright, and looked strangely formidable as I
approached them. I shouted to the man in
charge to pull one out and let me through, but
he either did not or could not hear, and so at
them I had to go. Luckily the mare imitated
the example of Mr. Sponge's " Multum in parvo "
and never rose an inch. We crashed through the
lath hurdles like paper and I pursued my headlong
career. Eventually I was able to stop the mare
and get her back to the paddock. Having furnished myself with a pair of strong new stirrup-
leathers, I rode her again in the last race of the
day and, in spite of the fact that she had never
seen a bank before and was a tearing, rushing,
star-gazing puller, she never touched a sod from
start to finish and won easily. The fences, therefore, very obviously cannot have been of the
dangerous height that the Irish jockeys fancied.

At the Cork Park Spring meeting in question I
bought a little entire horse named Canary, which
I sent to Warren Jackson's training stable at
Aghanesk. Warren Jackson invited me to come

over one morning and see the horse gallop. I accordingly started very early from Ballincollig and arrived at Aghanesk before breakfast, very cold and hungry. Warren Jackson himself, his friend and racing associate Peard, the vet., and Leland Hone were walking about outside the house when my jaunting car set me down at the door.

" Would you like a gallop? " was Warren Jackson's first question, after we had shaken hands and before I had even stripped myself of my overcoat. Now in those days a gallop over fences was the one thing that I loved more than all else on earth, so that to such a question there could be but one reply.

" I've a new course here that I want you to christen for me," he explained.

Full of interest I was taken out to inspect the new course, and I confess that I was absolutely staggered at what I saw. Never, surely, had fences of such colossal dimensions been seen on any steeplechase course—much less on any schooling ground. The banks were pretty near as high as hunting banks and yet of course had to be flown.

" I want you to put Obadiah round the course," Warren Jackson explained airily. " The horse is short of work and a gallop will do him good."

I wondered a little why a horse out of a regular training establishment should be short of work and also why—if he were short of work—one of the stable-lads or professional riders attached to the stable did not put him round the new course instead of a stranger who had no connection with the horse, and who rode no less than 12 stone 7 lbs. I also knew—having ridden Obadiah at Cork Park the week before—that he was a perfect fencer and required no schooling, so that the real work he should have been put to was a gallop on the flat by a light lad.

All this flashed through my brain in an instant, as did also a realisation of the fact that Warren Jackson's instructions to me were little short of an act of deliberate murder. Obadiah was the hardest puller in Ireland, and was in addition a " mad " horse, notoriously dangerous to ride; and I believe that Warren Jackson had only put me up on him at Cork Park because he could get no one else to ride him. To put such a horse over those immense fences, which were quite double the height of the revised fences at Cork Park, was, as I say, little short of an act of murder. I was not without a suspicion that the whole thing had been carefully planned out by Warren Jackson and Peard as an excellent " joke " at my expense, and my feelings, as I stood and watched the prancing and perspiring Obadiah being led up and down preparatory to his gallop, were decidedly mixed. However, I was young and foolish in those days and would far sooner have been flattened out than have let these humorists see that I was afraid. I examined one or two of the fences and noted that no horse had as yet been round the course. I also noted that—though the entire Aghanesk " string " was exercising—there was no disposition on the part of any of the stable-lads to accompany me over the new fences. That honour was to be mine alone. However, it was too late now to withdraw. I mounted, and, after giving the horse a quarter of a mile on the flat, turned him on to the steeplechase course. Obadiah was a very gallant horse, though, as I have said, excitable to the point of madness, and he had no idea of refusing anything. Twice, by a miracle, I got him successfully round the course (its circumference was very small) and, as I passed the group of disappointed onlookers, I shouted out : " Will that do ? "

" Oh, put him round once more," Warren Jackson shouted out in reply; and I did, or, at least, attempted to do so. This, however, was tempting Providence too high. At one of the fences, Obadiah, who had an immense stride, took off about twenty feet short, breasted the fence with terrific force and turned a complete somersault, mercifully shooting me clear. I was none the worse and was on my feet again in a moment, but not so poor Obadiah. He was badly injured, and, though they managed to get him to the stable, he never recovered, and, shortly afterwards, had to be destroyed.

The whole incident was regrettable, and, though it recoiled in a sense on to the heads of its originators, it was many a day before I ceased to regret the death of the unhappy horse who was victimised. The truth of the whole matter was,

196

BALLINCOLLIG

I believe, that the new banks had been built up by unsupervised workmen who modelled them on hunting banks, thinking that was what was wanted, and Peard and Warren Jackson thought it would be a pity to cut them down before they had got some fun out of them. The readiest form of fun which suggested itself to them was to break my neck. After the Obadiah episode, the banks were cut down to the usual height.

I ran Canary shortly afterwards at Tipperary Steeplechases. On the first day there were four starters in my race, and two of the other horses, ridden respectively by Messrs. Harty and Phelan, at one time in the race were at least a quarter of a mile ahead of me. Spurs, knees, voice and whip had no effect whatever on little Canary, who lobbed along at his own pace without taking the slightest notice of my various forms of encouragement. About half a mile from home, however, he suddenly lifted his head, had a look round, and then tucked his legs under him, popped over the Lilliputian fences as though they were not there and set off in pursuit of the leaders. He won by a head.

The next day there were eleven starters in my race and Canary started a hot favourite. Peard and Warren Jackson did their utmost to induce me to stand down in favour of a local rider named Norcott, even going to the length of assuring me that they knew for a certain fact that two of the jockeys in the race were starting with the sole object of knocking me over. As,

however, I had only bought the horse for the fun
of riding him, I refused to be influenced by a
sudden solicitude for my personal safety which I
had not noticed at Aghanesk. I rode most of
the race alongside of little Johnnie Beasley, who
good-naturedly gave me instructions throughout,
and told me exactly when to go through the ruck
and push to the front. This time I won by a
neck.

Canary was a wonderful little horse. He was
the laziest little beggar that ever ran, and stub-
bornly refused to win any race by more than a
neck. But he was as clever as a man, knew
exactly where the winning-post was, and timed
his effort better than ever Fred Archer did.

After Tipperary, Peard and Warren Jackson
persuaded me to put Canary into handicaps and
he never won another race. He broke down
within a year of the Tipperary meeting and I
sold him at Tattersall's for sixty guineas. Charlie
Cunningham had a look at him with a view to
purchase, but decided that he was too small to
be of any use to him.

The mention of Charlie Cunningham brings
back pleasant memories of one of the finest riders
that ever crossed a horse, and of one of the best
companions that ever brought gladness to the
heart of man. C. J. Cunningham had many
virtues and many attainments, but he was perhaps
chiefly remarkable for the fact that he was by
far the biggest man that has ever got into the
front rank of steeplechase riders. He was by

nature a 13-stone man, being well over six feet high and broad in proportion, but, by a most penitential system of wasting, he so reduced himself that he was able, on occasions, to ride as low as 11 stone 7 lbs. His success at Scottish and North-country meetings was unprecedented, and on a real bad horse he was, admittedly, without a rival. It is chiefly, however, on account of his personal qualities that he will be remembered and regretted in the North. At every race-meeting in Scotland, and indeed at many a social meeting in which racing had no part, there was a sense of incompleteness if C. J. C.'s cheery face and magnetic personality were missing. As a narrator of Scotch anecdotes he was unequalled, and his fund of these was inexhaustible and suited to all tastes. He killed himself by the systematic wasting of a big muscular frame that called for twice the nourishment it got.

In a more tragic way, but surely from the same cause, died the great Fred Archer. Archer was by nature a 10-stone man, and throughout the racing season he kept himself within the limits of 8 stone 7 lbs., saddle included. No constitution could stand such a strain indefinitely, and, in the end, he paid the penalty exacted by outraged Nature.

To the racing men of his day, Archer must always stand out as the foremost jockey of the century, if not of all time. It is always a difficult and a delicate matter to compare past giants with the popular favourites of the moment. The comparison is, in fact, impossible, as it is only in direct competition that pre-eminence can be established. But this much can certainly be said : that, during his riding career, Archer stood out more conspicuously from all his contemporaries than any former or subsequent jockey has done, not only by virtue of the fact that he always headed the list of winners, but also from his striking appearance and distinctive style of riding. Archer was a tall man and always rode very long. Nowadays jockeys present a more or less grotesque appearance, hunched up like monkeys on their horses' withers. No doubt the modern seat is justified by the relief afforded to the horse, but the result inevitably is that all jockeys have the same seat and look alike. In Archer's day the monkey-seat was not yet devised, and there was considerable latitude as to the length of stirrup, etc. which a jockey affected. Archer's seat was unique and unmistakable. Six inches taller than any other jockey of his day—with the possible exception of Webb—he rode as long as it is possible for a man to ride and yet touch the stirrups. His great length of limb made him no less conspicuous from all the other jockeys of his day than did his attractive, cadaverous face. In a field of twenty starters his appearance alone would instantly have arrested the attention of any foreigner visiting England for the first time. In a close finish his methods were equally distinctive. While the shorter jockeys worked their little legs against the saddle-flaps, Archer would seem literally to wind his

legs round his horse and lift him to the front by
sheer muscular force and determination. Nowadays such methods are made impossible by the
modern seat, and it may safely be said that
though that seat may be advantageous to the
horse, it cannot but be most disadvantageous to
the jockey, and makes it a physical impossibility
that we shall ever again see such finishes as Fred
Archer used to furnish us with when, on an
apparently beaten horse, he would, by sheer
muscular effort, force his way to the front through
the crowd of pigmies opposed to him, and win on
the post by a short head. Such exhibitions—and
they were frequent—were dramatic in the extreme,
and made Archer the idol of the public to an
extent never approached by any other jockey.
It used to be said—with some degree of truth—
that no horse, however bad, was ever out of the
reckoning in a five-furlong race if Archer were on
its back. On the other hand, it is not to be
denied that his driving power at the finish of a
race was so tremendous that he broke the spirit
of more than one good horse.

The most remarkable race that I ever saw
ridden was the race for the Gold Cup at Epsom
between Bend Or and Robert the Devil the year
following Bend Or's Derby victory, when the
latter, ridden by Archer, had won by a head.
Many people had criticised Rossiter's riding of
Robert the Devil on that occasion, and in the
Gold Cup next year, which was practically a
match between the two old opponents, Mr. Brewer
gave the mount on his beautiful horse to Tom

Cannon. Feeling and betting ran very high over the race, which was felt to be a duel between the Duke and the bookmaker, and, in a lesser degree, between the respective classes which the two principals represented. As the two horses came down the straight, the race appeared to be all over. Cannon was sitting perfectly still on Robert the Devil, who was leading by a length, while Archer was working at Bend Or with arms and legs. No one, 200 yards from home, would have taken 10 to 1 about Bend Or's chance. Then, to everyone's amazement, in spite of Bend Or's obvious distress, Archer was seen to be gradually gaining ground, and, when Cannon began to move in his saddle, a deafening roar of excitement went up from twenty thousand throats. Past the Grand Stand both jockeys were riding for all they were worth, the horses apparently dead level, and it was not till the numbers went up that we knew that Bend Or had again won by a head. Never have I seen anything approaching the reception that owner, horse and jockey got as the Duke led his horse in. Staid and sober men went mad and flung their hats in the air, not because of their winnings, but in sheer exuberance of spirits at seeing a favourite horse and rider achieve the apparently impossible. Of course Robert the Devil was a cur and Rossiter's riding in the previous Derby was vindicated, but, none the less, it is doubtful whether any other jockey that ever lived could have squeezed Bend Or's nose in front that day.

CHAPTER XIV

In 1885 my father died and my whole outlook in life was changed. A general election was impending. My brothers Claud, George and Frederic were already pledged to constituencies in England, and, at the time of my father's death, my eldest brother was the selected candidate for North Tyrone, the electoral division in which Barons Court was situated. His sudden accession to the title of course disqualified him, and, at the eleventh hour, I, as the youngest and only unattached member of the family, was thrust, an unwilling victim, into his place. I left the army and devoted all my energies to the more or less uncongenial work of electioneering.

The Nationalist candidate opposed to me was John Dillon, at that time one of the most prominent leaders of the anti-British movement in Ireland. John Dillon, it must be owned, was not a genial foe. I did my best to stretch out to him the hand of good-fellowship, but he did not respond, and, after a time, I abandoned the effort.

The election was prolific in incidents, generally of an amusing, but sometimes of a distressing character. One never-to-be-forgotten experience came very markedly under the latter category.

It is the privilege of the candidate at Parliamentary elections to sit, if he so wishes, in any of the polling-booths during the voting. In England, where the ballot is secret, this would be a dreary and profitless occupation, but in Ulster—with all the Roman Catholics under orders to vote illiterate —the situation offers many possibilities. Only once did I take advantage of my privilege. Happening to be in Newtown Stewart on the morning of the poll, and having nothing at the moment to do, I strolled into the polling booth and took my seat by the Presiding Officer. On the other side of the Presiding Officer sat the parish priest, who was acting as Personating Agent for John Dillon. Presently in came one of the gardeners employed at Barons Court, by name Carlin and a Roman Catholic.

" Can you read or write? " asked the Presiding Officer.

" I cannot, sir," stoutly replied Carlin, who was in reality an excellent scholar.

" Whom do you vote for? " asked the Presiding Officer, in continuance of the recognised formula.

Then began a very painful scene. Poor Carlin looked first at me and then at the priest. On the one side he saw—as he thought—instant dismissal from his employment, and, on the other side, all the purgatorial bans which the Roman Catholic Church can call down on the heads of those who go contrary to its orders. He scratched his head and he shuffled his feet, and he looked as if he wished the earth would open and swallow him.

POLITICS

The perspiration began to pour off his face. It was really a most distressing spectacle.

" Well," said the Presiding Officer impatiently. " Hurry up. I can't wait all day."

" Ah, well," said the poor fellow, with a look of agony, " I suppose I vote for his lordship over there," at the same time jerking his thumb in my direction. That was enough for me. My presence had obviously gained me a vote, but at too high a price. I fled the spot, and never again could any persuasion induce me to enter a polling-booth while voting was going on.

Outside, in the street, I met a strong supporter of mine of the name of David Nelson.

" Well, David," I said, " how are things going ? "

" 'Deed, sir, they're going right well," was his cheering reply; " I've voted twice myself already."

This was about ten o'clock in the morning, and there was a wealth of encouragement, to my mind, in the word " already " !

A little further down the street I noticed a small knot of my supporters in animated converse and joined the group. While we were discussing our chances, a farmer named Sproule came striding up to us, evidently pregnant with news.

" Did you hear John Porter died this morning ? " he inquired of the company generally.

" John Porter dead ! " cried one of the others. " Well, well, that's the sad affair."

" It's a queer thing the man couldn't have

205

waited till to-morrow," another remarked in an injured tone.

" He voted early," Sproule went on to explain; " 'twas on his way home from voting that he dropped dead."

" Ah, well," said the last speaker, in evident relief of mind, " a man can't live for ever, and there's others would be worse missed than John Porter, anyway."

Life and death on that day were considerations which were entirely secondary in importance to the recording of a vote against Home Rule.

Every kind of device was resorted to in order to ensure victory.

At one outlying polling-booth on the very fringe of the division, the Presiding Officer was a well-known Nationalist. To him entered two of my supporters whom I will call Henderson and Baird.

" Well, McCrossan," Baird inquired, " how are you getting on here ? "

" Oh, things are pretty slow," McCrossan replied; " there have only been two voters in during the last hour."

" Come out and have a drink, then," Baird suggested.

" Well, I don't mind if I do," said McCrossan; " but how about the blessed polling-booth ? I can't well leave that."

" Oh, Henderson here will take your place while you are away," said Baird.

" All right," said McCrossan, " I'm with you," and off he accordingly went with Baird, while

POLITICS

Henderson temporarily officiated as Presiding Officer.

After a time, McCrossan returned, much refreshed, and resumed his duties.

" Well ? " said Baird, turning to Henderson when they were clear of the polling-booth.

" It's all right," Henderson replied. " Five Nationalists came in while you were away, and I handed them all unstamped voting papers."

I did not quite believe this story when it was told me next day, but, at the counting of the votes, there, sure enough, was one box with five unstamped papers in it, on each of which there was a cross opposite Dillon's name. They were, of course, disallowed.

It might at first sight appear, from a superficial study of the above fragments, as though my election had been secured by methods which are not in general use and not officially recognised; but, on that score, I have no qualms of conscience, for it is quite certain that, for every point so scored by my over-zealous supporters, the other side scored at least two, and probably far more. In craft and subtlety they were streets ahead of us. For one thing, it was almost impossible for my Committee to find Personating Agents who could swear to the identity of the voters from the exclusively Nationalist districts. Men commissioned to make themselves familiar with these districts and their residents were apt to find themselves waylaid, and badly stoned or beaten by bands of politicians who viewed their enterprise unfavourably. The opportunities for personation, therefore, were almost unlimited. Hugh O'Kane, entitled to vote by his position on the register, might have been dead or he might never have existed in the flesh, but it was an absolute certainty that, on the election day, someone would slouch into the polling-booth and vote in the name of Hugh O'Kane, and then probably go on to another polling-booth and vote in another name. There is no doubt that, in my time, there were quite a number of electors on the register who had no existence except in patriotic imagination. In one townland alone, in my constituency, there were no less than thirty-eight Barney Devines on the register. It was, as I say, impossible to establish the identity of all these Barney Devines, whose right to vote the Revising Barrister had allowed, and vote they all did, dead or alive. The little unauthorised efforts to swell my majority made by well-wishers on my side were mere pin-pricks by comparison with the organised enterprise on the other side.

Although the Nationalists were admittedly ahead of us in various unrecognised branches of the electioneering art, I think we were but little behind them in the more legitimate fields of enterprise, as the following incident, which occurred during my brother's election, should show.

About six o'clock on the evening of the poll I was at Barons Court, resting after a very hard day, when a telegram arrived from Drumquin

urging the immediate despatch of some vehicle
to take several bed-ridden voters to the poll.
That was, of course, long before the days of
motor-cars. All the Barons Court carriages were
out except an antique vehicle known as the
Clarence, and for that there were no horses
available. My sister-in-law, the Duchess, and I
were the only two people on the spot at the
moment. Everyone else was away either voting
or helping others to vote. My sister-in-law, with
her usual promptitude and energy, grasped the
situation in a moment. We hurried up together
to the stables and there, with the help of one of
the garden boys, found an old cart-mare used for
bringing heavy luggage from the station, and
a four-year-old thoroughbred filly which was
out at grass. This most incongruous pair we
harnessed with some difficulty to the Clarence,
I climbed on to the box and away we started on
our six-mile drive. The cart-mare, whom I rib-
roasted most unmercifully, no doubt thought the
world had gone mad, while the filly alternately
galloped and kicked. Our progress was necessarily slow, for the cart-mare's best pace was
under five miles an hour, and it was 7.30 before
Drumquin was reached. Here I was met by a
small but enthusiastic knot of supporters, who
swarmed on to the groaning carriage and directed
me to the first house to be visited. Apparently
there were only three of these bed-ridden voters
to be carried to the poll. The first two were
safely got in and afterwards left to recover at

Dr. Corry's house hard by, while we went off to fetch in the one and last remaining voter. In this final journey the front of the Clarence was thickly covered with the stalwart forms of our friends, who clung to it like flies and supplemented my anæmic efforts at encouraging the horses with tremendous whacks from their sticks. The filly, being grass-fed and quite raw, was by now as deadbeat as the cart-mare and, in spite of these very direct appeals, our progress was slow. On reaching the house indicated, the old man on whom Unionist interest was, for the moment, centred, was found to be very frail and feeble, but dressed for the journey, and resolutely determined to register his vote against Home Rule, even if he died the next minute. My companions, however, assured him that a Unionist victory was the one tonic needed to set him on his feet again, and, on the old man concurring in a high falsetto pipe, they bundled him into the carriage and off we set once more for the polling-booth. By this time it was five minutes to eight : Drumquin was by far the most Nationalist district in the constituency, and outside the polling-booth a hostile crowd was assembled which did its best to prevent our old man from getting in before the clock struck eight. Our supporters, however, though few in numbers, were great in energy and zeal, and literally forced a passage through the crowd, carrying the old man with them. Amidst tremendous cheers he made his cross and was carried out again to the carriage with its two steaming and staggering horses. We got him safely home again, but I regret to say that victory did not prove the effective tonic that our supporters had anticipated, for he remained bed-ridden till his death.

To come back to my own 1885 election; when the votes were finally counted I had a majority of 453, the total electorate being between seven and eight thousand. I proffered my hand, according to custom, to the defeated candidate, but Mr. John Dillon refused to take it, and turned bitterly away with the threat that he would yet wrest the seat from me. On the occasion of the next election, however—six months later—he thought better of his resolve, and the Nationalists put up a Presbyterian of the name of Wylie to oppose me, the idea being that he would be able to detach from my support a certain number of the Radical Presbyterian farmers. Under the old political divisions of Liberal and Conservative, these Presbyterians had been pronounced and, in many cases, even bitter Radicals, but Mr. Gladstone's Home Rule Bill had—very much against the grain—thrust them into alliance with their old enemies the Conservatives against the common danger of Home Rule. Mr. Wylie was put up with the idea of reviving these ancient party animosities, and, in particular, of stirring up the old landlord *versus* tenant feeling. The ruse completely failed. Greatly as these sturdy Radicals may have disliked the idea of voting for a Tory, they disliked even more the idea of a Home Rule Parliament, and Mr. Wylie was defeated by some 360 votes. The announcement of the poll was quickly followed by the news of my three brothers' return in different parts of the country, and there were great rejoicings at Barons Court that night. During the two Sessions which followed on these elections, there were no less than four of us Hamilton brothers in the House of Commons and a fifth in the House of Lords—a legislative record which I should imagine few families had ever equalled.

Before the next election I had married, which made it necessary for me to retire from Parliament, and I did not stand again. My brother Freddie, who had so far represented one of the Manchester divisions, undertook to fill my place. His fight was a harder one than either of mine had been, for, in the meanwhile, the Nationalists had considerably strengthened their position at the Revision Sessions. In spite of this, however, he managed to defeat his antagonist, Mr. Dogherty by 47 votes. I shall never forget the desperate strain on our nerves during the counting of the votes on that occasion. When a box from a Nationalist district was opened, the ticks opposite Dogherty's name would surge ahead with a rush which it seemed as though nothing could check or overtake. Then a box from a Unionist district would come on the table and we breathed again as Mr. Dogherty's marks were gradually overhauled. When it was all over and Colonel King-Edwardes had announced the result from the balcony of the Town Hall, we all repaired in great glee to Sim's Hotel, where, on the first floor, a table had been prepared on which stood twelve bottles of champagne with the corks invitingly drawn. Mr. Dogherty had a more or less similar table prepared on the floor above, for—win or lose—the rule in Ireland is to celebrate the event in the wine that cheereth, or, at any rate, in the whisky that cheereth.

As we stood outside the door of our room, waiting for the expected guests to assemble, Father McConologue, Mr. Dogherty's election agent, mounted the stairs on his way to the refreshment provided on the upper floor. As he passed us, his eye rested approvingly on the spectacle of the twelve gold-necked bottles standing in hospitable array on the table within. Now Father McConologue was the bitterest Nationalist in all North Tyrone. He would invariably cross himself and spit when he passed any member of my family on the road, and black scowls were the only greeting any of us had ever been able to extract from him. My brother, however, in the bonhomie inspired by a victory which, half an hour earlier, had seemed out of reach, called out to him as he passed :

" Won't you join us in a glass, Father McConologue ? "

To our unbounded amazement, the priest first paused and then—after a moment's hesitation—replied :

" Well, I don't mind if I do."

It is possible that Mr. Dogherty's table above may have boasted nothing more sparkling than the wares of Kinahan or John Jamieson, and that the good priest knew that this was so, but—be that as it may—he readily joined us, the doors were closed and the juice of the grape passed with astonishing rapidity from the gold-necked bottles into glasses and thence to its time-honoured destination. At the end of half an hour spent in this pleasant relaxation, Father McConologue rose slowly to his feet and, in solemn but emotional tones, announced his intention of delivering himself of a speech. Loud applause greeted this announcement, for the twelve bottles were by now empty, and ten people only sat round the board.

The reverend gentleman's address consisted mainly of a passionate panegyric of the Hamilton family, and concluded with the following startling announcement, coming, as it did, from Mr. Dogherty's election agent :

" And I declare to you, gentlemen, that there's no man on God's earth that I'd so soon see representing North Tyrone as Lord Frederic Hamilton." Great indeed are the powers of Moet and Chandon !

At that time I was something of an idealist and was much given to tilting at social and political windmills, and one of the windmills against whose sails I was at the moment measuring my strength was the blood-sucking system of usury

214

known in Ireland as the Gombeen system. This
system did not operate to any appreciable extent
in Tyrone itself, but among the ignorant peasantry
of West Donegal it was reported to be rampant,
and to West Donegal I accordingly turned my
steps with a view to acquiring first-hand information on the spot. For the benefit of the uninitiated,
it may be explained that the Gombeen man is
the village moneylender who makes advances
at exorbitant rates to smallholders and shop-
keepers, and finally gets the entire country-side
body and soul into his clutches.

After some thought I determined to make the
village of Dungloe, in West Donegal, my head-
quarters, and I accordingly drove the intervening
sixty miles or so on an outside car and established
myself at the house of one McSweeney, a publican.
My first move, as was not unnatural, was to seek
out Father X., the parish priest of the place, with
a view to gleaning from him some particulars
of the worst known cases of Gombeen usury in
his parish. Father X. was entirely cordial, but
showed little enthusiasm over the special object
of my mission. He told me a number of excellent
stories, but always sidled adroitly off the main
track which led to the Gombeen system and its
local adherents.

Before I left—very little wiser than I had come
—he invited me to dine with him on the following
night, and I gladly accepted his offer, hoping that,
under the expanding influence of dinner, he would
become more communicative. In a sense my

hopes were realised, for, after the whisky had been succeeded by port, the good priest—though still disappointingly shy of the Gombeen question —made some amends by launching out into a furious tirade against the Land League and all its ways and apostles. As Father X. was the President of the local Land League, this outburst was not without its interest.

The dinner was a great success, especially at first, when conversation was brisk and reciprocal. The port, however, was good, and disappeared with a rapidity which soon became responsible for long pauses in the conversation. Lower and lower on his chest sank the good priest's head, till finally, with a flop, he himself disappeared bodily under the table and there remained. In serious alarm I rang the bell to summon the maid.

" I am afraid Father X. is not very well," I remarked, on her arrival.

" Och ! never heed him," she replied, with the utmost unconcern. " He'll be the well man in time for morning mass. Get you home now." So, much relieved in mind and on excellent terms with myself, I dismissed my host's sudden indisposition from my mind and trudged back through the night to McSweeney's hotel.

My first duty obviously was to return Father X.'s hospitality, but the matter presented some little difficulty, for not a drop of port was to be had for love or money in the village of Dungloe. Finally, after all my local inquiries had failed, I was forced to send off a special car to Gweedore, sixteen miles distant, with instructions to bring back two bottles of best port from the hotel, where, to my knowledge, the late Lord George Hill had laid down a cellar of very excellent wines in the hopes of bringing monied tourists into the country.

In due course the car returned with its two bottles, and my invitation went out to Father X. and was promptly and gratefully accepted. I carefully drew the cork of one of the bottles and instructed Biddy, the maid, to fill our glasses the moment the soup had been served and before she handed round the whisky. The little maid carried out my instructions to the letter, but, to my utter stupefaction, as she approached the priest, bottle in hand, he waved her away with the offended dignity of the confirmed abstainer.

" Take it away, Biddy," he exclaimed with a look of repugnance, " take it away. You should surely know that I never taste."

Having left my guest three nights before literally under the table, I could only sit and stare in blank amazement. Presently Biddy left the room, whereupon the priest gave a hurried and whispered explanation.

" You see, I'm President of the local Temperance Society," he told me, " and it would never do to let the girl see me drink-taking. But I see you've two bottles there on the table, and by your good leave I'll just slip the one with the cork in it into my pocket and take it home with me." Which he did.

It is impossible to leave the subject of Donegal and its Roman Catholic clerics without some reference to the famous Father McFadden of Gweedore. After leaving Dungloe, I spent some three weeks at Gweedore, and, during my stay there, I heard innumerable anecdotes concerning the exploits and peculiarities of the parish priest. My curiosity was aroused and I determined, at the risk of an unfriendly welcome—for Father McFadden was reputed a very bitter Nationalist— to pay the priest a call. Accordingly I set out one afternoon to cover the two miles of road which lay between the hotel and the priest's house. A neat maid responded to my ring, and, without inquiring my name, ushered me straight into the priest's sitting-room—a comfortable and luxurious room, the walls of which were lined with gaily-bound books of various descriptions. These books I examined with interest later on, but, on my first entry, I had eyes for nothing beyond the extraordinary figure with which I was confronted. I had come, as already explained, to call on the parish priest, but it seemed to me that I must have made a mistake and called on the M.F.H. instead, for the figure that rose to greet me was in full hunting costume, top-boots, leathers, scarlet coat and all. As there was, to my certain knowledge, no pack of foxhounds within a hundred miles of Gweedore, I could hardly believe my eyes, and felt that I must either be mad or in a dream. Father McFadden, however—for it was indeed he—quickly reassured me.

POLITICS

" You'll be surprised to see me like this," he remarked after shaking me warmly by the hand, " but the fact is I have just been giving a sitting to an artist who is painting my portrait. Come now till I show you."

He led me to an adjoining room, and there with pride showed me a life-sized portrait of himself in the costume in which he then stood, with the addition of a tall hat and a hunting crop. I admired the picture as much as I was able and then timidly inquired what pack of hounds he usually patronised.

" Hounds ! is it ? " he exclaimed. " Faith ! I've never crossed a horse's back in my life, but I just had the conceit to be painted that way. It's a pleasant change from the black, anyway."

We returned to the library, where, after a time, conversation turned to the cause of my long stay at that inclement season of the year (it was mid-winter) in such a wild district as West Donegal. I explained that I was collecting material for a crusade against the Gombeen men, and asked if he were in sympathy with my endeavour. He replied that he was, called the Gombeen men " dirty blackguards," and wished me every luck, but—as in the case of Father X.— I found the conversation adroitly turned aside the moment I began to press for facts. In spite of this disappointing reticence on the one subject as to which I particularly desired information, I found Father McFadden excellent company, and spent a very pleasant hour with him before returning to my hotel. Needless to say, he knew all about my stay in the district and, as he told me, had been expecting, and even hoping for a visit.

The peasantry of West Donegal are to a certain extent a race apart. They are reputed to be the purest Irish in the island, unalloyed by any admixture of immigrant blood.

There is good reason to suppose that the popular belief that West Donegal—in common with West Galway and Sligo—had a strong admixture of Spanish blood introduced into it by survivors from the Armada, is a fallacy. It is very doubtful whether there were any survivors in Ireland from the wreck of the great fleet. The evidence of the State Papers of the day goes to show that the natives killed all the survivors whom they found, and that the Government executed all those who escaped the natives. One man, named Loughlin McCabe, boasted that he himself had killed eighty Spaniards with a hatchet as they landed on the Donegal rocks from one of the wrecks. Fitz-william, who was Deputy at the time of the Armada, made a diligent search of the Connaught and Ulster coasts with a large armed force, but only succeeded in finding two Spanish and five Dutch boys, all of whom he dutifully hanged. Two brothers of the name of Hoveden, after a long search, collected a handful of survivors in Donegal, and sent them up to Dublin, where they were hanged. As a matter of fact the Spanish type, which is supposed to be an inheritance from the Armada, is very rare in Ireland. During my month's stay in West Donegal I hardly saw one who could truly be said to suggest a Spanish origin.

The people of the coast are a quiet, inoffensive race—poor physically and very poor in this world's goods. This latter is to a certain extent their own fault, for, at their very door, lies an inexhaustible supply of food, had they only the enterprise to grasp it. There is no better fishing-ground in the kingdom than off the Donegal coast, but it is impossible to induce the natives to tempt the waves in pursuit of it. The late Mr. E. T. Herdman, of Sion Mills, most generously furnished two of his protégés at Dungloe with a complete fishing outfit—boats, sails, nets and all. The men, who had pleaded their inability to equip themselves as their excuse for not fishing, were profuse in thanks, but when Mr. Herdman returned for his annual trout fishing a year later, he found that neither of the boats had so much as been in the water, the excuse this time being that the men had no one to teach them how to sail a boat. For all I know to the contrary, those two boats may still be lying high and dry on the shore.

CHAPTER XV

THE House of Commons, for the entry into which I had put myself to much inconvenience and a not inconsiderable expense, proved a disappointment to my expectations. It was not what I had pictured it. Like many another aspiring politician, I had entered the Parliamentary arena full of lofty schemes for the regeneration of mankind. I had pictured the House of Commons as being full of noble, high-souled patriots whose lives were devoted to the interests of their country and their fellow-men. I found it full of scramblers for salaried offices and mushroom titles. I myself was a mere brick in a buttress whose sole purpose was to maintain a number of paid officials in their billets. Outside of that one sphere of usefulness, I had no value and—in the party-political sense—no existence. Nobody wanted me except as a voter in divisions. If I voted regularly, and as I was told, for a certain number of years, and had a corresponding number of good marks against my name, then I myself (quite irrespective of merit) might hope to find myself on one of the lower rungs of the ladder of those who are paid. The demeanour of the two front benches struck

PARLIAMENT

me as unworthy. Of generosity, of desire to
facilitate the government of the country or
to further the interests of the empire I could
see little trace. No proposed reform, however
desirable, could rouse a spark of interest, unless
there were votes in it. On the other hand,
childish recrimination and insincere criticism of
every measure emanating from the other side
were in ceaseless evidence. It all seemed petty
and, in a sense, sordid. For, behind all this
wordy warfare, even I—inexperienced as I was—
could detect plainly enough the hungry greed of
the Opposition for the fat portfolios facing them,
and the avaricious tightening of the Government
grasp on those same portfolios the moment their
possession was threatened.

There were other phases, too, of Parliamentary
life that I quickly realised were outside my
mental grasp. When I saw Members of Parliament, who called themselves Englishmen, systematically taking the side of their country's
enemies, and yet being saluted by policemen and
going about the streets with whole skins, I felt
that I was in a world for which I was not fitted.

For a time the novelty of the situation made
some amends for my disillusionment. Mr. Gladstone was a source of ceaseless delight. His
splendid presence, his arresting voice with the
curious burr in it, his magnificent Homeric
periods, which sounded so superb and which
meant so little, fascinated me from first to last.
His courtliness to foe no less than friend was

even more captivating than his oratory. While
I was stumbling and halting through my absurd
maiden speech, Mr. Gladstone sat throughout
with his hand to his ear in an attitude of reverent
attention. My own front bench talked loudly
among themselves the whole while—a direct
snub which quickly reduced me to imbecile
incoherence. It was easy to understand, even
from a little incident such as this, the adoration
which the Liberal leader inspired in the minds of
his followers.

The best speaker of my day was unquestionably
Mr. Chamberlain. Gladstone was magnificent
and sonorous, but his utterances were cryptic
and left no sense of completeness. Chamberlain,
on the other hand, was clearness itself. He never
spoke for more than three-quarters of an hour—
admirable rule—there was no superfluous verbiage,
and every sentence he uttered was alive with
meaning. His voice was very clear and penetrating, and he was always the personification of
coolness, even in the midst of the violent vituperation to which his candid handling of cant and
humbug exposed him.

The Irish had a good speaker of the florid,
theatrical type in Mr. Sexton, but he always
seemed to speak with his tongue in his cheek,
and so failed to carry conviction. Engrossing
speeches, however, formed very occasional relief-
spots in a dreary sea of prosy and pompous talk,
and, at the end of six years, I withdrew moodily
and without regret from the field of party politics.

CHAPTER XVI

MOST people will remember the feverish rush of gold-seekers to Klondyke in 1897 and '98, the terrible tragedies of the Chilkoot and White Passes, and the lesser tragedies of the White Horse Rapids. These tragedies were, alas ! on an infinitely greater scale than the civilised world ever knew of. Unknown men swarmed up to try their fortunes in the new fields, sacrificing everything to the one mad desire to out-distance competitors and have the first pick of the golden claims which were waiting to be staked out. Hundreds found nameless graves in the snow, were trampled on by those who followed, and disappeared from the world unmourned and, in most cases, unidentified. At first the Chilkoot and White Passes shared the tragedies impartially. Later on the Chilkoot Pass was abandoned, and Skagway and the White Pass were the gates by which all who entered the Klondyke came and went.

The earlier pioneers had brought horses with them in hopes of out-distancing their rivals. It was quickly realised that the White Pass was impracticable for horses. They fell through the snow into bog-holes and could not be extricated. There were said to be 1500 dead and dying horses lining the short trail from Skagway to the summit of the White Pass at one time during the height of the rush. Dogs succeeded horses for the few who could afford them, but the majority tramped over the snow in single file, with set faces and with their packs on their backs, in many cases till they dropped. On the flat stretches, when the wind was favourable, sails were attached to the sleighs, to lessen the toil of haulage. When the Yukon River was reached, rough boats and rafts were put together and the adventurers dropped down the river to Dawson. In the White Horse Rapids, the hastily-constructed boats in many cases failed to bear the strain of the tumultuous waters, and many more nameless and friendless men dropped out of the competition.

In July 1899 I was asked by a small but enterprising syndicate, on the search for auriferous properties, to make the journey to Atlin, in the Yukon, to inspect and, if necessary, purchase a property, as to the possibilities of which the most exhilarating reports had been brought to London. The enterprise was one which appealed to my sense of adventure and I willingly accepted the offer. Twenty thousand pounds, the purchase price demanded for the property, was lodged to my credit in the Bank of Montreal at Vancouver, and off I set in company with my friend Fred Haggard, who was also attracted to the far North-West by the tales of fabulous riches which were afloat.

KLONDYKE

On arrival at Vancouver we took ship for Skagway in the old *Humboldt*, in company with a rough and cosmopolitan crowd all bound on similar errands to our own. In close quarters with the very mixed company in which I found myself, I experienced some little uneasiness from the fact that I was carrying £2000 in notes on my person, this being the deposit required to secure an option on the mine, in the purchase of which, we were assured, half the plutocrats in Europe were sending up their representatives to forestall us.

The only excitement during the voyage was furnished by the astonishing foolhardiness of our navigators. The British Columbian coast is generally fog-bound during the late summer months. A considerable part of the thousand-miles sail from Vancouver to Skagway is through ridiculously narrow channels between rocky islands and the mainland. In threading these narrows, which we did at full speed, we had to rely for our whereabouts solely on the time which it took for the echo of our siren to come back to us from the shore. As, in places, the channel was not more than 200 yards wide, this method of steering through a fog, coupled with our unabated speed, seemed to me little short of insane. I made observations to this effect to the skipper (an American), but he informed me laconically that, as a quick arrival at their destination was the first consideration with all who were bound for Klondyke, and as they were running in competition with another line of steamers, considerations of safety which ruled elsewhere had to be put aside. He reassured me, to some extent, by the information that, so far, there had been no accidents. Further north, in the more open waters, the same mad policy of full steam ahead, regardless of risks, was maintained. The sea off the entrance to the Lynn " Canal," as it is called, is thickly dotted with ice-floes thrown off by the Muir Glacier and other minor contributaries, and our progress was punctuated by continual shocks as our bow came in contact with these floes. An ice-floe, of course, is but a baby iceberg and some of these shocks were very severe. On our return journey, on the *Princess of Seattle*, we were all brought out of our bunks one night by a terrific shock which brought the boat to a standstill, quivering from stem to stern like a leaf, but no disaster followed and, after a time, we continued our precarious course.

Next morning I made inquiries from the ship's officers. " We struck a somewhat larger floe than usual," they explained, " but luckily it split." I asked what would have happened if it had not split, and was answered by an eloquent shrug of the shoulders.

Immunity from accident makes fools of us all. At the time I travelled there had been no accidents on the Skagway route. Within three years from the date of my journey, three ships went to the bottom—in two cases with all on board and in the third case with great loss of life. One, while steering by the siren, struck the rocks in a fog in one of the narrow channels. Another presumably struck an ice-floe which did not split, for it disappeared off the mouth of the Lynn Canal and there were no survivors to tell the world what had happened. Lastly, the gallant little *Princess of Seattle*, with her staff of bright and breezy American officers, turned turtle in Queen Charlotte's Sound and sank with all on board. She was really a river steamer, with far too much top-dressing for the open sea. The sea-voyage to Skagway, as already explained, is for the greater part in dead-calm waters between the mainland and the myriad islands that dot the coast, but Queen Charlotte's Sound is open sea, for which, under bad conditions, the *Princess of Seattle* was quite unfitted. However, she was fast, and, as that outweighed all other considerations with men who were racing one another for gold, Queen Charlotte's Sound was chanced; till, one day, a westerly gale caught the ship broadside on when she was half-way across the Sound and blew her over like a flower-pot.

No such disaster, however, overtook us during my trip, and, after a comparatively uneventful voyage, we entered the safe waters of the Lynn Canal.

The Lynn Canal has been pronounced by many critics to furnish the grandest scenery in the world. At the mouth stands Mount St. Elias, rising over 18,000 feet sheer from the water's edge, and backed by another giant, whose name escapes me at the moment, which is a thousand feet higher. The entire " Canal," which is about ten miles wide, is hedged in by giant peaks of eternal ice and snow, which sparkle in the sunshine with a hundred different lights and colours.

As we approached Skagway, Fred Haggard and I were considerably intrigued by the ceaseless attentions of an evil-looking passenger who hovered with unnecessary insistence in our neighbourhood. When we landed and found this same individual dogging our footsteps as we tramped the streets in search of lodgings, we had little doubt but that he knew of the £2000 I carried in my breast-pocket and intended transferring it by some means to his own breast-pocket. We eventually found a room which appeared clean, and we had just come to terms with the owner when we saw our villainous-looking shadow pass rapidly out of the house.

" Who is that ? " I asked of our landlord.

" I don't know his name," was the reply, " but he has just hired a room here for the night."

Our suspicions were now doubled. There remained no doubt in our minds that this was a " tough " on the track of our £2000. We had no arms and there was no lock to our door, but we pulled the chest of drawers across and, behind this barrier, slept peacefully till morn. Nothing happened. When we rose in the morning, the £2000 was still safely reposing beneath my pillow and the cut-throat tough had already left. We never saw him again. What his real object was in following us (for there is no doubt he did follow us) must for ever remain a mystery. The probability is that he had recognised us for English greenhorns, and hoped in some way to make profit out of us by acting as our guide and counsellor. It is practically impossible that he can have known of the money I carried.

When we arrived at Skagway, the White Pass railway had just been opened. Like everything American (Skagway and the White Pass are in U.S.A.), it had been engineered, built and opened with almost incredible rapidity, but with a corresponding lack of stability. The Alaskan country grows no big timber and the trestle-bridges and under-pins that held the track above the yawning abysses below were fashioned out of timber that was far too small for safety. The crankiness of the track was in everybody's mouth and, when we boarded the train next day, we were hardly surprised to find that all the passengers, without exception, stood throughout the short four-mile journey to the summit on the footboard next the cliff, ready to jump and cling when the train plunged down into the chasm below, as everyone expected it would. There were only two cars on the train, whose pace was between three and four miles an hour. As a matter of fact there was never any serious accident on the line, and, shortly after our visit, big timber was got up from San Francisco and the track put into proper condition.

At Bennet, which is in Canadian territory,

came the parting of the ways, those bound for Dawson taking to the Yukon River, while we who were for Atlin boarded the stern-paddler that was to carry us for 180 miles along the narrow, boomerang-shaped Takish Lake.

We were now in the province of Yukon and, during our eighteen hours on the lake, we had ample opportunity for studying the character of the country. The Yukon has a fascination of its own which lies mainly in its peculiar desolation. In place of the precipitous, forest-choked valleys of British Columbia, with their depressingly limited horizon, we were now among much flatter hills whose sides were only sparsely clothed with scrub, or with dwarfed and stunted fir trees clinging precariously to the patches of soil between the rocks. The colouring was simply gorgeous, the atmosphere clear as crystal and the horizon incalculably distant. Later on, when we were clear of the noisy steamer, the most noticeable features of this northern land were, perhaps, its intense silence and the depressing absence of bird life. A man lost in these parts, even though furnished with food supplies, and in spite of the vivid beauty of the landscape, might well be driven mad by the uncanny silence, by the absence of animal life and above all by the sense of illimitable vastness.

It was the evening of the day following our departure from Bennet before we reached the Taku River, where we had to disembark and cross on foot to Atlin Lake. The Taku River,

clear as aquamarine, came tumbling down from
Atlin Lake in a series of fascinating pools and
rapids which were more than my angling instincts
were able to resist. I had brought with me a little
hollow steel rod, the two smaller joints of which
were carried in the larger, and—for the moment
quite unmindful of graver issues—I hurriedly
put the rod together, attached my reel and line,
and cast an experimental fly on the waters of
this Arctic stream. My success was instantaneous. With my very first cast I hooked a
beautiful silvery spotless trout of about 1½ lbs.
From that time on it is no exaggeration to say
that, with every cast, I hooked a fish, sometimes
two, for I was fishing with three flies. Many of
them broke away, for I had no landing net and
had to haul them up kicking on to the shingle.
I stood throughout on the one spot without
budging. The sand-flies filled my eye-sockets
so that I literally could hardly see the water,
but in spite of the inconvenience of these attentions, so great was my excitement that I fished
on and on, heedless of the fact that all my fellow-
travellers had long since disappeared down the
trail through the forest. Finally, with a tremendous effort, I tore myself away from my
engrossing pursuit and made a desperate effort
to overtake the caravan. For some unaccountable reason I had with me an umbrella—
object of some curiosity and much derision, for
no such thing had ever before been seen in the
Yukon. The umbrella, however, was now to prove

its value, for I put all the fish I could carry
into it, seized the ends of the steels in a firm
grasp and, with the umbrella in one hand and
my rod in the other, and the flies still choking
up my eyes, set off best pace down the trail in
pursuit of my party. The trail was about a
mile and a half long, and when I arrived panting
and perspiring at the lake edge, there was the
little stern-paddler half a mile out, puffing its
way across to Atlin on the farther shore. While
I was anathematising my folly in having yielded
to the lure of the river, an unkempt figure in
greasy blue overalls and a black flannel shirt,
with three days' growth on his chin, came out of
the solitary tent on the wharf and remarked :
" I am afraid you have missed the boat." The
tone was so strikingly European that I stared in
some surprise.

" Come into my tent," he suggested, " and have
a smoke."

I accepted his invitation, sat down on an
empty packing-case and lit my pipe. The
stranger was greatly interested in my fish and
in my rod, which he gave me to understand was
the first trout-rod ever seen in Atlin. Men did
not visit those parts in quest of trout. After a
time, struck by the incongruity between my
host's speech and his appearance, I asked for
particulars concerning himself. As a result I
was told one of the saddest stories I have heard.

Smith, as I shall name my friend, had, it
appeared, been a medical student in Paris when

the Klondyke fever burst upon the world. He was badly infected and determined to risk his £600 capital in an attempt to make a quick fortune. Four other equally adventurous spirits joined him in the enterprise. Between them they raised £3000. Their plan was to reach Atlin from Ashcroft on the C.P.R., and so avoid the double duties at Skagway and Bennet by keeping throughout on Canadian soil. It was a mad scheme, for much of the country they had to pass through was unexplored and therefore almost certain to prove impenetrable. So in fact it turned out. Their way was continually blocked by fallen timber, round which they had to make long and wearisome circuits. The strength of man and beast gradually became exhausted. They started on their 1500-mile journey with twenty horses carrying themselves, their tents, food and camp equipment. Smith was the only one that reached Atlin. All the horses and his four companions died on the way, and he himself only just managed to stagger into Atlin with nothing in the world but a double-barrelled gun and the shirt on his back. When I met him, he was officially employed to check the baggage on the wharf at which the daily boat called. I suggested his writing to his people, who apparently had certain means, but he declared that he would die before he laid himself open to the " I told you so " taunts which his confession of failure would certainly bring upon him.

By the time he had finished his story it was quite dark, and, to his surprise no less than mine, we saw the lights of the little stern-paddler approaching from the far shore.

" There must be some miners coming out," Smith remarked. " You are in luck. It is more than a month since the boat made two trips across in one day."

True enough it was, as Smith surmised, miners who had missed the first boat and who were ready—as miners always are—to pay anything to get what they wanted. I left some of my fish with Smith and a promise to send him up some cartridges from Vancouver; but I never saw him again, although I made one memorable and very nearly fatal attempt to do so. It was in this wise.

After we had been in Atlin for a few days, I made the acquaintance of a New York lady named Mrs. Hitchcock, who was, as may readily be supposed, the only lady in Atlin, but who, having large mining interests in the country, had very pluckily resolved to come up to the Yukon and see about them for herself. I told her the story of " Smith," and she was so greatly interested that she organised a party to cross the lake and interview him with a view to philanthropic action. At the same time it was decided, while we were there, to test the fishing possibilities of the Taku River to the full.

On the morning arranged, the chosen party assembled at a narrow little creek that abutted upon the great lake, where lay the boat which was to carry us across the four miles of intervening and very agitated water. The party consisted of Mrs. Hitchcock, Haggard and myself, Bromley, our mining engineer, the young English parson attached to Atlin and two boatmen. With considerable difficulty the seven of us squeezed ourselves into the very limited space which the boat offered. We four passengers, so to speak, were wedged into the stern, where we sat packed together like herrings, while the two boatmen and the parson, who was acting as skipper, remained forward to see to the hoisting of the sail. When we were all in, I noticed with some concern that the stern of the boat was down to within two inches of the water. The creek where we had embarked, being sheltered from the wind, was as calm as a mill-pond, but, out in the open water, I could see big foam-crested waves chasing one another in quick succession down the ninety-six miles of the lake's length. I felt very uneasy. How in the name of reason could a boat be expected to carry a sail among waves such as those, when the water was lapping her gunwale in a dead calm? However, no one else seemed to share my misgivings, so I said nothing and we pushed off. In doing so one of the boatmen stumbled across a seat, and the lurch which he gave brought an ominous trickle of water over the stern. Then up spake Fred Haggard. "Mrs. Hitchcock," he said, "do you know that you are going to certain death out in the lake there?" Mrs. Hitchcock

expressed surprise and ignorance. She knew
nothing about boats. I did; and now that the
first word had been spoken, I loudly seconded
Fred Haggard's warning, and Bromley, who was
a composed and undemonstrative person, resolutely supported our view. Only the parson was
derisive. He had sailed this particular boat, he
said, across the lake a score of times in worse
weather than there was that day. "Yes," I
suggested, "but with two people in the boat,
and not seven." Still he sniffed and pooh-
poohed, but the weight of opinion was now very
decidedly against him and we put back. When
we were once more on shore, feeling slightly
ashamed of myself and the timid part I had
played, I got hold of Mackie, the owner of the
boat, who had so far uttered no word and shown
no interest in the discussion.

"Should we have got across?" I asked him.

"Not a chance," he replied calmly.

"Good heavens!" I exclaimed; "then why
did you let us start?"

"Well," he said, "you see I'm a Scot, and I
wouldn't have it said that I turned my back on
anything that others would face. But I was
right glad," he added, "when yon gentleman
spoke out."

With a distinct sense of grievance, I turned
away and sought out Johnson, the other boat-
man, who was standing some little way apart.

"Do you think we should have been swamped
out in the lake there?" I asked him.

"Sure thing," he replied, spitting unconcernedly into the water; "she couldn't have
lived two minutes in that sea, loaded the way she
was."

"But why didn't you say so?" I asked
irritably.

"Well, you see," he explained, "it's Mackie's
boat and I'm only hired for the day, so it wasn't
really my place to speak."

I then questioned Bromley and learned that
he too had known we were doomed the moment
he saw how close to the water was the gunwale
of the boat. So here were four of us, all grown
men and reputedly sane, going knowingly to a
purposeless and absolutely idiotic death because
we were all afraid to say that we were afraid!
There is no doubt that Fred Haggard saved all our
lives that day, for no one could have swum six
strokes in that icy water. His was a brave act,
and that is why I have recorded the incident.
The rest of us were cowards.

In all the financial enterprises upon which I
embarked in those days, my three close associates
were Fred Haggard, Alexander Hill, the most
honest and conscientious mining engineer that
ever assayed a sample, and Herbert-Smith, the
greatest and the straightest of all City lawyers.
We were all about the same age, and we used
to speak of ourselves as the four H's. Alas! of
that quartet, I alone remain. I could write a
volume about Alexander Hill and Herbert-Smith
—two of the finest characters it has been my lot

to rub shoulders with along the path of life, but
they are not in this story. Fred Haggard is,
and because he is in the story, and because for
over twenty years he played the Damon to my
Pythias, I hope that those who never met him
will forgive a short and humble epitaph to the
memory of one of the best. I travelled with him,
as I am now recounting, from London to the
Yukon and back; I travelled with him, as I
shall recount in the next chapter, from London
to the interior of Peru and back. I travelled
with him on a wild and very expensive goose-
chase into the heart of the mountain range that
separates Hungary and Roumania; I spent
three days and two nights with him on a filthy
tug which we chartered at Vancouver to take us
up a desolate inlet known as Frederick Arm, for
the inspection of a mine of doubtful value
belonging to our Syndicate. When, after a
horribly uncomfortable journey, we reached
this inaccessible spot, Bromley, who accompanied us, condemned the mine and Haggard
and I, as representatives of the owners, ordered
its immediate evacuation. So we took the eight
miners back with us on the tug and, at the water's
edge, we shot the beautiful young chestnut mare
that carried down their gear. It was a tragedy,
but there was no other way, so we left the poor
thing there, with its four hoofs sticking dismally
up in the air, for the coyotes to eat. It rained
during the whole of this trip; real straight solid
rain. We neither shaved nor washed nor changed

WHITE PASS.

a stitch of our clothing. We were wet through, and we ate and slept in the forecastle, or the cockpit, or whatever it is called, cheek by jowl with the crew and the miners, and with the cockroaches swarming round the swinging oil lamp on the low ceiling four feet above our faces. It was a trying experience, and one during which Damon might excusably have poleaxed Pythias; but, neither on that occasion nor on any other during our long, and occasionally uneasy, travels, did Fred Haggard and I ever quarrel. It is impossible to quarrel with a man who never loses his temper. He was often irritable to the extent of peevishness, but always with circumstances and never with me; and, so intensely acute was his appreciation of the humorous side of a situation, that his fits of peevishness died almost before they were born. The one that stands out in my memory as having lasted longest was in Vienna, when his tobacco-pouch was empty and he could not find a tobacconist. No one, of course, can in Vienna. There are none. But he could always find something to make him laugh, even in his own discomforts and privations, and no man that I have known had the same strange power of dispelling irritability in others. If I had been Prime Minister, on the point of em-broilment with other Powers, I should have sent Fred Haggard as my ambassador to smooth things over. If I had been a jeweller under orders to go round the world in a sailing-boat, I should have left my stock in the hands of Fred

Haggard. If I had been condemned to pass the rest of my life on a desert island with one man only for company I should have chosen Fred Haggard. No man can say more than this.

Atlin City in 1899 was a funny little straggling street of wooden houses standing on the edge of a lake four miles wide and ninety-six miles in length. It had no industry of its own, but was the focus-point of all the mining camps around. It subsisted on " mush " (porridge) and trout caught with a spinning-bait in the icy waters of the great lake. These trout weighed from twenty to thirty pounds and were " hawked " round every morning dangling from a pole carried by two men, who were the fish purveyors to the " city." They were as good eating as any salmon. Beyond these fish, Atlin produced nothing in the way of food. Everything else came up from Vancouver or Seattle. Beer was the price of champagne and everything else in proportion.

The mining camps were a great interest. Fiction, with a shadow of fact behind it—fact dating back in most cases to the Forty-niners— has painted the Western miner a savage desperado with knife or pistol always ready to hand. I, on the other hand, found him the salt of the earth. This is no exaggeration. With an experience of many countries and many nationalities behind me, I can truly say that I found human nature at its best in the mining camps of the great North-West. Nowhere else have I met with such disinterested kindness or seen such mutual goodwill and brotherhood among men— each man helping his neighbour as though it were himself. It needs the hardship and loneliness of the wilds to bring these qualities out of men. They lean together because the battle they are all fighting is a battle against cruel and adverse elements. So great was my attachment to, and trust in, these rough miners that I even made a practice of playing " poker " with them when they came into Atlin, and I continued to do so in the steamer the whole way down the coast to Vancouver. My playmates were perhaps a little more watchful of one another than the drawing-room poker-player, but there was no sign either of cheating or of knives and pistols.

It is not to be denied, of course, that there were occasional black sheep among these gold-seekers, as there will always be in every community, but for such the Atlin mining camps were far from healthy. Infringements of the local code were dealt with summarily and without mercy. As to the advisability of respecting this code I was very quickly " put wise." Just inside the entrance to each tent at a mining camp we visited, about six miles from Atlin, there stood one or more zinc buckets full to the brim with gold-dust and nuggets, and apparently offering exceptional opportunities to anyone with shop-lifting tendencies. I remarked as much to my companion, an old rugged miner.

" Yes," he replied, with suitable expectoration.

243

"We had one in this camp not long back with socialistic views as to the distribution of accumulated wealth. I reckon he was swinging from that pine tree yonder almost before his pockets were clear of the gold he'd pinched."

Such was the unalterable code of the North-West, and, though it may be stern, it is clear that it is the only way, where there are no bolts and bars, and where the whole of a man's earthly possessions lie exposed to a grasp of the hand. The penalty for gold-pilfering, at the time of my visit, was death without appeal, and, as this was universally known and recognised as being just, cases of gold-theft were very rare. In cases where summary executions did take place, the authorities were generally blind and deaf, recognising, as they did, that all communities must be governed by some code, and being powerless to administer effective justice themselves. The worst " tough " in the Yukon when I was there was a man named " Soapy " Smith. As far as I recollect, he was eventually lynched.

Gold mining throughout the Klondyke district was " placer " mining, *i.e.* the sifting of fragmentary gold out of alluvial deposits. In most cases the " dirt " is washed through sluice-boxes, the cross-bars of which catch the gold, while the lighter mud is carried away. In cases where the miner has no water-rights, he has to content himself with panning out the gold in a metal basin—a slow and tedious process and one calling for considerable skill.

KLONDYKE

Fred Haggard and I left Atlin on October 1st, having, after much haggling, reduced the purchase price of our Anaconda mine from twenty thousand pounds to two thousand, which, as it afterwards turned out, was exactly two thousand pounds too much. Every morning, for some days before our departure, when we wandered out into the rough, broad street that led down to the lake's edge, the snow-line on the hills across the lake had, during the night, perceptibly crept down, hard-cut and sharp as though pared by a knife. On October 1st it was very near the lake's level, although, so far, no snow to speak of had fallen in Atlin itself. The surface of the lake, too, had a film of ice on it as we cut our way across in the little *Atlin Queen*. For a week or so more the stern-paddler would force her way through the thickening ice, and then boat traffic would cease till the following May. A certain amount of coming and going took place through the winter months with " huskies " and sleighs, but this was toilsome and expensive, and few ventured it unless driven. The handful who had remained on in Atlin through the winter told me that, although it was often 40° below zero, the cold was not very noticeable unless a wind blew, and then no one ventured out except in complete sheepskin armour, face and all. The worst feature, they all agreed, was the deathly silence.

By the date of our departure the tales as to the ricketiness of the White Pass railway had become so accentuated that Haggard and I elected to walk down from the summit to Skagway, keeping with ease in front, or alongside, of the train. The only trying part of the walk was where the trestle-bridges had to be crossed. These were exceedingly narrow (the gauge, if I remember right, was only three feet) and exceedingly high above the chasm below. Although the sleepers were little more than a foot apart, the necessity for watching one's feet the whole while, and the consequent ceaseless view of the abyss below, after a time produced a sense of vertigo which was far from comfortable. Haggard, who had a bad head for heights, boarded the train for the transit of the trestle-bridges and so very nearly met his end, for the engine left the rails in the middle of the highest and longest trestle-bridge, and, when it pulled up, was not more than three inches from the edge of the bridge. With wonderful nerve and skill the engine was finally replaced on the rails by means of jacks, and the train proceeded on its funereal career. We were glad to get to Skagway.

CHAPTER XVII

IN the year following our trip to Atlin, the Syndicate which had sent us there, and which seemed generously inclined to thank us for having saved them eighteen thousand pounds rather than to blame us for having lost them two thousand, asked Fred Haggard and myself to make the journey to the interior of Peru for the purpose of inspecting and, if necessary, purchasing another gold-mine. The reports concerning this mine were more dazzling even than those which had taken us out to the Yukon. It was said to have furnished the old Inca kings with all the material for the golden tulips with which their gardens at Cuzco were at one time made so bright, but, since that day, to have lain dormant for three hundred years, waiting for some enterprising spirits (such as our Syndicate) to continue the process of gold-extraction.

We gladly undertook the mission, for the expedition promised some unusual experiences.

The first and not the least interesting of these experiences was a surreptitious visit which Haggard, Mrs. Haggard and myself paid to the forbidden town of Jacmel in Haiti.

Haiti is the mystery island of the world, for

—apart from its uncanny Voodoo worship and all the horrible stories connected with that cult —it is the only island in the world which has so far successfully resisted exploration by white men. One may say even more than this. It has even been successful in resisting exploration by the two black republics that nominally own the island, for these, in point of fact, know no more about the interior than does the Royal Geographical Society. Both the St. Domingo and the Haiti blacks live in continual mortal terror of the aboriginal Indians who occupy the interior, and with every reason too, for very rarely has anyone, either black or white, returned from any inquisitive excursions beyond the very narrow coastal limits over which the two black republics really hold sway. The few enterprising spirits who have succeeded in penetrating a short distance inland, and have returned alive, have learned nothing of the interior. How should they? Haiti is bigger than England and Wales combined.

Towards the end of the eighteenth century a French army of 40,000 men essayed the conquest and occupation of the island, but met instead the fate of all those who meddle with the mysteries of Haiti, for the entire army perished, partly from malaria, but mainly at the hands of the aboriginal natives, who—themselves invisible— harassed the invaders day and night with poisoned darts and arrows. Thus ended the last military attempt to subjugate the island.

Haiti would appear to be a land of surpassing loveliness. Slightly smaller than Cuba, but by far larger than any of the other West Indian islands, it is also by far the most beautiful, as seen from the sea. Range upon range of towering mountains rise up almost from the water's edge, completely clothed almost to their summits with a forest of emerald green, which, in the more distant ranges, gradually melts into a turquoise blue. The possibilities of the interior, both as regards scenery, climate and productiveness, are almost unlimited, but it is safe to predict that the interior will guard its age-old secrets for many years to come, except, perhaps, to the superficial eye of the aeroplane observer.

Haggard and I had an overwhelming desire to set foot on this forbidden island. The rule of the Royal Mail S.P. Co. is very strict as to no passengers being allowed to land, under any pretext whatsoever, owing to the fanatical hatred of the black republics for all the white races. Fred Haggard, however, was gifted with a persuasiveness of manner which few human beings could resist for long. In his informal, half-humorous, half-cynical style, he opened the attack on the captain on the day preceding our arrival at Jacmel. He was met with an immediate and peremptory refusal, at which Fred Haggard laughed good-humouredly, relit his eternal pipe and for the moment withdrew. Shortly afterwards, however, he returned to the attack and, long before Haiti was in sight, the captain had capitulated to Haggard's good-humoured persuasiveness, as everyone always did in the long run. It was arranged that, if we undertook not to whisper a word of our permit to the other passengers, Haggard, Mrs. Haggard and I might go ashore at Jacmel for two hours in the boat which carried the mails. He warned Mrs. Haggard, however, that there was considerable risk in what she was doing, and urged us, for our own sakes as well as his, to be extremely circumspect in our demeanour towards the people. This undertaking we gladly gave, and next morning—to the open-mouthed amazement of the other passengers—we slipped quietly into the gig which was to carry the mails across the mile of water which separated Jacmel and the S.S. *Atrato*.

When we landed, the second officer, who was in charge of the mails, and whose duty it was to see them safely to the Post Office, gave us an exact time for our return, saluted and went his way, leaving us three intruders to our own devices. We turned in the opposite direction to the Post Office and—feeling half brave and half foolish—commenced our wanderings.

The demeanour of the population towards us was interesting and peculiar. We were eyed with the greatest curiosity and with marked disapproval; that is to say, no one smiled at us, no one seemed pleased to see us; on the contrary, they seemed very far from pleased to see us; their looks were most distinctly unfriendly. On

the other hand, there was no attempt at active
hostility and we were not even mobbed. People
scowled at us, but they made no attempt to
follow us. Once or twice a burly negro showed
a disposition to hustle us off the footway, but
mindful of the captain's injunctions, we gave
way and there was no collision.

Our main object was to find the famous church,
of whose peculiarities we had heard so much,
but, as our undirected wanderings failed to bring
any such building within sight, we were at length
forced to make inquiries. In some trepidation
of mind, I approached the most benevolent-
looking old negro I could pick out, and taking
off my hat with a flourish, said :

" Ayez le bonté, Monsieur, de m'indiquer
l'église nationale."

To which, to my unmixed relief and no little
astonishment, he replied :

" Avec le plus grand plaisir possible, Monsieur.
La première à gauche, épuis la troisième à
droite," etc., etc.

There is something to my mind absurdly
incongruous in the French language coming from
negro lips. It seems at first the most grotesque
misfit imaginable, but it is quite certain that
no other language can the Jacmel negro either
understand or speak. We took a polite farewell
of our informant and, following his instructions,
soon came in sight of the church, which is remarkable for two things only—a fine bas-relief of the
Last Supper in which all the Apostles are black

except Judas, who is a white man; and a life-size figure of the Virgin Mary, who is a negress as black as coal. Having regaled our eyes for some time with these curious illustrations of the Jacmel interpretation of the Gospel story, we left the church and wandered a short way into the country, but the looks of the few people we met on the road were so very much more hostile than those of the townspeople, that after a short time we thought it best to retrace our steps towards the quay.

On our way back we had a piece of rare luck, for we passed the Admiral of the Haitian Navy. The Haitian Navy consisted at that time, and for all I know to the contrary still consists, of a single small obsolete war-ship, but what it lacked in tonnage it made up for in the magnificence of its Admiral, who was faultlessly arrayed in blue tunic and epaulettes, cocked hat and sword, and whose breast was resplendent with two rows of decorations. Repressing an almost irresistible impulse to shout out, " Yah! Massa Sambo," we took off our hats to this splendid figure, who haughtily saluted in return.

Curiously enough, the only attempt at a hostile demonstration while we were on the island was made by a white man, or, to be more accurate, by a man who was almost white. This man, as we afterwards learned, was a refugee from Jamaican justice, from which he had fled for safety to Haiti, where he was able to his heart's content to vent his spleen against the whole race of white men. We unfortunately arrived at the quay some quarter of an hour before the appointed time, and, while we were waiting there for the second officer, this madman (for he evidently was mad) commenced a frenzied harangue of the mob-orator type directed against us three intruders on the privacy of the island. Gradually he collected a crowd, as such people always do, and we could see only too plainly, by their flashing eyeballs, that he was working his audience up into a state of excitement little short of his own. We were very glad when the second officer arrived and we were able to push off out of hearing of the raving imprecations with which he pursued us.

Barbadoes and Jamaica I found uninteresting, and Colon inexpressibly dirty. Unluckily for us, we were detained at the latter place several days on account of a bloodthirsty rebellion which was raging in Colombia at the time. Eventually, however, the railway was pronounced clear and we were allowed to proceed. We reached Panama without coming in sight of either of the contending armies, and there took ship for Callao on the Chilian steam-boat *Aconcagua* (pronounced Ackongower). The sea voyage to Callao occupied at that time from ten to fourteen days owing to the many uncleanly and pestiferous ports at which the coasting steamers thought it necessary to call. Of these the most pestiferous and, at the same time, the most important was Guayaquil in Ecuador, the chosen home of cocoa,

Florida water, mosquitoes, yellow fever and sudden death. The town of Guayaquil has been built, owing either to *force majeure* or to the insanity of man, in one of the unhealthiest spots in the world. Not content with being mathematically on the equator, it is thirty miles up a sluggish river which, when the tide is out, leaves bare a broad expanse of stinking yellow mud, beloved of crocodiles but very bad for man. We left it after a stay of two days without regret, but with many unsolicited testimonials as to its unhealthiness in the shape of mosquito bites.

One little incident occurred on the way down to Callao which, small as it was, made me glad that I was an Englishman. A fire broke out one morning in the ship's hold, which shot forth a thin but ominous column of smoke through one of the hatches. The crews of the Chilian line of steamers are mostly dagos, but the officers are all European and our chief officer was an Englishman of the name of Lee. The moment the fire broke out, the crew came tumbling up from below, brandishing knives and gibbering like maniacs, and made a rush for the boats. Their rush, however, was stopped by the small but determined figure of Lee, who, revolver in hand, barred the way. A trial of nerve followed, which ended by Lee gradually driving the crew before him into the bows, where he held them. Beckoning to the third officer, he slipped the revolver into the junior's hand, told him to keep the crew covered and shoot the first man that rushed, while he himself dived down into the hold through the hatch from which the smoke was issuing. At the end of an hour he reappeared, black as a sweep from head to foot, but triumphant, for the fire was out. He had smothered it with mats. As we were carrying a desperately inflammable and, I believe, quite illegal cargo, there can be little doubt that Lee's prompt and determined action saved the lives of all on board.

We spent a week in Lima making preparations for our expedition into the interior, and during this week we were fortunate enough to be favoured with the only shower which Lima had enjoyed for seventy years. For five minutes it rained solid tropical rain. The terror-stricken inhabitants thought the end of the world had come, and I believe there is no doubt that the end of the greater part of Lima would most assuredly have come had the shower lasted another five minutes, for the town is largely built of mud. As it was, the rain produced some interesting effects. Both the dining-room and main staircase of our hotel were open to the air, and, by the end of the storm, the water was foaming down the latter with the force and effect of a miniature Niagara.

Along the six miles of flat, arid sand which separates the Andes from the sea throughout the length of Peru it never rains. Numbers of torrential streams, however, tumble down seawards from the Andes, and it only requires

intelligent irrigation to make this barren stretch
of waste land grow anything. The old Incas
clearly irrigated it, for the remains of their
aqueducts are still in evidence, but the modern
Peruvian is too indolent.

We spent two days at Chosica, 5000 feet up,
with a view to training ourselves gradually to
altitudes. On the afternoon of one of these days,
the four members of our party—that is to say,
Fred Haggard, Frank Merrick, the mining engineer, a herculean young doctor named Robert
Wilmot and myself—agreed that it would be
pleasant and exhilarating to walk to the top of
a conical hill which faced the inn. We set out
in cheerful mood. After some two hours' work,
during which our progress was disappointing, a
difference of opinion arose as to the best route to
take in order to reach the top with the least
difficulty. My three companions were firmly
persuaded that we ought to bear to the right,
while I was just as obstinately convinced that
the left-hand course was the best one. So heated
did the argument become that we finally agreed
to separate, I going my way and they theirs.

It need hardly be said that, after we had parted
company, I stretched myself to the utmost in
order to prove that I was right by reaching the
top first. With every ounce of energy that was
in me, I climbed and climbed towards my
objective till my limbs ached and my brow
grew very damp indeed, but without in any way,
as it seemed, lessening the distance which lay

AUTHOR AND PARTY ON PERUVIAN PAMPA.

ahead of me. Strain as I would (and there is
no doubt I strained very hard) the summit grew
no nearer. In some bitterness of spirit I pictured
the other three sitting smoking their pipes on
the summit and jeering as they looked down on
my futile efforts to negotiate the hill from the
wrong side; for I made no doubt now that they
had been right and I had been wrong. What
other conclusion could I come to? Finally, in
the shades of evening, fearing to be overtaken
by darkness on rocks which were becoming too
precipitous to be pleasant, I gloomily abandoned
my attempt to get any higher, and, in a dejected
frame of mind, commenced the descent. I
reached the hotel unpleasantly conscious of
failure, nor were my spirits raised by the sight
of the other three sitting happy and contented
under the verandah.

"Well?" Fred Haggard inquired, with a
touch, as I thought, of derision. "Did you get
up?"

"No," I replied shortly. "What was the
view like from the summit?"

"Oh, gorgeous," was the reply; "but the
finest sight was, of course, you, thousands of
feet below, trying to get up the wrong way."

Peals of laughter followed on this speech; the
laughter, in fact, was so sustained that I became
suspicious that something was in the wind.
Further inquiry elicited the fact that the others
had fared no better than myself and had, indeed,
abandoned the attempt as hopeless some time

before I did, as they had already been home a good half-hour.

The fact of the matter was that the summit of the " hill " which we thought to scale in an afternoon was 10,000 feet above where we stood, but the astonishing clearness of the atmosphere brought it down so close that our ambition was perhaps excusable. We made no further attempts to climb the Andes.

Next day we took the train to Oroya. The Oroya railway is, I believe, admittedly the finest example of railway engineering work in the world. It rises by a gradual incline of one in thirty-three to an altitude of 15,666 feet, and, in those days, ended at Oroya, a thousand feet down on the far side of the Cordilleras. Since then it has been extended to Cerro de Pasco.

It was amusing to watch the effect of the climb on the passengers. At 10,000 feet conversation was bright and brisk; cigars were being enjoyed and the magnificent scenery admired. At 12,000 feet conversation, though still sustained, began to lose much of its brilliancy. At 14,000, cigars were surreptitiously thrown away and an ominous silence reigned. On nearing the summit, this peaceful silence was abruptly broken, for several of the passengers rushed to the back of the cars and were violently sick. Personally, I had so far felt no particular discomfort. That was to come later.

We slept at Oroya and next morning started on our hundred-mile ride across the Peruvian

PERU

Pampa : Fred Haggard, young Merrick, our mining engineer, Don Miguel de Bezada, one of the joint owners of the mine, and myself. Robert Wilmot had returned to Lima. The weather was sunny and beautiful, but spoilt by occasional snow-storms, which in turn gave way once more to baking sunshine. The scenery was featureless but peaceful. The Peruvian Pampa is an undulating plateau covered with short, springy turf. It is absolutely treeless and bush-less, but intersected by many crystal streams and dotted with large lakes on which we could see the wild-fowl in their thousands. To north, south and west of us rose the glittering giant peaks of the Andes. Many of them at that time were unmeasured or, at any rate, only approxi-mately measured. I remarked on the peace and beauty of the scene to Don Miguel, but he shook his head disgustedly.

" It is an accursed region of evil spirits," he replied, crossing himself.

I disagreed with him and remarked that I thought it exhilarating.

" Exhilarating ! " he exclaimed; " why, I will bet you a sol that you cannot walk as far as that rock in front of us."

" Done ! " I promptly cried, and leaping off my pony, led him as far as the rock indicated. I won my sol, but I regretted my bet for the rest of that day and for the two days following. The exertion required to walk the short distance necessary was almost unbelievable. I remounted my pony with a violent headache which remained with me for the next three days. By the time we reached Tagasmayo, our first resting-place, I was a very sick man. I " shooed " a dozen hens off my bed, where they were peacefully roosting, and dropped on to it without even removing my boots. My head was like a furnace and my eyes were streaming. A cup of tea (without milk) was brought me, and I drained it and fell at once into a heavy sleep which lasted till morning. Another cup of tea in the morning, and I mounted the dejected pony which was to carry me the thirty-three miles to Junin, our next halting-place. That ride to Junin was one of the most trying experiences I have ever endured. The day was as beautiful as could be imagined and, across the dead-flat Pampa, Junin stood out quite clearly from the moment of our start. It looked no more than five miles distant, but hour after hour we rode and still this elusive village grew no nearer. Three miles an hour was the best the ponies could do. If you press them beyond that—in spite of the fact that they have been bred in that rarefied atmosphere—they bleed at the nose and fall down. We were denied the solace of smoking, for no pipe will burn at 15,000 feet. On and on we toiled in funereal silence. If I had been alone, I have no hesitation in saying that I should have lain down under a rock and, if necessary, died without any regret. I felt, in fact, that there was nothing I should enjoy so much as death. All the rest of the

PERU

party were bad, but none so bad as I was, for
no one else had been fool enough to walk three
hundred yards for a bet. Don Miguel, when he
left Oroya, had been a cheery little man, with a
smooth, rosy face like an apple. His face was
now like a medlar, lined with a hundred wrinkles.
His eyes streamed constantly, as indeed did all
our eyes. No one spoke. In fact I may say
that, from end to end of our hundred-mile ride
across the Pampa, no one of us spoke except
under necessity. We did not feel like speaking.
However, all things come to an end, and eventually we reached Junin after a ride of some eleven
hours. Once again I tumbled on to my bed (I
should have been sorry to tumble into it) after
a cup of tea, and fell instantly into a heavy
sleep.

Next morning I was so bad that there was
some discussion as to whether I had not best be
left at Junin. I insisted, however, on continuing.
Death, I felt, was infinitely preferable to Junin.
Haggard and Merrick between them lifted me on
to my pony, for I was almost too weak to stand,
and we continued our melancholy ride. Hope,
however, the greatest stimulant on earth, was in
my breast. I knew that, if I could remain in
the saddle, night would see me 5000 feet nearer
the sea-level and, beyond that, I cared for nothing.
After riding for about three hours we began to
descend. With every hundred feet we dropped,
life and the joy of living came back to me.
Indeed, even while on the undulating Pampa

itself, every hundred feet that we rose or fell made a perceptible difference to my comfort.

About 5 p.m., to my unspeakable relief, we reached the hospitable abode of Don Vincente de Bezada, who was to entertain us during our inspection of the mine. Don Vincente was a splendid specimen of the Spanish hidalgo, with a fine presence and a delightful charm of manner, and the entertainment which he afforded us was not only excellent in itself, but to myself extremely welcome, for no food had passed my lips since we had left Oroya three days before.

As an illustration of the extraordinary effect of high altitudes on the constitution, I may mention that, on that same day, as soon as we had washed and eaten, I went in the evening for a long solitary walk. I could hardly realise that, only that very morning, I had been too weak to mount my pony without assistance.

The much-dreaded " Soroche," or mountain fever, is always worst on the occasion of its first visitation. Every subsequent attack is milder. Residents in Lima, however, even though they may have crossed the Pampa before, contemplate a renewal of the experience with the utmost dread. Don Miguel, who had often crossed before, had gone through a three weeks' strict dietary training before he accompanied us.

The country in which our mine lay was the " 10,000 foot " country, pretty, hilly and tame, with a strong resemblance to Cumberland. Grass hills, clothed here and there with scrub, fenced

PERU

in clear streams tumbling down to the Amazon,
and looking as if they had been specially created
by Providence for the harbourage of trout. Most
of our common English birds, in rather gaudier
liveries, flitted about among the bushes. The
ubiquitous sparrow was of course there, in ceaseless evidence, as were also the chaffinch, the
blackbird and the robin, all a little disguised,
but still unmistakable for what they were. The
country was peacefully attractive and the climate
like that of our spring at its best. Of ploughed
land there was hardly any trace, for, though the
country was clearly capable of growing cereals to
any extent, the impossibility of transport to any
big market was sufficient to strangle all agricultural enterprise. Now that the railroad has come
to Cerro de Pasco, it is possible there may be a
little more cultivation, but even that is doubtful,
for Cerro de Pasco itself is as inaccessible from
Chuquitambo, where we were staying, as the top
of Ben Nevis is from Banavie.

It is a safe prophecy, however, that some day,
in the far future, the interior of Peru will be one
of the great food producers of the world. Its
vast extent, coupled with its unlimited water
supply and the ease with which climate can be
regulated by altitude, give it advantages which
no other country can rival. From 10,000 to 7000
feet cereals of all kinds can be grown; from
7000 to 4000 tea and coffee, and from 4000 to
2000 cocoa, sugar and cotton. Below the last-
named level lie the poisonous forks of the Amazon,

well adapted for rubber-growing, but not likely to be habitable for white men for many a century to come. At present the interior of Peru gives the world at large but little in the way of food, being shut off from civilisation by the Andes on the west and by the Amazon jungle on the east. The development of the country by railroads, however, is a perfectly simple matter. The supreme difficulty was bridged when Meggs built the Oroya railway. The rest would be child's play by comparison. The decline of the Andes is as gentle on the east as it is terrifying and precipitous on the west. If England or America took Peru in hand, it would not only become one of the greatest food and mineral producers in the world, but also one of the most perfect residential countries for colonists. At present it labours under two great disadvantages : its inaccessibility and the total absence of any authoritative government. The Peruvian Government concerns itself very little with what happens east of the Andes. How, indeed, can it be expected to repress outbreaks and quell disorder when it has no means of transporting its troops or police ? Below the " 4000 foot " level many of the Peruvian natives are dangerous and unrestrained by any law. Their priests exercise absolute control, and, in a desire to keep this control, they incite the natives to kill all strangers who have the temerity to come and spy out the land. While I was in Lima, I met a man named Hayward who had just returned from an expedition below the " 4000 foot" level. He was the sole survivor of the expedition, his four companions having been mobbed and killed by the natives.

At Chuquitambo the natives were not only civil but obsequious to the point of effacing themselves in the dust before every European that they encountered on the road. The Peruvian cholo of to-day is a placid person of the Esquimaux type, with a round, plum-coloured, hairless face. To my eyes they were all as exactly alike as a flock of sheep, but it is to be supposed that they are able to detect differences among themselves.

We bought the mine, as indeed we could hardly avoid doing in face of the genial hospitality of our host, Don Vincente. It is satisfactory to be able to record that after several years of uncertainty, the mine has at length proved a conspicuous success, and is to-day producing considerable quantities of gold.

I looked forward with unspeakable dread to our return journey, but was pleasantly surprised to find that I was not nearly so badly affected as before. At Junin we even found energy enough to stroll about and examine the place. Junin is a village of mud huts, remarkable only for its dirt and its church. The latter is a long, low, white-washed building with a thatched roof. It looks more like a cow-shed than a church on the outside, but inside it fairly makes the stranger gasp with astonishment. It boasts no fewer than three (I think there were four) carved Florentine altar-pieces, standing ten feet high and beautifully decorated—after their kind—in red and gold, blue and silver, etc. The old Conquistadores were certainly very wonderful fellows. Pizarro must have abandoned his ships at Colon and built an entirely new fleet at Panama. This in itself must have been a colossal undertaking. Then, from Panama to Callao, he had to face the ceaseless S.E. trade winds for 1000 miles ! How he did it no man knows. The conquest of the Incas was in itself no doubt a trifling matter, for they were not a fighting race. His chief claim to admiration is over his conquest of physical difficulties. The transport of those Junin altar-pieces over the Andes, in that rarefied atmosphere, stands out as an amazing achievement and one that seems out of all proportion to the results obtained. Why decorate a mud village nearly 15,000 feet above sea-level with these gorgeous examples of six-teenth-century Florentine work ?

The Peruvian Pampa is sparsely inhabited by cholos, lamas and sheep, none of whom seem to experience any inconvenience from the altitude. Their organisms have, no doubt, in the course of many centuries, adapted themselves to the con-ditions. If the natives are brought down to the sea-level they experience exactly the same symptoms as we do when we rise to their heights—violent headaches, sickness and running at the eyes.

Apart from other miseries, the track across the Pampa is made hideous by the constant sight of dead and dying lamas and donkeys. The

PERU

Peruvians—in common with most of the South American semi-Spanish natives—are absolutely callous with regard to the sufferings of animals. It is not so much that they are wantonly cruel; they are simply indifferent. Much of their cruelty comes from stupidity and the rest from traditional custom. All the copper from the Cerro de Pasco mines was in those days taken across the Pampa to Oroya on the backs of lamas and donkeys, who carried in stores on the return journey. A lama at those heights can carry 70 lbs. and no more. During this hundred-mile traverse, certain lamas would go sick and drop. Their burdens would then be shifted to other lamas and the sick beast left to die. Under the extra weight, other lamas would then, one after the other, drop and be left to die. One contractor that I spoke to told me piteously that he never crossed the Pampa without losing at least six lamas. I suggested the obvious expedient of taking with him half a dozen led lamas to take the burdens of those that went sick. He objected that this would be a great expense as well as quite contrary to custom. I could not make him see that there was less expense in taking with him spare lamas than in losing six on every journey. He was polite but quite obdurate. British and American residents in Peru told me that Peruvian customs with regard to animals were many hundreds of years old and were as unalterable as the laws of the Medes and Persians. No argument could induce the natives to change the customs of centuries.

On arrival at Oroya, we found Mr. Impett, the manager of the Oroya railway, awaiting us, and together we journeyed by the train as far as the summit, where, according to previous arrangement, he had in readiness for us a running trolley containing four seats and a very strong lever brake. Our baggage went on in the train, while we transferred ourselves to the trolley which was destined to carry us the rest of the way to Lima. Apart from all other considerations, the adventure was interesting from the fact that nowhere else in the world can a trolley travel 106 miles by gravitation alone. Such, however, was our purpose. After we had given the train half an hour's start, and protected our faces with thick veils, the wedge was kicked away from in front of our wheels and we instantly started gliding forwards with an ever-increasing speed. Impett took control of the brake and therefore of our speed, so that the rest of us were at liberty to give as much attention to the grandeur of the stupendous scenery through which we passed as our thick veils permitted of.

The relief of descent and the sense of returning vitality as more oxygen found its way to our starved lungs added materially to our powers of enjoyment as we skirted the giant precipices, or spanned the fathomless abysses of the Cordilleras. It was difficult to realise that the yellow, snowless peaks, to which we craned our necks as we glided along, were many thousands of feet higher than the ice-encrusted giants of the Rockies that had so awed our senses the year before; but we were helped to the belief by the memory of our depressing climb at Chosica. The permanent snow-line in the Andes is about 18,500 feet, and peaks of lesser magnitude show up from base to summit a uniform dull yellow. They are absolutely bare of vegetation and have the appearance of being built of sand. They are unspeakably grand, but more terrifying than beautiful on account of their nakedness. Over every valley, between the pointed yellow peaks, hovers a motionless condor vulture, looking like a kestrel in spite of its twelve feet of wing-span. In the lowest cleft of every valley roars a foaming torrent, along the edge of which are trees and a wild growth of heliotrope, which is the common Peruvian weed.

About an hour after leaving the summit, we very nearly ran into the train, which had been derailed by a rock avalanche, but which was hidden from our view by a sharp corner. It was that same sharp corner which had prevented the driver of the train from seeing that the track in front of him was covered with rocks and stones. As the track was, as usual, cut out of the side of a precipice, it was impossible for us to get our trolley past the train, and we had to wait in patience till the jacks had done their work and the train continued its careful career. The worst of it was that our pace had now to be restricted to the pace of the train, which was far too sedate for our tastes. At Matucana, however, which was the half-way house, both train and trolley came to a halt for half an hour, while those on board refreshed the inner man with such fare as the station provided; and, while we were so engaged, Impett had the trolley taken round and placed in front of the train.

Just as we were about to reseat ourselves, Impett turned to me and said : " Would you like to drive the rest of the way? " There was nothing, of course, that at the moment I desired so much, though my natural diffidence had so far prevented my making the suggestion; so, with a brief nod of acquiescence and with a doubtless unsuccessful attempt to conceal the elation I felt, I seated myself next the brake, signed to the cholo to remove the wedge, and off we started on the second stage of our journey, the two passengers in rear looking, I fancied, a little pale at the thought of my amateur guidance.

Now the driving of a trolley on the Oroya railway consists solely in the alternate application and release of the brake. The gradient throughout is a uniform gradient of three per cent., which is sufficient to give the trolley any speed required up to a hundred miles an hour. The nature of the track, however, forbids anything in the nature of excessive speed, except at short intervals. It is not merely that it is cut out of the edge of precipices throughout its entire length, but it also twists and turns round so many corners that it is very seldom that a clear view is obtainable for any great distance ahead. Such a view is, however, most essential to safety, for rock avalanches are perpetually falling on the track, and, though men are posted at regular intervals all along the line to cope with these avalanches, and to warn the trains if they approach before the débris is cleared away, we knew that such precautions would be quite inadequate to save us if we rounded a corner at full speed and found rocks just ahead of us on the track. The derailing of the train above Matucana was quite sufficient to prove to us that there was no real safety except in so sober a pace that a dead halt could be assured of in fifty yards. This was the regular train's invariable policy, and though, in the particular case cited, it had not been able to pull up in time to avoid being derailed, it had evidently pulled up quick enough to avoid being hurled over the precipice, as would inevitably have happened had its pace been less restrained. Another danger was to be found in the innumerable short tunnels, in which it was the inconvenient habit of the mountain goats to shelter from the sun.

My endeavour was to steer the middle course between blind recklessness and creeping prudence. Occasionally one could see ahead for half a mile or so, and then, with a glorious sense of exhilaration, we would shoot through the air for a time without any brake-restraint, till the next blind curve would approach, when caution once more had to be called into play. When we ultimately stepped off the trolley at Lima, I turned to

Impett and remarked with some pride : " Well, I think I did the second half in quicker time than you did the first."

" Yes," he admitted, with a sudden gleam in his eye, " you did. Would you like to come down again with me to-morrow and I'll show you what *I* call fast driving ? "

I politely declined this kind offer. Trolley-running on the Oroya railway has been responsible for many fatal accidents, as to which we had been furnished with full and gruesome details. We had also had it from many quarters that Impett was by far the most reckless trolley-runner in Peru. The sobriety of his pace during the earlier stages of our descent had no doubt been solely due to consideration for our untried nerves, and the gleam in his eye when he offered to show me what he could do in emergency was quite sufficient to determine my line of action.

It is a pity that the Peruvians hate us so. Much of this hatred can be traced back to an unfortunate occasion on which our representative in Lima paid an official visit to the President in knickerbockers and shooting-boots. This was, not unnaturally, construed into a deliberate insult to the Republic, and has never been forgotten or forgiven. It must be admitted, however, that altogether apart from the knickerbocker incident, the demeanour of the English residents towards the Peruvians is not such as to inspire love. The Spanish Peruvian is a great aristocrat, with an ancestry which, in many cases, dates back to

Pizarro. He and his kind have never crossed with the natives of the land they conquered, whom indeed they regard as little better than dirt, and, consequently, they still retain not only their pure Spanish blood, but their Spanish pride of race as well. They are not of the build to sit down tamely under an assumption of superiority on the part of the commercial class of a foreign country.

We had a comical illustration of our unpopularity in Peru on the occasion of a certain visit to the cinema theatre in Lima. It was during the Boer war, and we were given a representation of the battle of Spion Kop. The British army, consisting of about twenty fat swarthy men, in white duck uniforms with black belts (obviously the Lima police), were seen clambering painfully up a steep slope (obviously in the Andes) dragging a toy cannon behind them. Suddenly, from behind a wall, uprose three ragged-looking men with pitchforks and two women armed with mops, who fell upon the British army and—amidst deafening cheers from the Lima audience—hurled it headlong down the slope of the mountain.

In one particular respect the Spanish Peruvians are advanced far beyond the parent stock across the Atlantic, and that is in the matter of bull-fights. A bull-fight in Spain is one of the most unsporting, clumsy, debasing and beastly spectacles imaginable. A bull-fight in Lima, on the other hand, is a really beautiful and artistic performance. The picadors are mounted on exquisite little thoroughbreds, for which large prices are given, and which twist about and dodge the bull's rushes with all the agility of a polo pony. Any picador whose pony is, in the smallest degree, ripped by the bull's horns is hissed out of the arena. The bull, of course, is killed by the matador in the end, as in Spain, but there is none of the brutal mutilation of horses which so sickens anyone with the instincts of the sportsman who has to sit and look on at a bull-fight in Spain.

CHAPTER XVIII

THALASSA, THALASSA

I THINK I must have been born with the cry of the Ten Thousand in my mouth, for, from the moment when my infant fingers first fed ungrateful sea-anemones with little bits of seaweed, the sea in all its moods has beckoned me. To be on it, near it or in it—more particularly in it—has always seemed to me more to be desired than gold, yea, than much fine gold. In all latitudes, therefore, to which pleasure or duty has drawn me, the exploration of the local waves has been my first concern. The trouble generally is that, where the water is warm, there are sharks, and, where there are no sharks, the water is uninviting. The Mediterranean is, of course, an exception to this rule, but even this is now beginning to be invaded by sharks which find their way in through the Canal.

The most perfect bathing-place I have ever come across is at Port Antonio, Jamaica, where a large and deep lagoon is enclosed by a coral reef which is impassable to sharks. Here the water is so warm that bathers may swim about the live-long day in lazy comfort and without fear of losing a leg. A big hat, however, is a necessity on account of the sun.

The bay of Panama would be an ideal bathing-place were it not for the sharks and crabs. The crabs on the mainland are black, to match the rocks, which are also black, and they run quicker than any crabs I have ever met (or rather avoided). Fred Haggard, who shared my antipathy to crabs, always declared that the Panama crabs could run straight, which no decent crab should be able to do. They scared us when bathing even more than the sharks, for they were much more aggressive, and were not in the least frightened of us, which I believe the sharks were. We only bathed once from the mainland at Panama, and then without any guardian boat. Fred Haggard, Robert Wilmot and I swam out just far enough to feel brave and then, turning round, made for shore with a little more speed, I think, than was, strictly speaking, dignified, and with a good deal of superfluous splashing of the feet. We were all swimming in line when suddenly a simultaneous yell went up to heaven from three throats. We had swum into a bed of thick tenacious seaweed which had grabbed us all by the legs, and of course we thought that sharks had hold of us.

After that we bathed from the Pearl islands, which were infinitely more attractive than the mainland and much closer to our ship. Our only object in going to Panama had been to try to buy Panama hats, which—curiously enough—we were not able to do. There were none. It appears that the real Panama hats never find their way to Panama. They are all made at a place called Paita in Peru, where women sit in the sea and plait them under water. The hats are then all shipped direct to Europe.

We were held up for some ten days at Panama, owing to an unforeseen delay in the connection from San Francisco. During these ten days we remained on the good ship *Aconcagua* in preference to going to the only hotel which at that date offered hospitality to visitors in the town. We were anchored some six miles from the mainland and close to the Pearl island group, and every day we would row in one of the ship's boats to one or another of these lovely little islands and bathe, keeping the boat always between us and the open sea. We could often see the dorsal fin of a shark slowly cutting the water in the neighbourhood of the boat, but although, at first, this gave us a certain feeling of unrest, we soon got used to it, but of course always took care to keep in comparatively shallow water.

Apart from the bathing, the islands were most interesting to explore. They are inhabited by pure Indians of a very handsome type whose main industry is the culture of pineapples.

We did not find the natives very sociable. On one occasion, when Fred Haggard and I were accompanied by Mons. J. Henessey and the Comte de Vielle Castel, we ventured to pass the time of day to one of the ladies of the island who was engaged in pine-culture.

" Fine day, Jenny," one of our party remarked.

The lady responded with what the books term a dazzling and tooth-displaying smile. Such of the island gentlemen, however, as were working in the neighbourhood did not smile at all, but, on the contrary, began to gather round us with very hostile looks and with voluble comments on our behaviour which it was perhaps fortunate that we did not understand. Very soon a small crowd had collected, brandishing fists and agricultural implements in such very threatening style that we thought it best to beat a dignified retreat towards our boat. They pursued us to the very water's edge and, when we were fairly under weigh, indulged in such significant pantomime as to their intentions towards us that we decided that we would be safer in the future with sharks, or even with barracoutas, than with them, and we bathed from that island no more. No doubt they had at some time had trouble with cads from some ship in the bay and were unable to appreciate the strict conventionality of our British comments on the nature of the weather.

Thereafter we bathed from a smaller and more distant island. I had a most exciting hunt on this island for a humming-bird's nest which was very evidently situated in a biggish isolated bush, but without success. I was divided between a desire to find the nest and the fear of destroying it in tearing apart the clumps of foliage, and, in the end, I had to abandon the hunt. The two parent birds—very small and of a brilliant metallic blue—showed no trace of fear of me, but kept

buzzing round my head in most pugilistic
fashion.

Humming-birds are the most fascinating little
objects to watch. They do not fly like birds, but
like bees—perfectly straight and with incredible
speed. When attracted by a flower, they will
hover in front of it perfectly motionless except
for the beat of their wings, which is so rapid as
to be invisible, and which produces the faint
humming sound from which they derive their
name. Sometimes, while hovering, they will
make a perpendicular rise of twenty feet or so and
then fall back to their original position, and all
so quickly that the eye can hardly follow. Like
bees, too, they seem to have no perception of
the presence of man. At any rate, they show
no symptom of shyness.

It is not generally known that British Columbia
can boast three varieties of humming-birds—a
black one, a reddish one and another whose
distinctive colouring I have forgotten. They are
all three rather larger than the South American
varieties. I have seen the black ones at Rossland,
B.C., actually hovering over the snow—not of
course in mid-winter, but in April, when the
violets and crocuses force their way happily
through the thin layer of snow that is left and
form a brilliantly-coloured carpet with a white
ground. What happens to these British Columbian humming-birds in mid-winter, when Rossland
is four feet under snow, I have never been able
to learn.

The best places in South America that we struck for humming-birds were the Ecuador forests, which are ultra-tropical in their vegetation as well as in their steamy and oppressive heat. Almost more interesting than the humming-birds were the butterflies—very large and of the brilliant metallic hues which museums have made so familiar. These gorgeous insects, instead of fluttering, like our domestic British butterflies, within confidential reach of the collector's net, fly with the rapidity of a snipe and, even on smooth ground, would certainly leave far behind the fleetest entomologist that ever wore spectacles. In the dense tropical jungle, which is their habitat, it would, of course, be impossible to pursue them for five yards. How the professors secure them I cannot say. I can only imagine that they must be trapped by some species of sticky bait smeared on the tree-trunks. I believe that the scientific name for these fast-flying butterflies is *Ornithoptera*.

The small island to which we were driven by the menacing attitude of the natives was not so good for bathing as the large one, which boasted a horse-shoe bay, across the mouth of which our boat could patrol up and down to keep the sharks out. The smaller island had no such bay, and we consequently felt less secure. The rest of the group was too far distant to have any value for regular bathing.

I think there is very little doubt that the shark danger is greatly exaggerated. I once knew a certain Captain Montgomery in the Navy who had an amazing life-saving record. He was a magnificent swimmer and would go overboard to the rescue in any waters. He assured me that he had swum at times in seas that were infested with sharks and that they had taken no manner of notice of him. One has the evidence of one's own eyes, too, at places like Kingston, Jamaica, where small naked boys will dive all day long after sixpences thrown into the water. On one occasion when I was at Kingston the best diver was a boy who was nearly white, and one could follow the movements of his body, as he went wriggling down to the bottom with the greatest distinctness. And yet I have never heard of these boys being taken by sharks, although sharks are known to swarm round the ships. At the same time, there undoubtedly are, for some unknown reason, certain spots where the sharks are very wicked. One of these is, of course, Sydney Harbour, and another is Suez.

When I was at Suez it was very hot and I had an overpowering desire to bathe. The sea was as smooth as glass and of a marvellous transparency. Never have I seen any sea that looked so inviting. I was assured, however, that to bathe was to court certain death. Only three days before an Arab's legs had been taken off below the knee by a shark which attacked him while he was standing on the steps that led down into the sea washing his clothes. Residents at Suez, when they wish to bathe, have to take the train to the Ismailia salt lakes, on the surface of which a man may lie at full length and read a book, so great is their density.

One of the best bathing-places in Europe is at the Piræus, as Byron discovered over a hundred years ago. Modern bathers are accommodated by wooden steps which lead down into the water from a platform on to which open a long row of bathing-huts. Here in the blue waters of the Gulf of Ægina, the Greek gods and goddesses of the twentieth century disport themselves the live-long day, amidst surroundings which for scenic beauty it would be hard to rival anywhere. On all sides are seen, in their misty cobalt blue loveliness,

" The isles of Greece ! the isles of Greece !
Where burning Sappho loved and sang,"

conjuring up in the mind dim visions of the old heroes of the golden age. No wonder that W. E. Gladstone and Byron went mad over Greece. There is romance in the very atmosphere and in every line and curve of the wonderful seascape. There is romance too in the undying art of the Greeks and in every page of their absorbing history, which perhaps detracts from its value as mere history, but which nevertheless casts its spell over the reader and makes him loth to turn the eye of a too captious scrutiny on the facts. After all, history, even if not true, is none the less history in the absence of opposition, and he is but a poor historian who does not raise his own countrymen above the common level. So let us accept in simple faith the exploits of

THALASSA, THALASSA

the ancient Greeks as handed down to us by
Herodotus and Xenophon, for fear that, under
the lens, their glory might fade away as the
glory of the peerless Greek isles fades away on
close approach. From a distance they are the
softest, the deepest and the most heavenly blue
that the mind can picture, shimmering divinely
in the ceaseless sunshine. At close quarters they
are but piles of arid sand, almost naked of
vegetation. Even the mainland is indecently
bare of trees, and the glare is indescribable.
Greece suffers from perennial drought. Its rain-
fall is infinitesimal and its sunshine eternal and
desiccating, so that nothing grows but currants,
olives and marble. In spite, however, of their
disappointing character at close quarters, the
long-distance views are quite intoxicating in their
beauty, and none more so than the vast lagoon
into which Themistocles pushed out his fleet of
barges from the shelter of the Straits of Salamis
and scattered to the winds the naval power of
Xerxes.

> " A king sat on the rocky brow
>   Which looks o'er sea-born Salamis;
> And ships, by thousands, lay below,
>   And men in nations;—all were his !
> He counted them at break of day,
>   And when the sun set where were they ? "

I was looking upon the same view as Xerxes,
but I was sitting on no rocky brow, but on the
wooden steps that led down into the waters of
the Ægean Sea, and, very soon, shaking off my
poetic mood, I slid off the steps into the smooth,

283

warm sea and struck out from the shore. Some fifty yards out, an obese Greek was floating on his back and kicking up the water with his feet— a detestable practice in any waters, but particularly detestable under the poetic shadow of Salamis and Ægina. However, feeling at peace with all men, I overlooked his misdemeanour and as I passed remarked pleasantly and, as I hoped, grammatically : " τό ὕδωρ θερμόν ἐστί," which rendered into the English tongue means, " the water is warm."

I should perhaps here explain that, when in strange lands, I am always afflicted by a perhaps childish but, none the less, overmastering desire to address the natives in their own tongue. It is a harmless foible and occasionally meets with success. On this occasion it did not, for the obese Greek, who was either deaf or lamentably ignorant of his own language, replied in French and told me what time it was, as to which he evidently thought that I was inquiring. This was, of course, a little disconcerting, but I was not wholly discouraged, for it was evident to me that a man who was capable of the offence of splashing the water about with his legs was also capable of being ignorant of his own language. I accepted my first failure with resignation, but I was still none the less determined, if I could, to justify the expense to which my parents had been put in giving me a classical education, and, as it turned out, the opportunity was soon given me.

Having returned by the electric train to Athens,

THALASSA, THALASSA

I there took a taxi and visited some of the ancient and world-famous temples. My brother, in one of his books, has related with perfect truth how, on my return to the hotel, I attempted to remonstrate with the driver on the exorbitance of the fare demanded. A phrase which seemed to me to meet the case was " μὴ γένοιτο," an ejaculation very much in favour with St. Paul and which, in the English version of the New Testament is always translated as " God forbid ! " What could be more applicable ? " Μὴ γένοιτο," I accordingly thundered, with suitable gestures of protest. The man stared blankly and continued to hold up ten fingers in indication of the number of drachma demanded. I racked my brain to try and find some other suitable and objurgatory phrase from Homer or the New Testament with which to pulverise him, but I was able to think of nothing more scathing than ὣ ποποῖ, which, according to the lexicon, is an exclamation of surprise, pain or anger equivalent to " Oh, shame ! " With this parting shaft I withdrew haughtily into the hotel and told the hall-porter to settle with the man.

Some quarter of an hour later, while seated at luncheon with our local agent, Mr. Marino, a native of Athens, but a perfect English scholar, I determined to clear up the mystery of the cabman's ignorance.

" Why," I inquired of him, " did my taxi-driver not understand when I said μὴ γένοιτο ? Is the expression obsolete ? "

285

" When you said what? " he asked, with perplexed and puckered brow.

I repeated the words.

" Would you mind writing it down? " he said, still very puzzled. I did so.

" Oh ! ' *me jeneto*,' " he said at once, placing the accent on the first syllable; " well, of course he wouldn't understand you."

A long discourse on the modern pronunciation of Greek followed, in the course of which all my ideals were shattered. The one object of the modern Greek seems to be to violate all the hallowed dogmas of pronunciation as laid down by those admirable but unappreciated authors, Messrs. Liddell and Scott. There can be no other reason for their reckless disregard for the age-established quantities of vowels. Anaxagoras is now Anaxagōras; Demosthenes is Demostheenes; the Phaleeron Hotel at Piræus is pronounced Phalyuron, with the accent on the first syllable.

" But," I remarked to Mr. Marino, at the close of his painful explanation, " according to the way in which you pronounce all these words, Homer does not scan."

" No," he replied, with the utmost indifference, " of course he does not."

What more was there to be said? I turned my eye on the passing throng of ballet-skirted Athenians in the street; I thought of Miltiades and Aristides, and I sighed.

Mr. W. E. Gladstone, who was one of the finest Greek scholars in the kingdom, and an almost

THALASSA, THALASSA

fanatical admirer of Greece, paid a visit on one occasion to Athens and there delivered himself of a carefully prepared speech in the Athenian tongue to a large and deeply interested audience. They did not understand a single word he said. At the close of the meeting, one of those present was asked how he liked the speech.

" Oh ! it was magnificent," he replied; " such a wonderful voice, and such grand gestures ! But, as he spoke in *English*, I naturally did not understand what he was saying."

Modern Greek appears to me to come faster out of the mouth than any other language I have heard spoken. It sounds as if it was entirely composed of linguals and labials, with the linguals predominating. Two Athenians discussing politics sound to my ear exactly like two turkey-cocks gobbling at one another. Anything bearing less resemblance to the sonorous sounds we were at such pains to produce at school when reading Sophocles or Æschylus it is difficult to imagine.

With such an inherent enthusiasm for the sea, it was only in the natural course of things that I should have reared my family from a very early age to take to the water. The task was not a difficult one; in fact, with such goodwill did they take to the water that, after a few years of elementary instruction, a moment arrived—as it was inevitably bound to arrive—when the instructed began to show their heels, or, at any rate, the back of their heads, to the instructor. The instructor accepted the inevitable with becoming philosophy, and, from that time on, took his swimming exercise in dignified solitude, or, at any rate, in company with less adventurous spirits.

The family, especially the two girls, having permanently cast off my chaperonage, became daring in the extreme in their swimming ventures, and on more than one occasion gave me moments of acute parental anxiety. Their delight was to swim side by side straight out to sea, and the rougher the weather and the bigger the waves, the greater was their delight. At Minehead, three years ago, half the population of the place collected to see my son and youngest daughter swim out to sea in the face of the worst gale of the year, when no one else was dreaming of bathing. It was no mean undertaking, for the shore at Minehead shelves very gradually, and consequently the breaking waves extend for a long way out. The return journey was, of course, the most difficult, and the boy was smothered by one gigantic curling wave and badly knocked about before he could recover his equilibrium. On this occasion I had very little anxiety, for I knew that what they did was well within their powers.

Two years earlier, however, at Eastbourne, I had a very bad half-hour. My youngest girl had been ill for some time with swollen glands, and consequently unable to bathe. At length, on a certain fine morning, she was pronounced fit to take to the water. It so happened that there were very few people bathing when she made her appearance, and she consequently attracted some attention as she slowly walked into the water and commenced swimming outwards with her usual easy and indolent stroke. It was no doubt expected by the onlookers that, after covering some hundred yards or so, she would turn and come back, after the usual fashion of sea-bathers. As, however, she went steadily on and on, as though bent on swimming the Channel, the crowd on the beach began to get interested and, finally, excited. Smaller and smaller grew the black cap which she was wearing till, in the end, it disappeared altogether in the shimmer of sunshine on the water. The people now began to get restive. They stood up, chattered volubly in groups and craned their necks in an attempt to extend their horizon. I must confess that I did the same. We were all waiting for the moment when the black cap would once more become visible, as its owner turned to make her way homewards. We waited and waited, but there was no reappearance of the black cap. Nothing met our expectant gaze but an unbroken expanse of cold cruel sea. After a time one woman became hysterical, and ran up and down the beach wringing her hands and crying : " Can nothing be done ? Can nothing be done ? " Confident as I was in my daughter's swimming powers, I could not help being, to a certain extent, infected by the general panic and consternation. Visions of cramp and kindred calamities took possession of me. I mounted to the highest level of the sea-front, opposite the Grand Hotel, and from that point of vantage strained my eyes seawards. Not a sign was there of living being on the shimmering water that stretched away towards France. Then I must confess that my heart sank. I recalled with a pang many of the (so far unappreciated) virtues of my lost daughter. I realised with contrition the injustice of many of my past criticisms.

While still scanning the sea in this gloomy and reproachful mood, my eye chanced for one second to light on a tiny black speck far out on the horizon. Next moment, it had gone again, but I had seen all that I wanted to see. My mind was at peace and I returned leisurely to the beach and lit my pipe. When, some half an hour later, my daughter landed and strolled nonchalantly up the beach—happily unconscious of the wild consternation which she had aroused in the breasts of the good folk of Eastbourne—she was, I believe, much astonished at the torrent of abuse with which I greeted her. It was not till that moment that I myself realised how shaken I had been.

I think the best swimming performance of my two daughters was at Sidmouth four years ago, when they swam to Ladrum Bay against the tide. One morning after breakfast they announced their intention of attempting this swim. I told them it was impossible, as the tide would be against them, but they insisted that they could do it in spite of the tide, and so—after attempting in vain to dissuade them—I went down to the beach to arrange for a boat in which to accompany them. While I was so engaged, a young officer whom I knew, named Clarke, in the Hampshire Regiment, happened to come up, and I told him of what was in the wind, and asked his opinion as to whether it was possible. He expressed himself doubtful, but asked if he might form one of the party. Clarke was by far the best swimmer at Sidmouth, and many a morning I had watched his performances in the water with admiration. I was, of course, only too delighted to think that the girls would have so powerful a swimmer as escort.

Accordingly, as soon as preparations had been made, Clarke and my two daughters and my son entered the water, accompanied by me in the boat with their clothes and luncheon. The whole way across Sidmouth Bay the tide was adverse, but not violent, as the full force of the tide runs further out. Half-way across the bay Clarke was seized with cramp and had to come into the boat, and, shortly afterwards, my son, who was only a boy at the time, had to give up and also came into the boat. The two girls swam steadily on. When they got opposite the point on the far side of Sidmouth Bay, I thought that they must surely be beaten, for the tide here was running very strong, and I know that they swam hard at this spot for fully three-quarters of an hour without gaining a foot, for I had my eye on the shore. I think, if anything, they lost ground. So utterly hopeless did it seem that I strongly advised them to give up, but they indignantly refused, so I gave them some hot bovril from a thermos flask and on they went. Suddenly the tide must have changed, for they at once began to make headway, and, after that, it was all plain sailing. They made Ladrum Bay without any further trouble and without being either particularly tired or particularly cold. They were over two hours and a half in the water. Girls, for some mysterious reason, retain the heat of their bodies much better than men and, being less muscular, are not so liable to cramp.

CHAPTER XIX

DURING my mother's twenty years' residence at Coates in West Sussex we were naturally thrown into very close touch with the house of Wyndham at Petworth. Lord Leconfield was in fact my mother's landlord, and, as Lady Leconfield was one of her closest friends, it came about that much of our time was most enjoyably spent at Petworth House.

Petworth has always seemed to me, and still does seem to me—after a forty years' acquaintance and in the light of mellow judgment—to stand out as one of the most impressive country-houses in the kingdom. It is difficult to say in what exactly this impressiveness lies, but I think it is partly in the immensity of the house and partly in the sense of aloofness from the outside world which it inspires. This aloofness is not one of distance, for, in honest truth, the outside world is very close, being but just beyond the wall which separates the house from the town—a wall, however, solid enough to suggest a fortress and so high that even the Sussex hay-waggoner, perched on the top of his load, can get no glimpse of the sacred precincts within. Bidden guests pass through a gateway of dimensions which fit the wall and, at the end of a hundred yards, draw up between two large blocks of buildings, of which the block on the left is the residence of the Wyndhams, while that on the right contains the stables and offices, which are connected with the house by a subterranean passage. Through this passage all communications with the offices and stables pass unseen, so that the house itself, cut off from all menial sights and sounds, stands in a majestic silence which is certainly impressive. The house itself, too, is impressive. It is impressive in its great size; in the massiveness of the stone blocks of which it is built, and in its consequent appearance of unshakable solidity; in the vastness of the entrance-hall and staircase, and in the apparently endless chain of sitting-rooms—each with its own distinctive style of decoration and yet all blending into a harmonious whole. I always feel as though Petworth should be tenanted by dames and courtiers in eighteenth-century costume. Velvet coats and silk stockings would fit in so much better with the Gibbons room, the marble hall and the Louis XVI. room than knickerbockers and shooting-boots, or even than modern hunting costume. The eighteenth century, however, is adequately represented on the walls, where the matchless collection of pictures are a ceaseless joy to the eye.

The windows of the long chain of sitting-rooms which face west look straight out upon the park, without any intervening garden. This arrangement—although so unusual as to be almost unique—is not without its charm, for it adds to the general sense of aloofness and peace. Deer are more picturesque and less inquisitive than gardeners. Out in the park, beautiful with its hills and plains and valleys, the sense of aloofness and peace grows and grows at each turn. No matter in what direction the eye wanders, it can find nothing that does not please. To the south the barrier of the downs, to the west the beautiful valley of the Rother, to the north Blackdown, and to the east the rolling weald of Sussex, all aglow with that rich warmth of colouring which I always fancy is a peculiar feature of this favoured county. Small wonder that Turner thought Petworth one of the most beautiful spots in England.

No man ever fitted his surroundings better than did Henry Wyndham, second Lord Leconfield, for he himself looked exactly like a Vandyck cut out of the canvas. It is difficult to picture anyone who could more adequately represent in his own person all that one associates with the word " aristocrat." In manner, as in appearance, he was the typical *grand seigneur*, as conceived by painters and portrayed by novelists. In actual fact he lived up to his appearance and manner, for no one in West Sussex, north of the Downs, would have ventured to question his suzerainty over that little kingdom. The two Dukes were on the other side of the Downs, Parham was let and Cowdray uninhabited. Petworth and its owner, by virtue of possessions and residence, no less than by force of personality, stood out pre-eminent.

West Sussex is one of the few spots in the

country where hunting and shooting still walk hand in hand and where, as a consequence, the country squire dons knickerbockers and gaiters the one day, and breeches and boots the next. This is the spirit of the old country squire of eighty years ago, and it is refreshing to find it still lingering among the woods and wolds of Sussex. The head of the Wyndhams sets the example, for, throughout the winter, he hunts his hounds four days a week and beats his coverts the other two, and the whole of West Sussex —where it gets the chance—imitates the example thus set by its highest representative. In the happy days when I was " West Sussex," I had many a glorious day with Lord Leconfield, both in breeches and boots and in knickerbockers. The outlying shoots for which these last were donned were very delightful affairs in their way. Neighbours figured prominently on these occasions, and there was much " Sussex " talk. The whole atmosphere indeed was heavily charged with " Sussex," from the beaters in their white smocks, long wash-leather thigh-gaiters and wide-awake hats with red ribbons, to the red-faced, dewy-nosed " stops," contentedly gnawing raw turnips, and saluting each gun as he approached with a wide indefinite sweep of the arm. The woods with their copper-coloured bracken undergrowth and the russet leaves still hanging thick on the oak trees lent themselves harmoniously to the general scenic effect, and proclaimed at every turn the county to which they belonged. A further suggestion of old-world sport was imparted to the proceedings by the terrific detonations of Lord Leconfield's gun. He always shot with black powder and—despite constant evidence to the contrary—sturdily refused to believe in the efficacy of anything else. He himself ate no luncheon and he was very impatient of the delay occasioned by the necessary fortifying of weaker vessels. The retired colonel who, at the smell of the flesh-pots, rubs his hands and remarks : " By no means the least enjoyable part of the day's proceedings," was distinctly out of place at the Petworth shoots, for an interval of ten minutes was as much as the impatience of our host could tolerate. The sport, however, was always good.

Many of Lord Leconfield's social equals professed to be, and I believe honestly were, frightened of him because of his autocratic temper and of a certain grand manner, but there was really nothing to be frightened of in him, for he was not only one of the kindest of men, but also one of the readiest to admit error in himself if it were pointed out to him. He was quick to appreciate the humorous side of any incident, even if it were directed against himself. Curiously enough, the fear of him which some of his equals professed was not in the least shared by the farmer class, who would chat with him freely and on terms of perfect equality.

He was intensely " Sussex." Affairs outside of this sacred county had only a passing interest

for him.   On the other hand, he had an intimate
knowledge of everyone that lived, and everything
that went on, in his own county or, at any rate,
in the western half of that county.

No one that I have ever met has left upon me
the same impression of a little monarch ruling a
contented and loyal community.   Walter Francis,
fifth Duke of Buccleuch, had no doubt greater
possessions, but the very extent of those possessions and the fact that they were scattered
about here, there and everywhere prevented the
intimate relations between the over-lord and lesser
fry which was so noticeable at Petworth.   A man
cannot own a dozen country places and be well
known at each; or, indeed, at any, if he dis-
tributes his favours impartially.   Then, again,
in the Buccleuch possessions there were many
grimly Radical spots, whereas West Sussex was
fatuously Conservative.

Charles Wyndham, the present Lord Leconfield, married my great-niece, whose mother was
an Anson.   In most respects he has followed
closely in his father's footsteps, but is perhaps
rather less of a shooting man and more of a
hunting man.   The dignity of manner of his
father is tempered by the quick wit of his mother
(a sister of Lord Rosebery).   He is as whole-
heartedly " Sussex " as his predecessor, and takes
an even more active interest in county adminis-
tration.   He is less of the autocrat and more
of the country squire; less alarming and more
sociable.   The routine of Petworth is in the main

PETWORTH

unchanged. It remains one of the few spots in
England where one can forget that there has
been a war. Its *ménage* is pre-war; its atmosphere is pre-war. Its hounds (whose kennels
are in the park) still hunt the country four days
a week without subscription. Its entourage
remains—in all essentials—the same as I first
remember it forty years ago. New houses, those
hideous excrescences which have broken out in
so many lovely districts, like scorbutic eruptions
relieving an overcharged system, have no place
in the sleepy landscape on which the eye rests
from Petworth park.

CHAPTER XX

IN the early years of the twentieth century there was to be found four miles from Petworth a small but, in many ways, unique establishment. Here my mother, who was at that time approaching her ninetieth year, lived alone amidst surroundings which she grew to be as fond of as though they carried with them life-long associations. It was a very wonderful thing for an old lady of that age to live alone and yet be happy; and yet happy she undoubtedly was, with an irrepressible *joie de vivre* that many a girl of twenty might have envied. In her self-made garden, in her cows, her poultry, and even her pigs, she took a never-flagging interest, as well as in the personal welfare of all who served her and in the families of all who served her. And so she was never bored and always happy. This faculty of being perfectly happy, with no companions of her own class to talk to, did not prevent her welcoming with outstretched arms the sporadic visits of members of the little army that owed her their existence. At the time of her death in 1905 my mother could boast between 160 and 170 direct descendants, and it was seldom that a week passed without one or another of

Photo. W. & D. Downey.

FOUR GENERATIONS.

Standing: DUKE AND DUCHESS OF ABERCORN.
Seated: DOWAGER DUCHESS OF ABERCORN, MARQUIS OF HAMILTON AND
HIS DAUGHTER, LADY MARY HAMILTON.

these descendants passing a night or two under the roof of Coates Castle, as her residence was locally called, though it was in truth no castle at all, but just a castellated country-house of moderate size.

The majority of the aforesaid 170 descendants were grandchildren and great-grandchildren, and, in the ordinary passage of events, these grandchildren and great-grandchildren became engaged to persons of the other sex. On such occasions, the person of the other sex was—according to inviolable custom—taken down to Coates to receive the blessing of " Grannie." And to him or her, as the case might be, my mother became " Grannie " from that day on. No one dreaded the ordeal, for my mother had never been known to pass an unkind criticism on any single one of the many probationers who had come down to Coates seeking admittance into her sacred—but very widespread—family circle. She obstinately refused to see any of the failings which were occasionally so noticeable to less kindly-hearted critics, but pounced like a cat on the probationer's outstanding good points, and dwelt admiringly on these to the exclusion of all other comments; and so the probationer invariably went away as full of worship of " Grannie " as the chorus of grandchildren and great-grandchildren, who never wearied of singing of her incomparable sweetness.

Up to her ninetieth year my mother always insisted on attending the weddings of her descendants, and, on these occasions, she was always—

after the bride—the focus-point of all the love and homage that such family gatherings call forth. Shortly before her death, however, it was found that the strain of these functions was more than her strength was equal to, and thenceforward she was persuaded, much against her will, to stay quietly down at Coates and to let the post carry the messages of love and good-will with which her heart was charged almost to overflowing.

She retained her amazing vitality and keen interest in all family matters till the end, which came in her ninety-third year. She had gone through so many shaking illnesses from which she had always emerged smiling and apparently scathless that I think we had almost come to look upon her as immortal; and, when the end came, we felt as though the bottom had, literally, dropped out of the world. With regard to a certain small world this was no more than the truth, for, with the lowering of the blinds at Coates, there passed away the one golden link that held together some fifty families scattered here and there about the United Kingdom.

INDEX

INDEX

INDEX

Black, William, author of " Land of Lorne," 107
Blandford, Lord, 91
Blessed Shades, 18 *et seq.*
Boughton House, Kettering, a miniature Versailles, 133
Bowen, Edward, author of " Forty Years On," 102
Brewer, Mr., 201
British Columbia, humming-birds of, 279
Brocket Hall, early days at, 11
Buccleuch Scottish estates, enormous numbers of game on, 136
Buccleuch, fifth Duchess of, hospitality of, 130
Buccleuch, sixth Duchess of, 147
Buccleuch, Charles, fourth Duke of, his accumulation of country seats, 132; his army of labourers, *ibid.*
Buccleuch, Walter Francis, fifth Duke of, at Drumlanrig, 130; his hospitality, *ibid.*; his many possessions, 131; his valuable art collection, 133; his charity, 136; *grand seigneur* and country squire, 137
Buccleuch, William Henry, sixth Duke of, 136, 147; death of, 156; lovable disposition and happy married life of, *ibid.*
Buller, Charlie, 26; his fascinating personality, 27; sad end of, 29
Bull-fighting in Spain and Peru compared, 273–4
Burke, Micky, 170
Burroughs, Captain Kildare, 172, 173
Butler, Dr., headmaster of Harrow, 105
Byron, Lord, 282

C

Cambridge, H.R.H. the Duke of, 180, 181, 184, 185
Cameron of Lochiel, visit to, at Achnacarry, 86; first stag at, 86–90; a typical Highland chieftain, 90

Cannon, Tom, 202
Chamberlain, Mr. Joseph, 224
Chapman, A. P., 121
Chesterfield House, 36
Chilkoot Pass, Klondyke, the, 225
Chosica, an unsuccessful climb at, 256
Chuquitambo, 265
Clarence, Duke of, visits Barons Court, 44
Close, Pat, drawing-room acrobatics of, 176
Colchester, soldiering at, 162; " Spring-heeled Jack " at, *ibid.*
Copley, Catherine, marriage of, 31
Copley curse, the, 33
Copley, Sir Joseph, 33
Cork, drawbacks to hunting at, 190, 191; regimental races at, *ibid.*
Corry, Dr., 210
Costello, Mr., and the Duke of Abercorn, 112
Cricket in Dublin, 114
Cross, Dr., a doughty huntsman, 190; executed for wife murder, 191
Cunningham, C. J., 198, 199

D

Dalbiac, Mr., 164, 165; killed in Boer War, 166
Dalkeith, Earl of, 11, 148; death of, 152; endearing personality of, *ibid.*
Dalkeith, Lady, 74
Dawnay, Jack, 156
Dawson, Mr., Lord Mayor of Dublin, hostile reception of, in Derry, 182–4
Desborough, Lord, 103
Devine, Dan, 67
Dillon, John, 203, 211
Dinner in the Sixties a religious rite, 8
Dogherty, John, 69
Dogherty, Mr., defeated by Lord Frederic Hamilton, 212

INDEX

INDEX

Haiti, the mystery island of the world, 247; a French army annihilated in, 248; visit to, 250

Haitian Navy, the, 252

Hamilton, Lady Maria, 32

Hamilton, Lord, 32, 34

Hamilton, Lord Claud, 70, 80, 203

Hamilton, Lord Frederic, 35, 45, 60, 73, 74, 80, 81; at Harrow, 94; 203, 212

Hamilton, Lord George, 121, 203

Hamilton-Copley alliance, disastrous result of, 31–33

Hardy, Bob, 187

Harrow, at school at, 94 *et seq.*; "worship" of Baal at, 95; part-singing at, 95; "Forty Years On," national anthem of, quoted, 101; fight with a bully at, 105

Harrow, cricket at, 118

Henessey, Mons. J., 277

Herbert-Smith, Mr., 239

Herdman, Mr. Emerson T., 67, 221

High altitudes, effects of on the constitution, 258, 262

Hill, Alexander, 239

Hill, Lord George, 217

Hillingdon, Lord, 63

Hitchcock, Mrs., solitary lady in Atlin, 236, 237, 239

Hone, Willie, 115, 117, 118

Hounslow, soldiering at, 172 *et seq.*

House of Commons, the, a disappointing experience, 222

Howson, Mr., song-writer of Harrow, 102

Hunting in Co. Cork, drawbacks to, 199

Hussars, 11th, life in, 159 *et seq.*

I

Impett, Mr., manager of the Oroya Railway, an intrepid trolley driver, 268, 270, 272

In Memoriam, 300–302

Invergarry, deer-stalking at, 84–6

Inverness-shire, enervating climate of, 109

I Zingari Club, 26

J

Jackson, Warren, 193 ff.

Jacmel, a forbidden town in Haiti, 247

Junin, 260, 261; beautiful altarpieces at, 265; Pizarro and, 266

K

Kempster, Mr., 115

Kildare hounds and Ward Union, first riding over fence lessons with the, 125

King Edward, 140

King-Edwardes, Colonel, 212

King George at Drumlanrig, 141

Kingston, Jamaica, shark-infested waters of, 281

Klondyke, rush to, in 1897–8, 225; tragedies of Chilkoot and White Passes, *ibid.*; gold mining in, 244

L

Labrador retrievers, origin of breed from Langholm, 151

Lambert, Lady Fanny, 17

Lambert, Gustavus, Viceregal Chamberlain at Dublin, 17

Lambton, Lady Bee, and a pony race, 78

Lambton Castle, 72; its colossal hall, 73

Lambton Worm, the, 73

Land of Lorne, the, 107

Langholm, Labrador retrievers first bred at, 151; visit to, 148; improvements made by Lord George Scott at, 154; astonishing shooting at, 155–6

Landseer, Sir Edwin, at Ardverikie, 84

Lansdowne, Lord, 91

INDEX

Lawrence, Sir Thomas, 31
Leconfield, Lady, 293
Leconfield, Lord, 293, 296, 297, 298
Leconfield, Henry Wyndham, second Lord, 295
Leeds, Duchess of, 108
Letterbin, a model Irish village, 48
Leyland, Fred, at Harrow, 103, 104; punishes a bully, 105
Lichfield, Lord, 71, 108
Lima, a mud-built town and a tropical rainstorm, 255; bull-fights in, compared with Spain, 273-4
Lochiel. *See* Cameron of Lochiel.
Loch Laggan inn, 81
Lynn Canal, the, grandeur of, 229

M

McAnany, Paddy, 64, 66, 67
McBay, Alec, 64, 66
McConologue, Father, 213, 214
McFadden, Father, of Gweedore, visit to, 218-220
McLeod, Dr., and a wonderful charitable collection, 144-5
Mahaffy, Prof., 114
Manchester, the Duke of, 71
Marino, Mr., 285, 286
Merrick, Frank, 256, 259, 261
Middleton, Bay, excitability of, 126
Mid-Victorian girls, artificiality of, 5; pastes and powders unknown to, *ibid.*
Millionaires, self-made, and Society in the Sixties, 10
Mining camps, summary punishments in, 242
Mitchell, R. H., 25, 27
Montgomery, Captain, a swimmer in shark-infested waters, 281
Montgomery, Sir Hugh, 69
Morris, Charlie McPatrick, 68
Mount-Edgcumbe, 75

Mount-Edgcumbe, Earl of, 11, 75 *n.*
Mount St. Elias, 229

N

Newport, Lord, at Barons Court, 70
Nurse, the, and the slop-basin, 13

O

" Old Marquis," the, 30; his ill-fated first marriage, 31; marries and divorces Lady Cecil Hamilton, 33
Oroya Railway, a fine engineering work, 258; trolley driving on the, 270

P

Palmerston, Lord, Brocket Hall rented from, 11
Panama crabs, 276
Panama hats not obtainable in Panama, 276
Parliament, 222-3
Parliamentary elections in Ireland, 203 *et seq.*
Part-singing at Harrow, 96, 98
Pearl islands, the, 276
Pembroke, Lady, 108
Peru, 247 *et seq.*; its suitability for food production, 263; dangerous natives of, 264; unpopularity of the British in, 273; bull-fights in 273
Peruvian Pampa, the, one hundred mile ride across, 258; sparsely inhabited, 266
Peruvians' hatred of the British, 272
Petworth, 293; Lord Leconfield and, 295-7
Petworth House, 293; impressiveness of, 294
Philip McHugh island, 47
Pitt, William, at Bentley Priory, 30

INDEX

Piræus, the, an ideal bathing place, 282
Pizarro and the altar-pieces of Junin, 266
Politics, 203 *et seq.*
Ponsonby, Fred, 119
Popham, Judge, 15
Popham, Mrs., a charming singer, 14
Port Antonio, Jamaica, a perfect bathing place, 275
Prince of Wales (King George V), the, at Barons Court, 19; visit to Cork, hostile reception at, *ibid.*
Princess Mary at White Lodge, 186
Princess of Seattle turns turtle in Queen Charlotte's Sound, 229
Princess of Wales (Queen Mary), the, at Barons Court, 19; visit to Cork, hostile reception at, *ibid.*
Professional cricketers at Dublin, 115; at Harrow, 119
Professional jockeys and racing, 201

Q

Quasi-clerical bowlers, 114
Queen Alexandra at Dublin Castle, 18; her wonderful memory, 19
Queen Charlotte's Sound, *Princess of Seattle* turns turtle in, 229
Queen Mary at Drumlanrig, 141
Queen Victoria heads crusade against tobacco in the Sixties, 128

R

River Mourne, Ireland, 63
Rose, Sir Hugh. *See* Strathnairn, Lord.
Royce, Edward, and Gaiety burlesque, 177, 178

Russell, Lady Louisa, marriage of, to the first Duke of Abercorn, 35

S

Scot, the, generosity of, 144; innate honesty of, 145
Scott, Lord Francis, 155
Scott, Lord George, 153; introduces improvements at Langholm, 154
Scott, Lord Henry, 147, 155
Scott, Sir Walter, 132
Seven Sisters, the, 71 *et seq.*
Sexton, Mr., Irish M.P., 224
Shark-infested waters, swimming in, 281
Shaw, Alfred, 116
Shifner, Mr., a Harrow student, 95
Sixties, the, and the present day compared, 2; women and swimming in, 5; professional beauties in, 6; drawing-room conversation in, 7; high status of doctors in, 9; Society small in, 9; no glaring parade of wealth in, 10; fashions in, *ibid.*
Skagway, the, Klondyke, 225, 231
Society in the Sixties, exclusiveness of, 9
Soldiering, 159 *et seq.*
Soroche, the (mountain fever), 262
Southesk, Lord, 91
Spain, bull-fights in, compared with those in Peru, 273
Spanish Peruvian, ancestry of, 272
Spencer, Earl, 126, 127
Sports and exercises and the mid-Victorian girl, 5
Stewart, Baby, 25, 26, 27
Strathnairn, Lord, Commander-in-Chief in Ireland, 22, 23; his absent-mindedness, 24
Suez, sharks at, 281
Surtees, Robert, 3

310

INDEX

T

Tagasmayo, 260

Taku River, the, a fisherman's paradise, 233

Teck, H.S.H., the Duke of, his hospitality at White Lodge, 186

Tenant farmers of the Border counties, sterling qualities of, 137

Terry, Edward, and Gaiety burlesque, 177, 178

Thalassa, Thalassa, 275 *et seq.*

Tipperary Steeplechases, 197

Tobacco considered deadly to feminine organisms in the Sixties, 128; Queen Victoria leads crusade against, 128

V

Vaughan, Kate, and Gaiety burlesque, 177

Viceregal cricket in Dublin, 25

Viceregal days, 123 *et seq.*

Viceregal Lodge, Dublin, State Drawing-Rooms at, 16; country-house life at, 123

Victorian fops, 3

Vielle Castel, Comte de, 277

W

Ward Union and Kildare hounds, first riding over fence lessons with, 125

Webb, Fred, 200

Webbe, A. J., 118

West Donegal and the Armada, 220; indolence of peasantry of, 221

West Sussex, hunting and shooting in, 295, 296

Western miners, good qualities of, 242

White Pass, Klondyke, the, 225

Wilmot, Robert, 256, 259, 276

Winchilsea, Lord, 35

Winterton, Lord, 92; popularity of, 93

Y

Yukon, desolation of, 232

Yukon River, 226

www.ingramcontent.com/pod-product-compliance
Lightning Source LLC
Chambersburg PA
CBHW021216090426
42740CB00006B/240